T0333989

The Land Question in Neoliberal India

This book examines the land question in neoliberal India based on a cohesive framework focusing on socio-legal and judicial interactions in a point of departure from the political-economy approach to land issues. It sheds light on several complex aspects of land matters in India and evolves a critical and multi-dimensional discourse by mapping out exchanges between social and political actors, the State, elites, citizenry, and the legal battle and judicial interpretations on land as right to property.

Based on the themes of socio-legal policy and perspective on 'land' on the one hand and jurisprudence on the land question on the other, the volume discusses topics such as conclusive land titling; urban land governance; governance of forest land; land-leasing practices, policies, and interventions from the perspective of women; land acquisition policies and laws; how land matters interface with environmental issues; and judicial debates on 'compensation' against land acquisitions. It covers a wide range of case studies from all over India by bringing together specialists from across backgrounds.

Comprehensive and topical, this book will be useful to scholars and researchers of development studies, political studies, law, sociology, political economy, and public policy, as well as to professionals in NGOs, civil society organisations, think tanks, planning and public administration, lawyers, civil services and training institutes, and judicial and forest academies. Those working on rural and urban land issues in India, land management, land governance, environmental laws and governance, property rights, resource conflicts, social work, and rural development will find this book to be of special interest.

Varsha Bhagat-Ganguly has served as Professor at the Centre for Rural Studies, Lal Bahadur Shastri National Academy of Administration, Mussoorie; and Nirma University, Ahmedabad; and as Fellow at the Indian Institute of Advanced Study, Shimla (all in India). She actively researches on social and developmental issues. Apart from contributions to journals and books, she has edited three academic journals. Among her 14 publications are: *Protest Movement and Citizens' Rights in Gujarat* (2015); *Land Rights in India: Policies, Movements and Challenges* (2016, 2018); *Journey towards Land Titling in India* (2017); and *India's Scheduled Areas: Untangling Governance, Law and Politics* (2019). A forthcoming publication is *Electronic Waste Management in India: Opportunities and Challenges*.

The Land Question in Neoliberal India

Socio-Legal and Judicial
Interpretations

Edited by Varsha Bhagat-Ganguly

Routledge
Taylor & Francis Group

LONDON AND NEW YORK

First published 2021
by Routledge
2 Park Square, Milton Park, Abingdon, Oxon OX14 4RN

and by Routledge
52 Vanderbilt Avenue, New York, NY 10017

Routledge is an imprint of the Taylor & Francis Group, an informa business

British Library Cataloguing-in-Publication Data
A catalogue record for this book is available from the British Library

Library of Congress Cataloging-in-Publication Data
A catalog record for this book has been requested

ISBN: 978-1-138-58373-3 (hbk)
ISBN: 978-0-367-49509-1 (pbk)
ISBN: 978-1-003-04238-9 (ebk)

Typeset in Sabon
by Apex CoVantage, LLC

To all land dependents –

for their land rights and well-being through effective land governance

Contents

Figures

Tables

Contributors

C.R. Bijoy is with the Campaign for Survival and Dignity, a national coalition of Adivasi and forest dwellers' organisations (www.forestrigthsact. com). His areas of engagement and interest are in non-State and State-led processes addressing human rights issues; land and forest rights; self-governance and autonomy, particularly of tribals or Adivasis; forest dwellers, and indigenous peoples. He has published more than 60 papers in books, research journals, and popular magazines.

Sonali Ghosh is an Indian Forest Service officer with more than 20 years of work experience in forest and wildlife conservation in India. She has a dual master's degree in wildlife science and forestry and a PhD in geography from Aberystwyth University, UK. She has worked as a field manager in the country's finest Protected Areas (Kaziranga and Manas) and has travelled extensively and written about forests and people's livelihood issues in Northeast India. A WWF-PATA Bagh Mitra awardee, she has also served as a scientist (on secondment) at the UNESCO Category 2 Centre on World Natural Heritage Management and Training for Asia and the Pacific Region at Wildlife Institute of India, Dehradun. She is member of IUCN World Commission on Protected Areas, World Heritage and Ecosystem Management groups.

Amlanjyoti Goswami is a faculty member at the School of Governance at Indian Institute for Human Settlements, New Delhi and also heads the Legal and Regulation Team. He works on law, policy, and governance, including research in land acquisition, decentralisation and knowledge epistemologies. He studied sociology and law at the University of Delhi and has an LLM from Harvard University. He has played key roles in the revision of municipal corporation and town and country planning acts, worked on cultural and creative economy issues, and provided policy inputs to the Planning Commission on the XII Plan.

Pallavi Harshe is a development professional based in India engaged in research and teaching, specifically from a gender and caste perspective. She has been working with the Society for Promoting Participative

Ecosystem Management (SOPPECOM), Pune, and is involved in various capacities to ensure land rights to rural women farmers and entitlements to single rural women.

Deepika Jha is at the Centre for Land Governance, School of Governance, Indian Institute for Human Settlements, New Delhi. She has a master's degree in planning, with specialisation in regional planning, from the School of Planning and Architecture, New Delhi. She has been studying land records modernisation and e-governance initiatives in urban and peri-urban areas in different states/union territories of India. She has also worked on identifying best practices followed by different states in land records administration and any persistent gaps in the systems.

Seema Kulkarni is one of the founding members and currently Senior Fellow, Society for Promoting Participative Ecosystem Management (SOPPECOM), Pune. She coordinates gender and rural livelihoods activities within the organisation and has undertaken various research projects and programmes concerned with decentralisation, gender and land, water, and sanitation. Several articles/book chapters on these have been published. She is actively associated with the women's movement, is a member of the national-level network Mahila Kisan Adhikaar Manch (MAKAAM), Forum for Women Farmers' Rights, and anchors the network at the Maharashtra level. Her recent publication as co-editor is *Ecologies of Hope & Transformation: Post-Development Alternatives from India* (2018).

Chandra Bhushan Kumar is an Indian Administrative Service officer with more than 25 years of working in areas of public policy and governance. As a district administrator, he served in tribal-dominated areas of Arunachal Pradesh and Andaman and Nicobar Islands, wherein specific insights on administering scheduled areas were acquired. A mathematics and law graduate, he also has a master's degree in public policy from Syracuse University. He subsequently completed his PhD in human geography from Aberystwyth University, UK, wherein he examined the water governance issues of the megacity of Delhi.

Kaye Lushington is with the Legal and Regulation Team at Indian Institute for Human Settlements, New Delhi. She is a lawyer by training from ILS Law College, Pune, and has a master's degree in development studies from TISS, Mumbai. She has examined land record modernisation efforts in various states of India, with a focus on status of modernisation initiatives, extent of integration of survey, land records and registration functions in these states, changes in relevant legislation, and ease of property transactions. Her key area of interest is urban governance, higher education and its regulation, and intellectual property rights and their relevance and application in cultural knowledge production.

Shiju Mazhuvanchery is Professor, Christ Academy Institute of Law, Bangalore, India. A teacher for more than 18 years, his research interests include environmental law, constitutional law, and competition law. He was one of the rapporteurs for the High-Level Segment of the CoP 11 of the Convention on Biological Diversity held in Hyderabad in 2012. He is a member of the Green Growth and the Law Working Group of the Green Growth Knowledge Platform – a joint initiative of the Green Growth Institute, OECD, World Bank, and UNEP. He is also on the editorial board of the *Indian Journal of International Law* and is a regular contributor to the *Yearbook of International Environmental Law.*

Malabika Pal is Associate Professor of Economics at Miranda House, University of Delhi, India. She has worked as Associate Professor in Law and Legal Studies, School of Law, Governance and Citizenship, Ambedkar University, Delhi. Her research interests are in the fields of law and economics and international finance. She is a recipient of the National Scholarship and the Ford Foundation Scholarship. She has recently published Economic Analysis of Tort Law - The Negligence Determination, Routledge 2020.

Ray Sharat Prasad is a practising lawyer, associated with a reputed Delhi-based law firm, with a specialisation in real estate and the hospitality sector, and has advised several multinational and Indian companies for more than 15 years on Indian and cross-border transactions. He continues to contribute to urban development–related policy documents. He has assisted the Ministry of Housing and Urban Affairs (MoHUA), Government of India, in drafting the Real Estate (Regulation and Development) Bill, 2013, and has been a part of the stakeholders' consultation process on the 'single window approval system' organised by MoHUA in 2014.

Rita Sinha is an Indian Administration Service officer and has served for 37 years. She was the first secretary of the Department of Land Resources (DoLR), serving from January 2008 to July 2010, when she retired. She has been part of programmes initiated by the DoLR – NLRMP (National Land Records Modernization Programme) when conclusive land titling was conceptualised and the first two national titling acts were drafted; The Land Acquisition Act, 1894, was amended; and the R&R Bill, 2009, and The LA (Amendment) Bill, 2009, were presented to Parliament, both of which lapsed in February 2009. She was a member of Technical Advisory Group (TAG), for LGAF (Land Governance Assessment Framework) by the World Bank. She has sustained her interest in land-related issues and has contributed to a few academic journals.

Foreword

In rising and transforming India, there is growing albeit competing demand for land for high-value agriculture, infrastructure, housing, urbanisation and industrialisation. At the same time, the slow pace of updating and digitisation of land records, coupled with lack of conclusive land titles, insecurity of land tenure, and informal tenancy, continue to affect investment and economic growth. Hence, there is a felt need for appropriate land policies which will ensure efficient, equitable, and sustainable uses of land for accelerated, diversified, and inclusive economic growth in India. During the past five years or so, the Indian government as well as some state governments have undertaken several new land policy initiatives such as agricultural land leasing reform, real estate regulatory reform, and fast-track digitisation of land records which are likely to impact economic growth positively and significantly. But there are still huge implementation challenges with respect to all these initiatives. Besides, effective implementation and codification of customary land laws in the Northeast and other tribal areas, promotion of women's collective farming on the pattern of Kudumbashree in Kerala, improvement in land acquisition law, and proper regulatory frameworks for inclusive and sustainable uses of land would be essential. This volume edited by Varsha Bhagat-Ganguly and entitled *The Land Question in Neoliberal India* discusses some of these important aspects of land policy reforms which have far-reaching implications for accelerated, inclusive, and sustainable economic growth. I am sure the book will be of great value to social scientists, lawyers, policy makers, and others engaged in policy discourse on land issues.

Tajamul Haque
Ex-Chairman, Special Cell on Land Policy
NITI Aayog, Government of India

Acknowledgements

Among various land issues, land acquisition, land value, and revenue are known because of their relevance in the day-to-day lives of people in India. The problem of land acquisition entered into the public domain mainly because of the hue and cry by social activists regarding large-scale displacement and lack of rehabilitation and resettlement of the large number of displaced populations across India. Land as a property and permanent asset has made people aware about its various uses, mainly for housing, industrial purpose, and economic growth of the country. A very few scholars have been able to bring the land question (including land reforms, land governance, land records, land titling system, land acquisition, and land rights) comprehensively to the public domain and public knowledge.

I took almost 12 to 15 months to mobilise contributors from different disciplines – law practitioners, senior civil servants, academia, researchers, and social activists working on land issues. I thank all the contributors for readily agreeing to write. They have not only responded to my persistent editorial queries, but some of them also prepared papers within a short time span without compromising the quality of this volume. It is not easy to work on a subject that is multi-dimensional and to be inter-linked with newer themes of socio-legal and judicial interpretations while mapping changes in neoliberal India. I deeply appreciate their academic rigour, hard work, and patience and am grateful for their contribution for shaping the volume that makes a mark on the existing body of work on land issues in India. I also thank them for going through the draft introductory chapter and giving feedback for its improvement.

Special thanks go to the anonymous reviewer of the manuscript. Much credit goes to the reviewer for the content of this volume.

Dr Nupur Chowdhury is the first to be thanked, for she introduced me to many academics as potential contributors to the volume. I was able to discuss the volume with her in detail, and she responded very thoughtfully to each point of discussion.

I am grateful to Dr Tajamul Haque for writing the foreword to this volume based on his vast experience and deep knowledge of land issues and their close association with agrarian relations, and resource rights, and how socio-political and economic relations are altered with land struggles.

Abbreviations

AMRUT	Atal Mission for Rejuvenation and Urban Transformation
APCRDA	Andhra Pradesh Capital Region Development Authority
APCRDAA	Andhra Pradesh Capital Region Development Authority Act
APDR	Association for Protection of Democratic Rights
BAPL	Bengal Aerotropolis Project Limited
BDO	Block Development Officer
BJP	Bhartiya Janta Party
BRTS	Bus Rapid Transit System
CAFA	Compensatory Afforestation Fund Act
CAG	Comptroller and Auditor General
CBA	Cost-benefit analysis
CCI	Competition Commission of India
CLR	Computerisation of Land Records
COC	Committee of creditors
CPI (M)	Communist Party of India (Marxist)
CRZ	Coastal Regulation Zone
CSE	Centre for Science and Environment
DDA	Delhi Development Authority
DFO	District/Divisional Forest Officer
DILRMP	Digital India Land Record Modernisation Programme
DoLR	Department of Land Resources
EIA	Environmental Impact Assessment
EIC	East India Company
EPA	Environment (Protection) Act, 1986
EWS	Economically weaker sections
FAO	Food and Agriculture Organization
FAR	Floor Area Ratio
FCA	Forest Conservation Act, 1980
FDI	Foreign direct investment
FRA	Forest Rights Act/The Scheduled Tribes and Other Traditional Forest Dwellers (Recognition of Forest Rights) Act, 2006

FTL	Full Tank Level
GIFT	Gujarat International Finance Tec-City
GMC	General Motors Corporation
GNIDA	Greater Noida Industrial Development Authority
G.O.	Government Order
GOI	Government of India
HIG	High income group
HMWSSB	Hyderabad Metropolitan Water Supply and Sewerage Board
HRIDAY	Heritage City Development and Augmentation Yojana
IBC	Insolvency and Bankruptcy Code, 2016
IFA	Indian Forest Act, 1927
IIHS	Indian Institute for Human Settlements
IMEG	Independent Multi-disciplinary Expert Group
IMF	International Monetary Fund
INR	Indian rupee
IRA	Indian Registration Act, 1908
ISFR	India State Forestry Report
JFM	Joint Forest Management
JLG	Joint Liability Groups
JNNURM	Jawaharlal Nehru National Urban Renewal Mission
LA	Land acquisition
LAA	Land Acquisition Act, 1894
LARRA	Land Acquisition, Rehabilitation and Resettlement Authority
LFG	Left Front Government
LGAF	Land governance assessment framework
LPG	Liberalisation, privatisation, and globalisation
LPP	Land pooling policy
LPS	Land pooling scheme
LWE	Left wing extremism
MALLA	Model Agricultural Land Leasing Act, 2016
MMRDA	Mines and Mineral Regulation and Development Act
MoEF	Ministry of Environment and Forest
MoEFCC	Ministry of Environment, Forest, and Climate Change
MoHUA	Ministry of Housing and Urban Affairs
MoRD	Ministry of Rural Development
MoRTH	Ministry of Road, Transport and Highways
MoTA	Ministry of Tribal Affairs
MPD	Master Plan for Delhi
MPEB	Madhya Pradesh Electricity Board
MRTS	Mass Rapid Transit System
MTALA	Maharashtra Tenancy and Agricultural Lands Act, 1948
NCLT	National Company Laws Tribunal
NCMP	National Common Minimum Programme
NCRB	National Crime Records Bureau

NDA	National Democratic Alliance
NEC	Northeastern Council
NEFA	North East Frontier Administration
NER	Northeastern region
NGT	National Green Tribunal
NIC	National Informatics Centre
NLRMP	National Land Record Modernisation Programme
NLUP	New Land Use Policy
NMDC	National Mineral Development Corporation
NOC	No Objection Certificate
NREGS	National Rural Employment Guarantee Scheme
NSSO	National Sample Survey Organisation
NT	Nomadic Tribes
NTFP	Non-Timber forest products
NTPC	National Thermal Power Corporation
NLUP	New Land Use Policy
OBC	Other Backward Classes
PESA	Panchayats (Extension to the Scheduled Areas) Act, 1996
PIL	Public Interest Litigation
PLFS	Periodic Labour Force Survey
PPP	Public-private partnership
PSP	Public/semi-public facilities
PSU	Public Sector Undertakings
PVTG	Particularly Vulnerable Tribal Groups
RBI	Reserve Bank of India
REIT	Real Estate Investment Trust
RFCTLARR	Right to Fair Compensation and Transparency in Rehabilitation & Resettlement
RFCTLARRA	Right to Fair Compensation and Transparency in Rehabilitation & Resettlement Act, 2013
RoI	Returns on investments
R&R	Rehabilitation and resettlement
ROR	Records of Rights
SA	Schedules areas
SC	Scheduled Castes
SCM	Smart City Mission
SEBI	Securities and Exchange Board of India
SECC	Socio-Economic Caste Census
SERPP	Society for Elimination of Rural Poverty Programme
SEZ	Special Economic zone
SFR	State Forestry Report
SIA	Social impact assessment
SIMP	Social Impact Management Plan
SKJRC	Singur Krishi Jomi Raksha Committee/Committee to Save the Farmland of Singur

SPV	Special purpose vehicle
sq. mts.	Square metres
sq. yds.	Square yards
SRA&ULR	Strengthening of Revenue Administration and Updating of Land Records
SUCI	Socialist Unity Centre of India (communist party)
TDR	Transferable development rights or tradable development rights
TMC	Trinmul Congress
TML	Tata Motors Ltd.
TOD	Transit-oriented development
TWAIL	Third World Approaches to International Law
ULB	Urban local body
UNECE	United Nations Economic Commission for Europe
UNESCO	United Nations Educational, Scientific, and Cultural Organisation
UPA	United Progressive Alliance
UPOR	Urban Property Ownership Record
USF	Unclassed State Forests
UT	Union Territory
WPA	The Wildlife (Protection) Act, 1972
ZDP	Zonal development plan

Glossary

Abadi Deh (states of Haryana, Punjab) / Lal-dora area Inhabited Site of Village. Abadi deh is also known as lal-dora area.

Bargadar Land tenant, sharecropper

Conclusive titling A title system which confers absolute title, not open to challenge

Deed Any document sealing an agreement, contract, etc. A sale deed is a document evidencing a particular sale-purchase agreement. A title deed is a document which gives the holder the title to property.

Deed-based register Public repository where documents for providing evidence of land transactions are lodged, numbered, dated, indexed, and archived.

Devasthan land A village, portion of a village, or *land* held under a *devasthan inam* given for cultivation in exchange for service that a person provides during an annual religious procession.

Encroached gairan/grazing lands Grazing land or community land is a part of the common property resource of a village. The major purpose of grazing lands is to ensure common land for grazing of the cattle of the village. As a part of the movement by dalits to get land rights, the dalits in Marathawada even today continue to possess grazing lands and cultivate them for their personal use.

Encumbrance A burden on a property, generally one that affects the ability to transfer title, or one which affects the condition of the property. Examples are liens, mortgages, taxes, easements, water rights, etc.

Hadki Hadvala Collective *inam* land given to Mahars

Inam land (state of Gujarat) Land which was given away as a grant, typically free of rent and held hereditarily in perpetuity. Different categories exist within *inam* lands, depending on the purpose/type of grant and the prevalent revenue system.

Jamabandi (states of Punjab, Haryana) Record of Right (RoR); land record maintained by Revenue Department

Khas Mahal Land (states of Bihar, West Bengal) A category of government land which is leased out to individuals for various purposes and is non-transferable

Khazan land   Reclaimed wetlands, salt marshes, and mangrove areas, where tidal influence is regulated by the construction of embankments and sluice gates

Land acquisition   Acquisition of land by the government for public purpose, under eminent domain.

Land reforms   Umbrella term for tenancy reforms, including 'land to the tiller', land ceiling regulations, and zamindari abolition

Mouza   Administrative block

Mutation   Process of legally changing a parcel's owner in the Record of Rights. It can occur after sale-purchase, inheritance, gift, partition etc. Mutation typically follows registration.

Patwari   A village accountant or registrar

Poramboke land (state of Tamil Nadu)   Land which is not assessed in revenue records. Originally, these were uncultivable lands (hence outside revenue accounts) which were set aside for public use. It has now typically come to mean government land in villages.

Presumptive titling   A title system in which one is presumed to be the owner, unless proven otherwise

Rayat/ryot   Landowners

Record of Right (ROR)   Land record in which various rights and liabilities in respect of every piece of land are noted

Registration (deed based)   Recording a transaction deed for land or property between buyer and seller; buyer and seller get a registered sale deed; State gets stamp duty.

Shajra-nasb (states of Haryana, Himachal Pradesh, Punjab)   Genealogy tree of each land-owning family in a village

Shamilat Deh (state of Haryana)   Part of village outside abadi deh, which is considered as jointly owned by the village community. Public facilities, including grazing land, etc. are often located in Shamilat Deh.

Survey/Resurvey (state of Gujarat)   Operations conducted towards settlement, or recording and preservation of connected rights. A 'resurvey' is used when an area has existing records, and these are being updated.

Title-based Register   The Title Register serves as the primary evidence of ownership, within a title-based registration system.

Wajib-ul-arj (state of Himachal Pradesh)   Part of the Record of Rights, which documents the rights and liabilities of various parties, based on local customs. It includes customary rights on common lands, including grazing rights, as recorded during settlement operation.

1 Introduction

Varsha Bhagat-Ganguly

This volume expands the discourse on three important aspects of land in India: 'land question', 'neoliberal India', and 'socio-legal and judicial interpretations'. Regarding the 'land question',[1] instead of using land issues as a generalised term or land regime which is implicitly expressing the State's supremacy, it proposes an overarching term to make 'land' more cohesive and comprehensive. The 'land question' incorporates 'land' as a property; as a resource; as a medium to sustainable development – environmentalism, conservation, protection, rejuvenation, and afforestation; and how people relate to 'land' – as wealth, social status, power, socio-cultural identity, and land rights and land use. The land question also incorporates its multi-dimensional and systemic associations, such as land record, land titling, land governance, land acquisition, land markets and land economics, land rights, land use and closely linked to the agrarian question, and so on.

Neoliberal India has dealt with the 'land question' in varied ways, and these find different expressions and variations from different segments. Several government departments as well as actors within the Planning Commission (NITI Aayog 2014 onwards), industry and trade bodies, national and state legislatures, civil society organisations, political parties, and political groupings press their opinions and agendas on land legislation (Sud 2012: 84). Two broad sets of views exist with regard to the liberalisation of land – (1) proponents of using land as a resource for economic growth versus (2) land as an asset and valuing associated non-monetised concerns. This volume captures shifts and trends in the thinking and doings of the Indian government post-1991 (neoliberal India) on the land question (popularly known as introducing the structural adjustment programme [SAP]/New Economic Policy [NEP]) and how Indian citizens and others have responded to shifts in land policies and laws. 'Neoliberal' India refers to pluralistic dimensions and three intertwined manifestations of neoliberalism: an ideology, a mode of governance, and a policy package (Steger and Roy 2010: xi). In India, it is believed that 'neoliberalism' has set its roots as an economic ideology[2] with connotations of a market-friendly political agenda (free-market, foreign investment, worldwide flow of goods, etc.), facilitating a 'paradigm'[3] and decision making provided by the ruling political parties since the late 1990s; and changes in policy regime that are endorsed by elites.

The attempt to understand social, legal, and judicial interpretations of 'land' is multi-dimensional. 'Social' broadly refers to a collage of opinions, responses, and actions by a variety of actors and organisations on 'land'. The volume explores whether the social, legal, and judicial interpretations are inter-linked and have circularity, that is, one directly affecting the other, and if they do so, which are the visible forms; or though they are not clearly inter-linked, whether they are influential with regard to one another. For example, protests against land acquisition led to enaction of a new law, RFCTLARRA, 2013 (*Right to Fair Compensation and Transparency in Rehabilitation and Resettlement Act*). Nielsen and Nilsen (2014) mention that such a 'right based agenda' as a hegemonic process shows how law making is a complex and contradictory practice seeking to negotiate a compromise equilibrium between subaltern groups vulnerable to marginalisation and capable of mobilisation, and dominant groups whose economic interests are linked to spaces of accumulation through market-oriented reforms. The judicial interpretation regarding land acquisition, principle of eminent domain (ED), and public purpose vary case to case – in some cases approving land acquisition by the State following the principle of ED, while in other cases granting supreme importance of land management by Adivasis through local governance institutions, that is, Gram Sabha. Chowdhury (2014) calls such range of variations in judicial interpretations 'judicial activism to judicial adventurism'. This volume maps out changes, challenges, opportunities, and manifestations in the social, legal, and judicial domains that signify neoliberal India, which is distinctly different from the political economy approach to 'land' issues.

Debates over land as property – origin and continuity

India chose the Constitution as a path to democracy and development; every elected ruling party was expected to be bound by the provision of the Constitution. The Right to Property was enshrined as a fundamental right in the Indian Constitution in 1951, which was in tune with the Universal Declaration of Human Rights, 1948. However, it seems that the Constituent Assembly[4] did not envision the country as socialist, unlike communist-socialist countries where all property belongs to the State (Sathe 2017: 20). With the first amendment to the Indian Constitution, that is, insertion of Article 31-A and 31-B, it was considered the beginning of a tussle between the Judiciary and the Legislative, induced by the Parliament echoing the then social ethos and sentiments. The Parliament defined 'Estate', which was expanded by further Constitutional amendments, which covered 'entire agricultural land in the rural areas', including waste lands, forest lands, and lands for pasture or sites of buildings. Introducing Schedule Nine[5] and Article 31-B[6] through subsequent amendments was another attempt to usurp judicial power, which is interpreted as 'autocratic power was sustained by democratic processes' (Salian 2002: 234). Land entered the concurrent list of the Indian Constitution: the laws, administrative procedures, and institutional mechanism for land governance and land use remained state-subject, and thus dealings with the land question vary across the states in India. The higher Judiciary was made the arbitrator to maintain the just balance between private rights and public interests.

The tussle between the Judiciary and the Legislative is also visible with the 44th Constitutional amendment in 1978 which shifted status of the Right to Property to Constitutional Right, with effect from 1979, wherein the Right to Property accepted doctrine of individual right to property; conversely, a denial of common land and communal holding of land (Salian 2002: 233; Sathe 2017: 21). Consequently, the property loser could approach the High Court and not Supreme Court in case of a conflict. This is one of the reasons for huge variation in judicial interpretations regarding land acquisition and public purpose; 'public purpose' is not yet defined in a way which is accepted to all. Simultaneously, with respect to land – land acquisition for public purpose from a person cultivating land – the government needs to pay compensation at market value (Sathe 2017: 21). This amendment also reveals a conflict between the Fundamental Rights and the Directive Principles (which asks the State to promote economic equality – abolition of *Zamindari*) (Sathe 2017: 22) regarding land as property. Redistribution of land became a seed for a gamut of land reform measures, including law making, tenancy reforms, evolving land administrative structures/machinery, and introducing government programmes for poverty alleviation and social justice.

The said Right to Property as a fundamental right was not absolute, as though the State could take the property for public purpose; it was subject to the law of reasonable restrictions in the interest of the general public, that is, after compensation was paid. Such amendments by parliamentarians are seen as reflections of social aspirations. Mitra (2017: 36) describes that property rights were driven by mixed feelings and ideological stances in the first 30 years of independence – distributive justice as well as populism, which eventually led to abuse of land acquisition laws. When land acquisition started occurring at unprecedented levels post-1991,[7] several protests took place in different corners of India. This phase showed stalling of land redistribution or land reforms, changes in land use, booming of land markets, efforts for digitisation of land records, and conclusive titling; negligible changes in land governance and procedures were made. Such inter-linkages between social sentiments and actions against land acquisition; the role of the Judiciary as main arbitrator and reviewer of Constitutional amendments; the administrative machinery selectively following and enforcing the rule of law, by the Legislative or Judiciary; and actions by the Legislative to deal with the land question are explored in this volume.

Resistance of land dependents against land acquisition, withdrawal or continuation of development projects in response by the Executive – with or without judicial intervention – enaction of a new set of laws echoing public demands and aspirations, such as the *Forest Rights Act*[8] (FRA) for recognition of forest rights of forest dwellers) while sometime evading public policy (*Forest Conservation Act, 1980*; *Special Economic Zone, 2005*; *Compensatory Afforestation Fund Act* (CAFA), *2016*)[9] reveal different patterns of criss-cross and conflicts between the (Indian) Society, the Legislative, the Executive, and the Judiciary in neoliberal India. Judicial interpretations seem to follow mandates of the State/present development paradigm sometimes and issue orders that contradict the spirit of the law and overlook the Executive's wrongdoings. For example, the interim order on 13 February 2019 regarding FRA calls for evicting hundreds of thousands of forest dwellers whose claims have been rejected by the authorities. In the cases of Niyamgiri – mining project of Vedanta[10] and Singur[11] – land acquired in Singur for the Tata Motors Factory, the Supreme Court reinstated the importance of democratic institutions and processes – the importance of *Gram Sabha* (village assembly) and the return of 1,000 acres of agricultural land to ensure the livelihood of small and marginal farmers were established, respectively. Such judgments echoed social voices and concerns.

Unfolding the land question in India

The 'land' has several connotations – land as a resource is closely linked to a factor of production (labour, capital, and economic enterprise) and leads to disputes and conflicts. The 'land' as territory refers to both, relations and ownership – whether land exclusively belongs to the government or belongs to citizens and how do they relate with land. Land as property has multiple dimensions – ownership at an individual level, communal level, and state level. At the individual level, the ownership of land could be through two routes – earned and through succession. Individual ownership of land through succession is largely addressed by personal laws while the State deals with it through a mix of laws and procedures related to registration and stamp duty for earned property. As property, it is directly linked to land acquisition and land market (emotional value, real estate value, and compensation). Land has been closely associated with its use (for agriculture, housing, and productive asset), its value and land market, and its acquisition. Ownership of land in India has been presumptive in nature; thus, the land record and titling are stressed upon, as they are the main evidences of landownership and could also be used in the courts during litigation. Land as a productive asset played a significant role in an agriculture-based economy (capital and labour, government earning land-based revenue), which led to land reforms through various laws and administrative measures (land redistribution, introduction of a ceiling on extent of landownership, tenancy, and tenurial rights/land to the tiller). Those who do not own land, but whose livelihood and identity are associated with land, are demanding ownership or rights to land (access, use, management) (Bhagat-Ganguly 2016).

When Adivasis[12] are losing their lands, the issue of land alienation (Centre for Equity Studies 2016) under development discourse occupies important space. Land as resource and resource rights,[13] land grabs, and need for land pooling are newly enunciated issues.

Many researchers believe that hundreds of land laws create confusion and conflicts because of contrasting provisions. Various departments – rural development, commerce, agriculture, forests, fisheries, ports, revenue, etc., administer matters of land. Until the 1980s, land was a very important component for revenue generation for the government; tax and revenue collection were ensured through classification of land (cultivable, waste, fallow, shallow, marshal, etc.) and under which region it is – scheduled areas, national security areas, or any other. These aspects are largely taken care of by the land governance or administration system. The construct 'land question' aims to discuss all the aforementioned issues/ dimensions together, which are closely associated with one another; some are dealt with through a bundle of laws, while some are guided by administrative procedures.

In traditional parlance, land administration or governance (of late called 'land management') was considered to be the important system to deal with different dimensions of land, such as land record system, land title system, land-based revenue earning, and compensation value against land acquisition by the State, following legal and procedural mandates. The term 'land administration' was coined in 1993 by the United Nations Economic Commission for Europe (UNECE) in its Land Administration Guidelines. In 1996, a UNECE document mentions that a land administration system should ideally: guarantee ownership and secure tenure; support the land and property tax system; constitute security for credit systems; develop and monitor land markets; protect state lands; reduce land disputes; facilitate land reform; improve urban planning and infrastructure development; support land management based on consideration for the environment; and produce statistical data.[14] Land records encompass different types of land, survey and settlement process, records of rights (RoRs), customary rights, tenancy arrangements and tenurial rights, conversion of land, change in land use, and spatial data.

The World Bank felt the need to develop a land governance assessment framework (LGAF) as a diagnostic instrument in the early 2010s in India. The manual of LGAF (The World Bank 2013: 6) describes the need for a systematic assessment of land governance arising from three factors: (1) sustainable growth and poverty reduction; (2) better coordination among land governance institutions, leading to a reduction in the gap between legal provisions and their actual implementation; and (3) dealing with the technical complexity and context specificity of land issues and the consequent change which may be resisted by powerful stakeholders benefiting from the status quo through a participatory and deliberative process.

The manual further elaborates that the LGAF allows identifying key areas of good governance practices, such as:

> (i)   how property rights to land (at group or individual level) are defined, can be exchanged, and transformed; (ii) how public oversight over land use, management, and taxation is exercised; (iii) how the extent of land owned by the state is defined, how the state exercises it, and how state land is acquired or disposed of; (iv) the management of land information and ways in which it can be accessed; (v) avenues to resolve and manage disputes and hold officials to account; and (vi) procedures to deal with land-related investment.
>
> (The World Bank 2013: 6)

The LGAF and the land question apparently have almost a similar set of contexts and concerns in neoliberal India, such as land property rights, need for updated and efficient land records system and conclusive land titling system, strategy for meeting demands of land – coming from industrial units and private enterprises as well as demands for land reforms and hue and cry against large-scale land acquisition. However, 'land' being an asset for landowners, and 'estate' or 'property' as a resource for the State have evolved several contours of meanings, which are not a concern of the LGAF. Thus, poverty alleviation and institutional mechanisms are stressed upon (neoliberal features) but not the agenda of land redistribution, changes in land use, concerns of land dependents, and just land markets that the 'land question' aims to address.

Earlier land records were used for revenue purposes;[15] these increasingly have given way to three needs: availability of modernisation of land records (computerisation and digitisation); adoption of a conclusive land titling system; and modes and scale of land acquisition in neoliberal India. The land record system is a state-specific mechanism, while the land acquisition is a concurrent responsibility – the union and states in India. Not many states have been able to update land records based on the survey and settlement process because of many technological reasons. With increasing demands for land and consequent land acquisition, availability of land and identification of landownership become difficult with outdated land records. Moreover, a conclusive land titling system with outdated land records and redistribution of land under land reforms are not possible as they go against increasing demand for land for private entities, broadly for industrial development and urbanisation. Thus, the land question is larger than the land administration system, LGAF, and land acquisition–related issues, as the term gives equal weight to social and legislative ideas and expressions.

The land question and neoliberal India

The decade of the 2010s has witnessed several collective actions or uprisings in different parts of the country, raising issues of 'land' by a variety of communities, such as farmers, forest dwellers, and pastoral communities, for recognition of rights and for state support, communities like Jat and Patel, asking for reservations in government jobs (implying/enunciating a need for access to equitable livelihood opportunities) and educational institutions. These actions across India signify economic and socio-political dynamics revolving around land – some landed communities do not wish to have their land acquired, some wish to make land more productive and sustainable, while those who are already alienated from the land ask for government jobs.

The land question, linked to land governance and land acquisition,[16] is at the heart of different collective actions or upsurges in independent India which have addressed different land issues. For example, Tebhaga and Telangana during the late 1940s advanced the agenda of tenancy reforms, and the Naxalbari uprising in the late 1960s put forward an agenda of land reforms and cultivation rights of peasants and landless people. The Nandigram and Singur protests in 2007 onwards fought against coercive land acquisition by the state government for industrial purposes, and later land conflicts in Chhattisgarh and Jharkhand signify struggle against land grab, land acquisition, and change of land use (forest land) for mining purposes.

The land question thus symbolises the nature of association with land – agrarian relations, shift in economy – agrarian to industrial, as space and urban/regional planning, change in perspective about land use as a resource for economy, that is, from land as social identity to commodity, and perspective towards development of the country, which tilts towards economic growth rather than equitable and sustainable development. When the collective actions or uprisings are recognised as attempts to alter socio-political and economic relations, the land question acquires a much wider landscape, a landscape that captures multiple dimensions through different voices (social actors and organisations) on dynamics of social and developmental processes, legal regime and regulations, judicial interpretations, and role of diverse institutions engaged in planning and implementation of land policies in neoliberal India.

In the discourse on the land question in neoliberal India, how people relate with 'land', how the Legislative turns into political agenda, how the Judiciary arbitrates, role/s of the State, and how the existing land governance system responds – these issues occupy centre stage. This volume explores Chatterjee's (2008: 56) idea of passive revolution:

> The characteristic features of the passive revolution in India were the relative autonomy of the state as a whole from the bourgeoisie and the landed elites; the supervision of the state by an elected political leadership; a permanent bureaucracy and an independent judiciary; the negotiation of class interests through a multi-party electoral system; a protectionist regime discouraging the entry of foreign capital and promoting import substitution; the leading role of the state sector in heavy industry, infrastructure, . . . relatively greater influence of industrial

capitalists over the central government and that of the landed elites on the state governments.

In this context, it is necessary to understand that how people have related to and whether having knowledge of or have expressed concept, approach, strategy, mandates, functioning and implementation and monitoring mechanism of the existing land governance system, and solutions to newer problems of 'land'. This is an attempt to understand how 'civil society' and 'political society' (Chatterjee 2008) interact with each other for different aspects of 'land'.

Neoliberalism as an ideology, governance, and policy

To expand the discourse on the land question and neoliberalism as an ideology, governance, and policy, a few trends/illustrations are shared here based on the 'new sociology of governance' – who organises the core ideas and strategies; how the core ideas and strategies get organised into fairly simple truth-claims that encourage people to act in certain ways; how and by whom the ideas are operationalised; and which are the agencies (including the State) that further the ideology supported through governance; and role of elites in furthering the ideas/dictating political objectives.

Rose (1999: 16) looks at governance in the liberalised era and describes its characteristics – a useful substitute and analogue for regulation, administration, management, and the like. Governance is normative as well as descriptive – it could be good[17] or bad. He refers to the 'new sociology of governance' that tries to characterise the pattern or structure that emerges from the interaction of a range of political actors. Referring to strategies, good governance implies to disperse power relations among the whole complex of public service, judicial system, and independent auditors of public finances, coupled with respect for the law, human rights, pluralism, and a free press. The 'governmentality':[18]

> Sees continual attempts to define and redefine which aspects of government are within the concept of the State and which are not, what is and what is not political, what is and what is not public, private and so forth.
>
> (*op. cit.*)

The elites are believed to be codifiers and advocates of neoliberal governmentality, which is rooted in entrepreneurial values such as competitiveness, self-interest, and decentralisation. It celebrates individual empowerment and the devolution of central state power to smaller, localised units (Steger and Roy 2010: 12; Das 2015). In this way of functioning, the State pursues profits in the name of developmentalism (or politics of developmentalism) rather than traditional lines of pursuing the public good by enhancing civil society and social justice. Most bureaucrats choose to develop entrepreneurial identities – where they see themselves as self-interested actors responsible to the market and contributing to the monetary success of slimmed-down state 'enterprises' (ibid.); a very few consider themselves as public servants and guardians of a qualitatively defined 'public good'. This behaviour of public servants is mostly hailed by elites, including political leaders, in the name of developmentalism. Regarding land, capital/finance from the market in the name of public-private-partnership (PPP) is stressed upon as a main strategy. They promote employment of technology as a solution to existing problems, which are taken from the world of business and commerce, and set quantitative targets and outcomes as indicators of efficiency. This model mostly leads to shrinking space of political governance (popularly phrased as 'best-practice governance'), the introduction of 'rational choice' models that internalise and thus normalise market-oriented behaviour. Thus, a shift – citizen turning into an 'idealised consumer' vis-à-vis the land question, especially how one related to land and its use, reveals that use of technology and service delivery–related solutions are promoted by the Executive. The NLRMP (National Land Record Modernisation Programme), launched in 2008, and introducing the Land Titling Bill, 2008, and Land Titling Bill, 2011, in the parliament are good examples of this paradigm. In this initiative, land records are reduced to the purely economic and transactional – providing services such as availability of land records online, mutation entries done digitally, etc. The entire process of digitising land records ignores socio-historical aspects, and the longstanding problem of wide gaps among textual, spatial, and actual land records. Citizens as consumers are happy with the service delivery through technology, which itself is indicative of selective elites availing benefits; not every citizen has access to the internet nor has adequate knowledge and skills for using such digital technology.

The Legislative studies examples of other countries and plans to execute them in India, but this largely turns out to be a crude attempt to define and introduce 'corporate governance' (Bijoy 2008) since PPP (public-private partnership) is given utmost importance. Enacting and creation of SEZs (special economic zones) is one of the prime examples of a neoliberal agenda, that is, urged for improved infrastructure, establishing industrial and commercial units/facilities, and belief that would generate jobs and growth of allied industries/businesses. The Indian government enacted a law – *Special Economic Zone, 2005* – and aimed to create 500 SEZs for exports and attracting forest investment, under a broader agenda of economic growth. As per the report of the Department of Commerce, Government of India (2015), approximately 491 SEZs have been formally approved, notified SEZs are 352, in-principle approvals are 33, and operation SEZs are 196, with 3,864 approved units in India covering 51,055.73 hectares of land. 'The total area (including IP approvals) covered by SEZs is 0.058 percent of total land area and 0.317 percent of agricultural land' (Parwaz 2016:

139). The recent announcement to revamp SEZs to house a wide range of companies (Suneja 26 May 2019) is an indicator of determinedly boosting entrepreneurial identity.

Chakravorty (2016: 54) talks about 'taking state' and 'giving state' in the context of land. The 'giving state' redistributed under land reforms measures; the prime objective of 'taking state' was to enhance public welfare through various development projects. The problem was that the population that benefitted from the development project was fundamentally different from the population that was displaced. As land prices increase with better infrastructure and development, peculiar consumerism is encouraged through the process of urbanism and selected spatial development. The Legislative and the Judiciary seem to associate themselves with such developmentalism, which is reflected in their attitude and behaviour, in the form of increased efficiency of land markets, evolving regularising norms, and improving land administration (*The Draft Model Guidelines for Urban Land Policy 2007:* 2). The Indian government focused on urban development – as a machine for economic growth of the country – and initiated various measures for expansion of the land market: launching of a land-pooling policy/voluntary land-pooling scheme as an alternative to forced land acquisition, and reclassification of zones and land use wherein the State's role as a facilitator for private entities became obvious. Such initiatives by the State are a mix – they are service delivery as well as containing 'rights'[19] component (Bhagat-Ganguly 2016: 38–39).

The New Economic Policy (NEP) has been a front-runner in changing the policy regime[20] on many counts, especially liberalisation of land. Unfolding policy regime is also unfolding of politics of developmentalism (Solomon 2008) and, when land is seen as a 'conceptual entry', it helps reveal a subtle, often stealth-like and quiet but extensive form of political consciousness[21] and viewed from the lenses of social identity, status, and wealth, reveals extensive forms of socio-political consciousness and how this consciousness influences policy regime (Bhagat-Ganguly 2016).

The reviews of three policy documents – Five Year Plans (pre- and post-1990); Draft Urban Land Policy, 2007; and Draft National Land Reforms Policy, 2013[22] – reveal three important points related to developmentalism in neoliberal India: (1) the gap between what policies aimed at and what are anticipated and unanticipated outcomes, especially in the context of controlling land values/markets and 'housing for all' – overtly for economically weaker sections, and covertly for clearing of slums, supporting real estate, land markets, and fulfilling aspirations of urban elites; (2) land rights of different stakeholders in urban areas; mainly how and why four groups – metro elite, land developers, retailers of 'branded' products, and international donors (Solomon 2008: 720) – have become influential in making the cities competitive on land use; and (3) understanding political economy of land policy, that is, how the given policy and government programmes/ schemes bring in private players in order to attract investment and how the language of development is being appropriated to facilitate private entities. Mostly the citizenry knows very little about land use, how valuation is done, the impact of land pooling, whether these programmes have legal backing and thus are not legally binding to the government or the landholders/land aspirants, and whether budget allocations are justified when cost-benefit ratio analysis is undertaken.

Tenancy reforms/tenurial rights are recognised as an important policy-making area associated with the land question, which is treated independently from land reforms[23] in the neoliberal era. Since the 1950s, land redistribution across all states in India is skewed in favour of influencing people;[24] now land use, records of rights (RoRs), and land titling are crucial for economic growth. Until now, tenancy is not legalised in most of the states in India; West Bengal with *bargadar* (land tenant, share cropper) system is one of the exceptions. The Model Agricultural Land Leasing Act, 2016 (MALLA) has not seen the light of day. Absence of a sound institutional framework facilitating land leasing had been viewed as a major obstacle for private investment in agriculture, resulting in poor productivity in the neoliberal era; insecure land tenurial rights that resulted in tenants becoming subject to multiple forms of exploitation by money lenders, landowners, and traders of agricultural commodities is considered less important.[25] Although tenancy laws differed from state to state, they were generally found to be very restrictive in the sense that they had almost prohibited agricultural tenancy. The tenancy arrangements are primarily informal in nature, leaving tenants insecure (Mani 2016). A recent trend of reverse tenancy, which refers to small landholders leasing their land to big landholders, also is an important issue of land policy in the context of social structure, political economy, and agriculture and allied activities increasingly becoming loss-making ventures, especially for small and marginal landholders. Therefore, small and marginal landholders are forced to lease-in land to make up for the loss in the crop production sector. Large numbers of small and marginal landholders belong to Scheduled Castes[26] (SCs) and Scheduled Tribes (STs).[27] One of the schools of thought on tenancy argues that forced tenancy of wage labour and peasants is a variant of 'hunger leasing',[28] and such tenants are subjected to multiple forms of exploitation by money lenders, landowners, and traders of agricultural commodities (Mohanakumar 2014); newer culture is emerging in the relations between these stakeholders. The Model Agricultural Land Leasing Act, 2016 (MALLA) is silent on reverse tenancy and secured tenancy rights of land dependents[29] through legalised leasing, and continues to be an abandoned group in policy making.

Organisation of the volume

The volume is organised on two themes: (1) socio-legal and policy perspective on 'land', and legal initiatives (programmatic and regulatory mechanism); and (2) evolving jurisprudence on the land question. Through these themes, the volume expands discourse on the land question, focusing on socio-legal and judicial interpretations – what happened in neoliberal India? How did neoliberal India pose herself vis-à-vis other continents/countries[30] related to the land question – whether the Indian government learnt and adopted some global best practices regarding land governance, land records, and land titling, to name a few, or found indigenous technology-based, all-encompassing/holistic solutions to the chronic and inherently complex problems of the multi-faceted land question? What has happened as the role, behaviour, and attitude of the State changed – from a welfare state ensuring the larger common good to facilitating private entities and market forces? How the citizenry – a mix of consumers and proponents of right to land – have received and responded to different land policies shaped with neoliberal ideology? Does this imply a higher degree of conflict, dispossession, and violence? Whether newer institutional mechanisms, procedural and legal modifications, newer solutions based on technological advancement, and evolution of polity have been tried out, to ensure the larger common good? Whether the character of the Judiciary changed or remained the same or shifted to judicial activism to judicial adventurism is strengthened. Could the State and the Judiciary take cognisance of how the land question and rights to land are being articulated from gender, class, caste, and regional perspectives, and from the perspective of marginalisation/deprivation, and how did they respond to the concerns, demands and aspirations of these cross-cutting, inter-twined perspectives while ensuring development of the country?

Socio-legal perspectives on 'land' and legal initiatives

> There has always been a debate whether land in India was collectively owned by the community or whether individual ownership was the most common form of landed property. The Indian peasant has for centuries enjoyed the right of permanent and hereditary occupancy of land. This was assured by the State and recognised by the superior landlords. . . . Apparently, *owning* land was possibly not in itself a very meaningful thing. Having a right or claim on a share of its produce was the crucial issue. Land came with a hierarchy and range of rights and obligations. It was a time when the central question revolved around rights *on* land rather than rights *to* land. In this respect, therefore, the debate today seems to have altered irretrievably.
>
> (Singh 2016: xiv)

This theme narrates the politics of land and rights to land in neoliberal India from the lenses of landholders and land dependents on an individual basis and from different social group/communities for public/government land. The land question with different components creates multiple axes on which debates on land laws (broadly legal regime and reforms); justiciability of laws of social control; the skill set or know-how of technicality of law; process of policy or law making and interests of the State and elites; developmentalism and politics of developmentalism; technology and technocracy adopted by the Legislative, the Executive, and the Judiciary; how access to information ensures rights to land; and some similar concerns are expanding.

Several instances of people's protests against development projects followed by legal cases in the High Courts and the Supreme Court substantiate the point in case. Indian government started using land as a resource and by expanding land markets, especially in the regime of property rights – private landownership. Private property is an essential concept in market-driven (Gangopadhyaya 2012), rule of law economics; land value depends on who buys/acquires the land or who grabs and appropriates land.[31] In this rule of land economics, small-landholder, socio-economically backward, single women and such vulnerable groups/communities face a dual-edged sword. These groups may get a better price for the land compared with the compensation offered by the government, mostly against loss of their asset and traditional source of livelihood. They compare returns from agricultural activity and may find selling of land comparatively lucrative and an opportunity to explore a new livelihood activity. The private entity that receives land from the government or buys the land, in most cases, retains its advantageous status, as the land economics work in its favour – with asset building that is productive, infrastructure facilities, long-term business opportunities, and tax revenue–related other benefits. This is applicable to SEZs, establishment of industrial estates, and infrastructure building or other development projects, to name a few; on the other hand, economics-oriented cost-benefit analysis undermines socio-cultural,[32] vulnerability,[33] and relative deprivation[34] framework in a neoliberal regime.

Five chapters are presented under this theme, covering different types of land issues (of urban areas, forest land, and cultivable land), in different parts of India.

Chapter 2 by Amlanjyoti Goswami, Deepika Jha, and Kaye Lushington[35] examines some of the key policy and legal developments in India on establishing conclusive land tilting legislation, at the central and state levels, within the scope of India's Constitutional Federalism. It explains that implementing a Torrens-like system of land records in the country requires a shift in the Common Law system, from presumptive deeds-based systems to conclusive title-based regimes. Therefore, practical realities of land record systems and institutions need to be mapped out. As against neoliberal impulse – to reduce land records to the purely economic and transactional, and the focus on titling and ownership, excluding tenure aspects – the chapter discusses alternatives. The chapter examines whether meaningful incremental efforts to set up more comprehensive and accurate land records systems and processes would be better than the present top-down measures of title legislation.

Ray Sharat Prasad, a practicing lawyer, begins Chapter 3 with a shift in the governance model in neoliberal India. The State expects to achieve the twin objectives of sustainable economic growth and fulfilment of the socio-economic aspirations of all such actors, including those of the urban poor, through the trickle-down effect. The chapter looks at various interventions and initiatives taken by the State and examines whether they have had the desired trickle-down effect and fulfilment of the socio-economic aspirations of all, in the complete absence of the State's redistributive role, or whether achieving the objectives will remain a myth.

In Chapter 4, C.R. Bijoy, through a combination of academic and social action, explores how *Forest Rights Act, 2006* (FRA) has provided an opportunity for the right to forest resources through evolving forest governance. After providing historical background of forest governance to enactment of the FRA[36], the chapter narrates how this law pertinently pioneered the introduction of a non-centralised democratic land and natural resource governance, by the transfer of power directly to the communities at the level of habitation, perhaps an unprecedented model never attempted anywhere in the world. Yet, while implementing this law, the administrative arms continue to resist through blatant acts of commissions and omissions over a decade. The chapter captures lessons drawn for the emergence of another paradigm of land and resource governance as if people matter.

Chapter 5 by Seema Kulkarni and Pallavi Harshe studies the main features of the *Model Land Lease Act, 2016*, a solution proposed by the NITI Aayog, aiming to prohibit the formalising of land leases across the country. It then critically examines the Land Lease Bill introduced by the Government of Maharashtra in 2017 through an exploratory study of lease agreements and practices in the Osmanabad district of Maharashtra State. After the mention of salient provisions of the bill in the neoliberal state, the chapter delves into whether it holds the potential for providing a security of tenure for the landless and women's collectives. The chapter concludes that, by and large, the Land Lease Bill and the Model Act, on which it is based, is silent on the rights of the tenant, and therefore in its present form does not address the concerns of these groups.

Sonali Ghosh and Chandra Bhushan Kumar, belonging to the civil services – Forest and Administrative Services, respectively – have authored Chapter 6. The chapter begins with how the Northeast region (NER) of India has been an area of complex intrigue for natural resource conservation planners and policy makers in post-independence. The authors coin the term 'hybrid neoliberalism' – how neoliberalism and conservation have merged in policy and practice through devolved initiatives. This chapter elaborates the bio-cultural narrative of the NER and its neoliberal connect: first, by discussing multiple meanings of natural resource conservation, as absence of its appreciation affects the process of land acquisition in the pre- and post-neoliberal eras; second, by analysing the question of public purposes in the overall discourse of development of the region and to examine whether neoliberal thinking has introduced newer shades of development; and third, by suggesting a pathway for future engagement for natural resource conservation.

Evolving jurisprudence of the land question

Land acquisition being in the concurrent list, the Central Government is able to acquire land for different development projects under the colonial law *Land Acquisition Act, 1894* (LAA) and now *The Rights to Fair Compensation and Transparency in Rehabilitation and Resettlement Act, 2013* (RFCTLARRA). Different ministries and authorities, such as the National Highways Authority of India, National Highways & Infrastructure Development Company Ltd., and State Public Works Departments, are empowered with new institutional mechanisms, such as the launching of the Bhoomi Rashi[37] portal for national highway (NH) projects. The process starts with the appointment of a revenue functionary of the State Government as Competent Authority for Land Acquisition (CALA) for each NH project. It ends with the taking of physical possession of the land by the implementing authority and disbursal of compensation to each affected/interested party.

Land acquisition is linked with a few critical processes related to land – change in land use, land grab, land value booming, or expansion of land markets. The discourse on land acquisition mainly revolves around use of 'eminent domain' and 'public purpose' for acquiring land by the state; displacement, R&R (rehabilitation and resettlement) and compensation; relocation cost and solatium; procedure for acquiring land; and land pooling as an alternative to land acquisition. Several protests, social conflicts,[38] and legal cases[39] against acquisition of land as well as for higher compensation have taken place. However, the Judiciary and its interpretations largely focus on the term 'estate', which has resulted in substantial variations in judicial orders/verdicts – sometimes the state-specific, sometimes instance/project specific, and sometime community/customary rights.

Some judgments of the Supreme Court have become more debatable in the neoliberal era, which show greater importance and acceptance of technocracy for economic growth of the country; the critiques focus on social justice, equitable resource distribution, and resource rights of different stakeholders, for instance, Narmada Bachao Andolan[40] and others who fought against the building of a dam and R&R of the project affected population – the Sardar Sarovar Project and Narmada Sagar Project that affected four states – Gujarat, Madhya Pradesh, Maharashtra, and Rajasthan. The judgment of the Supreme Court on Nirma Cement Plant,[41] with 1.91 MTPA (million tonne per annum) capacity at Mahuva Taluka, Gujarat State, is also an example of resource rights (Bhagat-Ganguly 2016). Both verdicts hailed the importance of economic growth – through the building of large dams and the cement industry, respectively. Another set of judgments has been hailed by civil actors and critiqued by the industrial lobby that has reinstated the importance of democratic institutions and processes, for instance, the Niyamgiri judgment and Singur verdict.

Chapter 7 by Rita Sinha, a senior bureaucrat, who was instrumental in introducing NLRMP as the secretary of the Department of Land Resources (DoLR), delves into the historic process of land acquisition – from colonial regulation introduced in 1824 to the RFCTLARRA, 2013. The chapter traces the origin of land acquisition laws and captures the manifestations and behaviour of the State by looking at land acquisition in India through the old act – the LAA, 1894 and newly enacted law, RFCTLARRA. It focuses on two issues that have risen to prominence in the neoliberal era: (1) was there a justification for the historical continuity of colonial land acquisition laws effectively into the neoliberal era, and (2) is the RFCTLARRA in tune with India's neoliberal policies or is it a step backwards towards putting restraints on government from making land available to private enterprises? By examining relevant sections of RFCTLARRA to understand the neoliberal state's agenda of displacement, R&R, compensation, and solatium, through the existing land administration system, the chapter concludes that RFCTLARRA has retained overarching powers of the State to enable it to continue accruing land for private companies to achieve its neoliberal agenda.

Malabika Pal, an academic, compares some landmark judgments of the United States and India to understand use of eminent domain, linkages between economic growth and land acquisition, and public use and just compensation in Chapter 8. This chapter shows the absence of constitutional interpretation of two terms – 'public use' and 'compensation', and interpretation by the Legislative and Judiciary in both countries. To capture neoliberal design of development, the chapter scrutinizes the reasoning in landmark judgments like *Kelo* and *Singur* and argues about 'just compensation' using the standard proposed by Frank Michelman – to include demoralisation costs – that helps to incorporate considerations of justice along with efficiency.

In Chapter 9, Shiju Mazhuvanchery, an academic teaching law, looks at land as one of environmental media, since land regulation plays an important role in environmental protection. Though neoliberal policies have permeated the even field of environmental regulation, land regulation is considered as the weakest link in modern environmental law. The chapter delves into the discourse on environmentalism and whether it is still viewed as an opposition to the injustices of capitalism and how the land question has been viewed in the given model of capitalism and sustainable development. As market-based instruments and cost-benefit analysis are important components of present-day environmental regulation, part of the neoliberal precepts, this chapter discusses land regulation as a means for environmental protection in India. The chapter analyses various statutes and case law in order to understand whether there exist linkages between various environment and land-related regulations and how environmental regulations have addressed land issues in neoliberal India.

The contributions show that the State, being a 'taking' and 'giving' State, has explored newer options for using land as a resource for economic growth, with neoliberal precept; however, there seems little progress on comprehensive solutions to the complex, long-standing problems related to the land question. The agenda of social justice or broadly called concerns for marginalised communities, concerns for development project–affected persons, are duly addressed through policy and legal initiatives, but the very thin existence of an institutional mechanism makes it difficult to achieve success with the land-related agenda. Every new initiative of the State on the land question has not been successful nor has significant headway been made despite huge budgetary provisions; this situation in a way leads us to think more deeply about the neoliberal precept and its limitations. Existing legal and policy frameworks may lead to limited success on the land question, as socio-historical factors ask for 'suitable' initiative, not entrepreneurial every time. Not every people's struggle is able to stall development projects; either the Executive's interventions or judicial interpretations have played a role in support of the neoliberal state. This indicates a need for deeper study with regard to state-centric theoretic concerns in the context of socio-political-economic and human geography – how complex restructuring of the policy-making process takes place in the face of 'globalisation' and 'localisation' (Peck 2001).

Notes

1 Levien (2012: 933) refers to the land question as 'agrarian questions of labor and capital are, consequently, now rejoined in "the land question"'.
2 The processes of liberalisation, privatisation, and globalisation (LPG) had begun worldwide before the 1990s; they became official post-1991 in India when a new economic policy was enforced. The LPG is also known as the D-L-P formula of neoliberal policies: (1) deregulation (of the economy), (2) liberalisation (of trade and industry), and (3) privatisation (of State-owned enterprises) (Steger and Roy 2010: 14), with a market-friendly political agenda or 'paradigm'[2] (free-market, worldwide flow of goods; availability of services and labour; idealised images of a consumerist, foreign investment; and facilitating decision making by the ruling political party) that rose to prominence in the 1980s at the global level and in the 1990s in India (ibid.: 10).
3 Related policy measures include massive tax cuts for domestic and foreign corporations willing to invest in designated economic zones; removal of controls on global financial and trade flows; regional and global integration of national economies; downsizing of government and reduction of social services and welfare programmes; replacing welfare with 'workfare'; lower interest rates by banks to keep inflation in check; and the creation of new political institutions, think tanks, and practices designed to reproduce the neoliberal paradigm (Steger and Roy 2010).
4 In the Constitutive Assembly Debates (1947–51), land rights focusing mainly on ownership were discussed at length and depth among representatives from different parts of the country. As part of prevalent socialist development paradigm, they also stressed a need for agrarian reforms and consequently land reforms focusing on tenancy reforms for poverty alleviation and social justice. Following

this, different land laws were enacted or existing laws were amended as part of land reforms introduced in the 1950s and 1960s.

5 The Legislature made void laws offending fundamental rights, and they were included in Schedule Nine, and later, the list was extended from time to time (Salian 2002: 234).

6 Article 31-B declared that none of the acts or regulations specified in the Ninth Schedule nor any of the provisions thereof shall be deemed to be void on the ground that they are inconsistent with Part III, notwithstanding any judgments, decree, or order of any court or tribunal to the contrary. By further amendment, the list was extended (*op. cit.*).

7 Land as a critical resource to expedite the development of India was promoted in the 1970s and 1980s through adoption of 'technocracy' or simply said 'techno-managerial approach' by the late Prime Ministers Indira and Rajiv Gandhi, respectively, which prepared grounds for globalisation, privatisations, and liberalisation (LPG). This approach became a norm for development of the country. The social processes and aspirations which were the driving forces for political agenda and action were gradually replaced by technological and managerial solutions; consequently, the focus on social justice and equitable distribution of land was subdued post-1991.

8 Officially, *The Forest Dwellers and Other Traditional Forest Dwelling Communities (Recognition of Rights) Act, 2006.*

9 This Act legalises land grabbing or change in land use by private entities and government authorities.

10 *Orissa Mining Corporation vs. Union of India and Ors.* [2013] 6 SCR 881, writ petition (civil) no. 180 of 2011, judgment on 18 April 2013.

11 *Kedarnath Yadav vs State of West Bengal & Ors.* Civil Appeal No. 8438 of 2016 (arising out of SLP (C) Np. 8463 of 2008), dated 18 January 2008.

12 Popularly called tribals, officially – the Scheduled Tribes.

13 Land rights incorporates land ownership, access to land, and control and management of land. For more details, see Bhagat-Ganguly 2016.

14 Available at www.fao.org/in-action/herramienta-administracion-tierras/introduction/concept-land-administration/en/ Accessed on 9 December 2018.

15 In most states of India, land revenue collection stopped in the late 1980s or early 1990s; a few states have continued to collect a very negligible amount of land revenue – not more than a few hundred thousand per annum.

16 Chakravorty (2013) and Sathe (2017) deal with land acquisition and the price of land. They argue that land acquisition has not always been opposed as some farmers are willing to sell land if a just price is offered. Chakravorty (2016) provides details about four types of land markets and links them with RFCTLARRA and how it will affect the land market. This volume recognises these writings as important contributions to expanding discourse on the land question in neoliberal India.

17 The World Bank defines 'good governance' as 'the manner in which power is exercised in the management of a country's economic and social resources for development' (quoted in IFAD 1999: 1).

18 This concept was originally introduced by Michel Foucault (1969) and is applied to elaborate neoliberal governmentality; governance and governmentality have concern with the State and with 'Stateness' as their common denominator. Foucault touches upon the core of the relationship between pedagogy and politics, and a relational conception of society and its institutions connecting the political and the subjective realms (Amos 2010: 3).

19 Any right is considered an aspiration of citizens, a vision of good society and how it comes to play during interaction among different stakeholders. Any right

is an enabling factor for the well-being of citizens. Though any 'right' is primarily projected as a claim that focuses on 'need/s', it could be a means to access and achieve justice.

20 Public policy is an instrument that is used for achieving the development goals of the country; it is a regime that marks a triangle – aspirations of civil society in the form of public discourse that is reflected through a political agenda, usually of the ruling political party, and facilitated by administrative mechanisms – structure and procedures.

21 Solomon (2008: 720) refers to Massey (2005) in the context of spaces of politics revealed via ethnographic explorations of land economy and institutions. I refer to Chatterjee (2017: 9), 'something *new* in the way governmental authorities began to negotiate with population group'. In the changed scenario, a political fixer gets things done at a government office on behalf of a local community. For the political society, such a phenomenon is novel, and they need to learn to articulate self-interest from the perspective of right, which also ensures a larger common good.

22 Though the policies are not implemented, they are mentioned here as indicative of entrepreneurial ethos of the then governments. Such initiative/s could be taken up by the ruling party as and when found to be promising, may or may not be in modified form.

23 Repeal of the *Urban Land Ceiling Regulation Act, 1976* (ULCRA) was successfully implemented in the neoliberal era, as suggested by the National Commission on Urbanisation in pre-neoliberal India.

24 At the time of independence, there were three main systems of land tenure, namely *zamindari*, *ryotwari*, and *mahalwari*. The *zamindari* system covered about 57 percent of the total privately owned agricultural land, followed by the *ryotwari* system (38 percent) and *mahalwari* system (5 percent), respectively (quoted in NITI Aayog 2016: 38).

25 See Terms of Reference of the expert Committee on Land Leasing, number (iii). The other terms of reference are: (1) to review the existing agricultural tenancy laws of states, including hilly states and scheduled areas; (2) to examine the distinctive features of land system in erstwhile *zamindari*, *ryotwari*, and *mahalwari* areas; (3) to suggest appropriate amendments, keeping in view the need to legalise and liberalise land leasing for much-needed agricultural efficiency, equity, occupational diversification, and rapid rural transformation; (4) to prepare a model agricultural land-leasing act in consultation with states; and (5) any other related matter.

26 As per the Agriculture Census (2015–16), of the total of 36 states and union territories (UTs), marginal landholding among the SCs living in six states had no landholding and six states had negligible holding (fewer than 500 units/hectare). Of the rest, three states reported fewer than 3,000 SC farmers, four states reported fewer than 100,000 SC landholders, and 14 states had landholders ranging from 100,001 to 1,000,000. Only three states had landholders in excess of a million: Bihar (1,823,000 landholders), West Bengal (1,569,000 landholders), and Uttar Pradesh (3,601,000 landholders). Among SC small landholders, seven states had no landholding and six states had negligible holding (fewer than 500 units/hectare). Of the rest, three states reported fewer than 3,000 SC farmers, four states reported fewer than 100,000 SC landholders, and nine states had landholders ranging from 100,001 to 1,000,000. A total of nine states reported landholders between 1,000,000 and 3,000,000.

27 As per the Agriculture Census (2015–16), of a total of 36 states and UTs, marginal landholding among the STs living in six states had no landholding and six states had negligible holding (fewer than 500 units/hectare). Of the rest, four

states reported fewer than 1,000 ST farmers, and four states reported fewer than 100,000 ST landholders. Nine states had landholders ranging from 100,001 to 500,000, and five states had 500,001 to 1,000,000 ST landholders. Among ST small landholders, six state STs did not have landholding, and two states had negligible holding (fewer than 500 units/hectare). Of the rest, three states reported fewer than 3,000 ST farmers, four states reported fewer than 100,000 STs landholders, and nine states had landholders ranging from 100,001 to 1,000,000. A total of nine states reported landholders between 1,000,000 and 3,000,000, and three states had ST small landholders ranging between 300,001 to 500,000.

28   The author (2014: 6) discusses hunger leasing with reference to usury capital – characterised as a pre-capitalistic form of surplus appropriation, and petty producers and small peasants are major victims of usury capital.

29   The 'land dependents' is a construct; the term is expanded to include dependents on private land as well as common lands. It incorporates tenants, sharecroppers, those who have taken land on lease for their livelihood, agriculture labourers, pastoralists, workers in the mining sector, persons engaged in fishing, and unorganised labour in different industries that are engaged in land-based activities, for example, brick making and construction (Bhagat-Ganguly 2016: 6).

30   For example, the Philippines, Brazil, and China for expansion of the land market; Uganada for land reforms; and Australia and the United Kingdom for land titling systems.

31   When the government acquires land for a development project, compensation for the land is paid as per the prescribed value as if the land sale had taken place between two private parties; however, the value of the land may be much more than what the government pays. In the event the land transaction cannot be legal because of the absence of land titling or land records, then there is a higher possibility of appropriation of land or land grab.

32   Loss of land conceptualised as 'risk' of various types. In the context of displacement, the IRR (impoverishment risks, risk management, and reconstruction) model developed by Michael Cernea (1990) is widely acceptable, which mentions eight risks – landlessness; joblessness; homelessness; marginalisation; food insecurity; increased morbidity and mortality; loss of access to common property and services; and social disarticulation. Of them, loss of community ties resulting in uprootedness and alienation on socio-cultural counts are of greater concern.

33   This is social (includes economic and political) vulnerability, which is different from biophysical (referring to climatic) vulnerability. This framework is applied in the broader context of structural inequality and social justice, risks, and need arising for transformative social protection because of poverty, displacement and deprivation, and loss of livelihood.

34   The relative deprivation framework is primarily a social psychology concept that evolves in three stages – cognitive analysis based on comparison, appraisal in terms of loss or gain, and disadvantages perceived as unfair and manifesting into resentment and resistance – at individual as well as at group/community levels. Social movement theory considers this framework relevant in terms of manifestation of resentment or resistance that is inter-linked with mass mobilisation and resource mobilisation, and also has a greater potential for turning into collective action or protest (Fahey 2010; Pettigrew 2015).

35   The authors work with the Indian Institute of Human Settlements (IIHS), and their views are personal. The chapter is based on the research studies conducted by IIHS in different states of India.

36   Officially named the *Scheduled Tribes and Other Forest Dwellers (Recognition of Rights) Act, 2006.*

37 Visit http://bhoomirashi.gov.in/WriteReadData/la.pdf for more information. This is a portal developed by MoRTH (Ministry of Road, Transport and Highways) and NIC (National Informatics Centre), and comprises the entire revenue data of the country – of upto 6.4 lakh villages, more than 900 notifications issued for land acquisition, etc. Bhoomi Rashi portal has been instrumental in reducing the time taken for approval and publication of notifications pertaining to land acquisition.

38 As per the Land Conflict Watch Portal, a land conflict is defined as any situation that has conflicting demands or claims over the use or ownership of land, and where the public is one of the contesting parties. These conflicts can also be over naturally occurring land resources such as forest, underground water, fish stock, etc. The conflict may arise as a result of development projects such as mining, building infrastructure, industry, urban development schemes, conservation schemes in protected areas, or because of land grab and encroachment.

On 6 March 2019, in 671 conflicts, a total of 7,470,306 people in 2,427,456 hectares are reported to be affected in India. www.landconflictwatch.org/ (Accessed on March 6, 2019).

39 As per a study conducted by the Centre for Policy Research, 1,269 cases were involved in litigation under the *Land Acquisition Act* during 1947–2016, while 280 cases were decided under the *LARR Act, 2013*, for the period January 2014 to December 2016 in the Supreme Court of India (CPR 2017: 12).

40 *Narmada Bachao Andolan vs. Union of India and Others* [2000] 10 SCC 664, judgment on 18 October 2000. The Supreme Court allowed an increase in Sardar Sarovar Dam's height and *pari passu* for R&R.

41 *Khimjibhai Lalubhai Baraiya vs. Union of India* SLP (C) No. (s) 15016, 32414, and 32615 of 2010 at Gujarat High Court. The Supreme Court Order dated 18 March 2011, petition for Special leave to Appeal Civil No.9s) 14698/2010 (from the judgment and Order dated 26 April 2010 in SCA No. 3477/2009 of High Court of Gujarat).

References

Amos, Karin. 2010. *Governance and governmentality: relation and relevance of two prominent social scientific concepts for comparative education*. University of Tübingen. Retrieved from www.scielo.br/pdf/ep/v36nspe/en_v36nspea03.pdf accessed on 9 March 2019.

Bhagat-Ganguly, Varsha. 2016. *Land rights in India: policies, movements and challenges*. London and New York: Routledge.

Bhagat-Ganguly, Varsha. 2016. 'Tracing journey of legislative processes for land acquisition and resettlement in India from rights' perspective', *Journal of Land and Rural Studies*, 4(1): 36–48.

Bijoy, C.R. 2008. 'SEZ: corporate statehood defined', *Labour File*, 6(4–5): 22–24.

Centre for Equity Studies. 2016. *The extent and nature of individual tribal land alienation in fifth scheduled areas in India*. New Delhi: Centre for Equity Studies.

Centre for Policy Research (CPR). 2017. *Land acquisition in India: a review of Supreme Court cases 1950–2016*. New Delhi: Centre for Policy Research.

Cernea, Michael. 1990. *Impoverishment risk, risk management, and reconstruction: a model of population displacement and resettlement*. Washington, DC: The World Bank.

Chakravorty, Sanjoy. 2013. *The price of land: acquisition conflict consequence*. New Delhi: Oxford University Press.

Chakravorty, Sanjoy. 2016. 'Land acquisition in India: the political economy of changing the law', *Area Development and Policy*, 1(1): 48–62. doi:10.1080/237 92949.2016.1160325

Chatterjee, Partha. 2008, 19 April. 'Democracy and economic transformation in India', *Economic and Political Weekly*, pp. 53–62.

Chatterjee, Partha. 2017. 'Prelude: land and the political management of primitive accumulation', in Anthony P. D'Costa and Achin Chakraborty (eds.), *The land question in India: state, dispossession and capitalist transition* (pp. 1–15). Oxford, UK: Oxford University Press.

Chowdhury, Nupur. 2014. 'From judicial activism to adventurism – the *Godavarman case* in the Supreme Court of India', *Asia Pacific Journal of Environmental Law*, 17: 177–189.

Das, Raju J. 2015. 'Critical observations in neo-liberalism and India's new economic policy', *Journal of Contemporary Asia*, 45(4): 715–726, http://dx.doi.org/10.108 0/00472336.2014.1003143

Fahey, Tony. 2010. *Poverty and the two concepts of relative deprivation*. Working paper series, WP10/1. Dublin: University College Dublin.

Foucault, M. 1969. *Archaeology of knowledge*. London: Routledge.

Gangopadhyaya, Shubhashis. 2012. 'Developing the market for land', *Review of Market Integration*, 4(2): 197–220, https://doi.org/10.1177/0974929212465680.

Government of India. 2007. *Model guidelines for urban land policy (draft)*. New Delhi: Ministry of Urban Development, Government of India. Retrieved from http://www.cmamp.com/CP/FDocument/GuidelinesULP.pdf accessed on 25 March 2020.

Indian Institute of Human Settlements (IIHS). 2017. *Land records modernisation in India: an institutional, legal and policy review*. New Delhi: IIHS.

International Fund for Agriculture and Development (IFAD). 1999. 'Good governance: an overview', *Executive Board–Sixty-Seventh Session*. EB 99/67/INF.4, document 35370. Retrieved from www.ipa.government.bg/sites/default/files/pregled-dobro_upravlenie.pdf accessed on 29 September 2019.

Levien, Michael. 2012. 'The land question: special economic zones and the political economy of dispossession in India', *The Journal of Peasant Studies*, 39(3–4): 933–969.

Mani, Gyanendra. 2016. 'Model agricultural land leasing act, 2016: some observation', *Economic and Political Weekly*, 51(42). Retrieved from www.idsj.org/wp-content/uploads/2017/05/WP-173.pdf accessed on 23 March 2019.

Massey, D. 2005. 'The prison house of synchrony', in D. Massey (ed.), *For space*. London: Sage.

Mitra Madhumita Datta. 2017. 'Evolution of property rights in India', in S. Pellissery et al. (eds.), *Land policies in India, India studies in business and economics* (pp. 35–50). doi:10.1007/978-981-10-4208-9_2

Mohanakumar, S. 2014. *Tenancy relations in India: observations from a field study*. Working paper 173. Jaipur: Institute of Development Studies.

Nielsen, K.B. and A.G. Nilsen. 2014. 'Law struggles and hegemonic processes in neoliberal India: Gramscian reflections on land acquisition legislation', *Globalizations*. doi:10.1080/14747731.2014.937084

NITI Aayog. 2016. *Report of the expert committee on land leasing*. New Delhi: Government of India.

Peck, Jamie. 2001. 'Neoliberalizing states: thin policies / hard outcomes', *Progress in Human Geography*, 25(3): 445–455. https://doi.org/10.1191/030913 201680191772

Pettigrew, Thomas F. 2015. 'Samuel Stouffer and relative deprivation', *Social Psychology Quarterly*, 78(1): 7–24.

Rose Nikolas. 1999. *Powers of freedom: reframing political thought*. Cambridge: Cambridge University Press.

Salian, Shushant. 2002. *History of the removal of the fundamental right to property*. Working paper no. 0041, Centre for Civil Society, pp. 232–255. Retrieved from https://ccs.in/sites/default/files/files/wp0041.pdf accessed on 5 March 2019.

Sathe, Dhanmanjiri. 2017. *The political economy of land acquisition in India*. Singapore: Palgrave Macmillan.

Sazzad, Parwaz. 2016. 'A study on special economic zone implicated land acquisition and utilisation', *International Journal of Development and Conflict*, 6: 136–156.

Singh, Chetan. 2016. 'Foreword', in Bhagat-Ganguly Varsha (ed.), *Land rights in India: policies, movements and challenges* (pp. xiii–xvii). London and New York: Routledge.

Solomon, Benjamin. 2008, September. 'Occupancy urbanism: radicalizing politics and economy beyond policy and programs', *International Journal of Urban and Regional Research*, 32(3): 719–729. doi:10.1111/j.1468-2427.2008.00809.x

Steger, Manfred B. and Ravi K. Roy. 2010. *Neoliberalism: a very short introduction*. Oxford: Oxford University Press.

Sud, Nikita. 2012. *Liberalization, Hindu nationalization and the state*. New Delhi: Oxford University Press.

Suneja, Kritika. 2019, 26 May. 'New SEZ policy bats for easy exits and flexibilities in leases', *Economic Times*. Retrieved from https://economictimes.indiatimes.com/news/economy/policy/new-sez-policy-bats-for-easy-exits-and-flexibility-in-leases/articleshow/69509265.cms?from=mdr accessed on 1 October 2019.

The World Bank. 2013, October. *Land governance assessment framework: implementation manual*. Retrieved from http://siteresources.worldbank.org/INTLGA/Resources/LGAF_Manual_Oct_2013.pdf accessed on 24 March 2019.

Part 1
Socio-legal and policy perspectives on 'land'

2 Approaches and methods of land title legislation in India

Far from reality or close to the ground?

Amlanjyoti Goswami, Deepika Jha, and Kaye Lushington[1]

The task of modernising land records has received renewed attention in the past decade, building on earlier initiatives in pre-liberalised India. The rationale for such efforts has been twofold. First is the need to increase efficiency in land-based transactions, including in transitional situations of land acquisition, rehabilitation, and resettlement; rural-urban spatial and demographic changes; creating conditions for better urban planning as well as for augmenting State revenues through registration of deeds that provide evidence of transfer of property. Second is the more distributive goal of ensuring better access to the common citizen, of an updated and digitised land record that is real time and does not suffer from wear and tear inevitable in paper-based systems. Such an updated record could then be used for welfare schemes, subsidies, and other measures.

These recent measures mark a departure from the colonial era when land revenue itself was the focus, and periodic and frequent updation through the colonial administration was necessary to ensure accurate measurement, crop record, and collection. With the shift from the largely agrarian context and the decreasing significance of land revenue for the State's finances, land records too had fallen into disrepair and had become archaic. This was sought to be addressed through measures to modernise record systems, from the 1980s onwards. From around the first decade of this century, there have been newer methods and goals articulated to bring about greater efficiency in land-based transactions, centring on questions of ownership of land. The greater salience of real estate in peri-urban and urban areas has also added weight to such questions. In other words, while the legacies of the colonial era (and still further back to Mughal times) persist in the structure of land administration as well as land record formats, new attention to goals, such as Torrens and title-based systems, call for fundamental shifts in the structure itself, which the system is currently unable to absorb or accommodate. One of the most important shifts advocated is from the deeds-based presumptive system (predominant in Common Law countries) to a conclusive title-based system (first attempted in Australia and now being advocated as a model to follow). This therefore entails a quick overview of the structural differences inherent in such shifts and the accompanying difficulties of doing so. In such light, the State's modernising impulse of creating more accurate digital land records needs to be distinguished from the State's neoliberal impulse of focusing on title legislation based on the Torrens system.

This chapter has three parts. It begins with describing the current legal structure of maintaining land records in India, followed by a description of the proposed conclusive titling system and the anticipated changes. The second part of the chapter traces the policy shifts towards the conclusive titling system at the national scale, and then via the legal and technological initiatives at the state level. The third part details the challenges in achieving conclusive titling, including legal, institutional, and technological aspects.

Presumptive title and a deeds-based registration system

India has a presumptive system of proving title. Its origin is located in colonial era legacies, when the primary purpose of maintaining land records was to collect revenue or property tax. The person mentioned in these records was presumed to be the owner for the purpose of revenue collection, and hence the title so conferred was incidental to revenue. The entry in the land record is not conclusive proof that the person is the title-holder, and such entries may be open to challenge by interested parties. Further, the registration of an instrument is only proof of the transaction (legal fact) having taken place and does not stand as direct proof of ownership/title to a property as it does not indicate that the parties entering into the specific transaction are at the first place legally in a position to do so.

The Supreme Court also re-emphasises this position. In *Suraj Bhan vs. Financial Commissioner and others* (2007 (6) SCC 186), the Supreme Court held that

> It is well settled that an entry in revenue records does not confer title on a person whose name appears in the record of rights. It is settled law that entries in the revenue records or *Jamabandi*[2] have only 'fiscal purpose' i.e. payment of land revenue and no ownership is conferred on the basis of such entries. So far as the title to the properties is concerned, it can only be decided by a competent Civil Court.

The Indian Registration Act, 1908 (IRA), the relevant law for the system of registration of instruments, is based on a deeds-based registration system in which the registered deed serves as evidence of the transaction having taken place and not as proof of title. A failure to register transfer of property (subject to exceptions) as per the IRA can render the transaction inadmissible as evidence. As per section 35 of the *Stamp Act, 1899*, instruments that are not duly stamped are neither admissible as evidence, nor can they be registered by a public official. *The Transfer of Property Act, 1882*, deals with the types of transfer of property that confer formal property rights in the form of ownership, lease rights, mortgage, and so on. It is presumed that the transactions once registered are genuine, but this is only a presumption unless challenged in a court of law. The *Indian Evidence Act, 1872,* reaffirms this presumption with respect to registered documents. The situation regarding boundaries and spatial details is more complicated. While sections 21 and 22 of the Registration Act provide legitimacy to the survey and settlement process, maps and surveys (which provide clarity on boundaries and area-specific detail) do not require mandatory registration along with property documents, even as the *Evidence Act, 1882,* does recognise details in maps as facts.

It is pertinent to note that section 17 of the Registration Act, although mandating compulsory registration of a sale deed on land, does not require registration authorities to verify the history of the land or its ownership and encumbrances from the seller. Under the *Transfer of Property Act, 1882,* too, there is no reference to verification of the previous legal status of the seller. This is primarily based on the principle of *caveat emptor* in law, or 'let the buyer beware'. Accordingly, the principle puts the buyer at caution by placing the responsibility on the buyer to make the relevant enquiries in relation to the land.

It appears that all these laws, of colonial origin, came to terms with the basic inadequacy of efforts that seek to make all records completely accurate and free from any doubt. Given this basic indeterminacy, courts were given the power to adjudicate on claims arising from disputed ownership or boundary, apart from other litigation issues arising from land.

Under the current presumptive system of land records in India, subsequent to a registration of the conveyance deed, a quasi-judicial process of mutation needs to be undertaken. This mutation entails verification by revenue officers that a genuine transaction has taken place as per the registered deed, which is then followed by an updation of the land/revenue record, commonly known as the Record of Rights. The mutation-registration link is the vital connection, which enables verification of the status of such property and vires of persons entering into transactions, subject to the 'let the buyer beware' rule and determination, if any, by the courts if there is a legal challenge to title. This connection requires active cooperation of the Revenue department of the state, and in particular coordination between the registration and revenue functions. Linkages with the survey and settlement function (within the Revenue department) further buttress the presumed accuracy of the record, so long as updation is timely and accurate.

Principles of conclusive titling and the Torrens system

While India follows a presumptive system, the ultimate aim of the Government of India (GOI) flagship programme on land records modernisation introduced in 2008 is to usher in a conclusive titling system with title guarantee (DoLR 2008–09: 2). Within the conclusive system of titling, the GOI advocates the Torrens system, with 'mirror', 'curtain', and 'indemnity' as its core principles. It is necessary to understand what each of these terms means, and what the transition from a presumptive to a conclusive system would entail.

As documented by DoLR (2008–09: 8), the 'mirror' principle would require that the cadastral records mirror the ground reality. This would need accurate textual and spatial records, which are further updated on a real-time basis.

The 'curtain' principle would ensure that the title is a true depiction of ownership status, and references to past records would not then be necessary. It would essentially draw a legal curtain over past transactions or rights, thus making sure that tracing the chain of title through a series of previous transactions would no longer be required.

The 'indemnity' principle would provide a guarantee to the correctness of the title. Any loss suffered by a titleholder on account of defect of title will be monetarily compensated by the State. In addition, the National Land Record Modernisation Programme (NLRMP) also targeted having a single window to handle all land records, including textual records, spatial records, and registration records (DoLR 2008–09: 8).

In the shift to a system of conclusive titles, the registration process would also change from a deeds-based system to a title-based one. Under the current legislative framework in India, the sub-registrars register conveyance deeds which record a transaction of property, and these act as evidence of the transaction (though not of the property title). In the proposed title-based registration, the title of the property itself would be registered and thus serve as conclusive evidence of the proof of title. In other words, 'deeds systems provide a register of owners, focusing on "who owns what", while title systems register properties representing "what is owned by whom"' (Williamson et al. 2010). In effect, this also means that with conclusive titling in a title-based system, when a transaction would take place, the current concept of *caveat emptor* (or buyer beware) would in effect turn into a state guarantee of title.

Tracing policy shifts towards conclusive titling as a goal

The gradual policy shift towards conclusive rather than presumptive titling as part of the land records modernisation agenda began in 1989 when Mr D.C. Wadhwa recommended these changes as a part of the One-Man Committee on Records of Rights in Land in 1989 (Wadhwa 1989; Zasloff 2011). After a decade, it was the 'India: The Growth Imperative' report by McKinsey Global Institute (2001) which brought the issue back into focus. The report listed land market distortions, including unclear ownership of land, as one of three major barriers to economic growth in India, claiming that it accounted for the loss of almost 1.3 percent of economic growth every year. Subsequently in 2002, a GOI attempt for disinvestment of some hotels under the Indian Tourism Development Corporation revealed that while the hotels had operated for several decades, none of them had clear titles or ownership papers (Zasloff 2011). By 2004, the need for clear titles was highlighted in the National Common Minimum Programme (NCMP), a document outlining the minimum objectives of the Central Government in 2004. Nayak (2013) notes that the move towards conclusive titling was supported by the World Bank and also reflected in the Eleventh Plan (2007–12), which recommended the formalisation of land rights, repeal of ceiling laws, and reform of tenancy laws.

The landmark moment in the policy shift was the introduction of the National Land Records Modernisation Programme (NLRMP) in September 2008, which for the first time stated the ultimate objective as implementing the conclusive land titling system, with title guarantee. The NLRMP Guidelines 2009 highlighted the important steps to reach conclusive titling: computerisation of registration, its integration with land records, automatic mutation following registration, integration of textual and spatial data, conducting cadastral surveys, building record rooms, and bringing legal changes (DoLR 2008–09: 32). However, of all these preconditions, the focus of the scheme was clearly on conducting surveys/resurveys, as INR 16 billion of the initial allocation of INR 31.48 billion was reserved for 'survey/resurvey and updating of survey and settlement records' (DoLR 2008–09: 41). Based on the recommendations of the Eleventh Plan, the earlier land record modernisation schemes of the Central Government[3] were also combined into the NLRMP.

The introduction of the NLRMP also triggered a series of other policy conversations and initiatives at the Central Government level. In November 2008, the Ministry of Urban Development set up a task force on a property title certification system. Based on the recommendations of the task force, the Jawaharlal Nehru National Urban Renewal Mission (JNNURM) had incentivised states to introduce a property title certification system in urban local bodies as part of its optional reforms (Ramanathan 2009). However, this remained limited in implementation.

In 2008, the Government of India (GOI) proposed a draft Model Land Titling Bill, as a possible legislative solution to ensure conclusive titling. A subsequent draft was also proposed by the GOI in 2011. Since land is a subject under the State list of the Constitution, it was imagined then that the draft Model Land Titling Bill would be adopted subsequently by various states. However, it did not see much traction from the states. The Government of the National Capital Territory of Delhi did propose a land titling bill in 2009, but it was later shelved because of various procedural and constitutional reasons. In 2008, the Government of Rajasthan had introduced an ordinance on titling in urban areas (GOI Expert Committee 2014: 3) but was subsequently unable to get the necessary legislation passed, and the Ordinance was allowed to lapse. In April 2016, the Rajasthan Legislative Assembly passed land titling legislation for urban areas and thus became the first state to have an enabling legal framework. However, this Act never used the term 'conclusive'. The details of such state-level interventions are discussed in the next section.

In December 2013, the GOI also set up an expert committee, which submitted its report on a roadmap to land titling in India, in February 2014. The said committee reviewed four models of land titling – Systematic, Incremental Compulsory, Incremental Optional, or the Systematic Selective Model – and recommended that a systematic model of land titling is most suitable for India, under an independent authority. This indicates a shift outwards from the Revenue department, which is significant. It also recommended that selective systematic land titling may be undertaken in urban areas, and recommended that pilot projects can be taken up for such titling (GOI Expert Committee 2014: 8–10).

It was subsequently through the *Real Estate (Regulation and Development) Act, 2016*, [RERA, section 32(h)] that the term 'conclusive titling' first found mention in a statute. Under the RERA, the Real Estate Regulatory Authority can make recommendations to the appropriate government to undertake measures to 'facilitate digitisation of land records and system towards conclusive property titles with title guarantee'. The state government can also notify that real estate promoters must obtain insurance regarding 'title of the land and building as a part of the real estate project' [Section 16(1(i)].

By the end of 2016, the NLRMP was made into a Central-sector scheme and placed under the umbrella of 'Digital India', and was renamed as the Digital India Land Records Modernisation Programme (DILRMP) (DoLR 22 September 2016). The DILRMP continues to place focus on moving towards a system of conclusive titling with the mirror principle, the curtain principle, and title insurance.

State-level approaches to conclusive land titling

To understand the movement towards a conclusive title regime, it is important to look beyond the national-level policy and legislative initiatives, towards the ways by which various states have tried to introduce conclusive titling or improve the records system. This is also significant since land records come under the State List in the Constitution (Entry 45, Seventh Schedule of the Constitution) and, while the Central Government can prod and push through incentives (and model templates), it is ultimately up to the states to enforce action. Given political economy realities, including realities of institutional administration, states are more aware of the situation on the ground, and their measures to ensure a more accurate land record is reflective of such awareness.

While in principle all states agree on the need to ensure a more accurate land record, efforts in the states seem to follow two broad patterns: a legally enforceable conclusive titling legislation or incremental improvements in land records management. The first set of initiatives recognises that a legislative route is necessary for any changes in the titling system and uses it to push through a series of radical changes in the administrative, judicial, and procedural systems, using a top-down approach. The second set of initiatives recognises that land records systems are not in a reliable condition and need to be improved for an updated and accurate set of records, through computerisation of textual records, digitisation of spatial records, and integration of the two.

Through legislation

The underlying conditions of land governance vary between states, and a one-size-fits-all titling model may be inadequate in terms of the local context. A shift towards a titling system would require new and complex laws and also a nuanced understanding of the different legal conditions that the titling system will bring. This variation of underlying conditions among states is reflected in the varied types of title legislation drafted or enacted in India. For instance, Maharashtra in its 2018 Amendment Bill has sought to implement a titling system by means of amending its Revenue legislation, whereas Andhra Pradesh, Rajasthan, and Delhi have sought a route of independent enactments.

Some states have attempted to introduce conclusive titling legislation, at least at some point, and four of these proposed/approved/pending attempts have been looked into detail vis-à-vis the Draft Model Land Titling Bill 2011, for a more nuanced understanding of how some states have tried to envision a conclusive titling legislation.

The Draft Model Land Titling Bill 2011[4] drafted by the then Central Government was an attempt to create a template for states to establish a system of conclusive titles. It is a 'model' and not an actual bill. It advocated an altogether new institutional framework comprising a Land Titling Authority, Title Registration Officers, a Land Titling Tribunal, and a Land Titling Fund. The notified provisional title record would turn into a conclusive title record on completion of a three-year challenge period.

Delhi survey, registration, and recordal of title of immovable properties in Urban Areas Bill, 2009 (Draft)

The bill was apparently cleared by the Delhi Cabinet in 2010 but was not tabled in the Legislative Assembly. Subsequently, as per news reports, it appears that the Central Government had clarified that the Government of the National Capital Territory of Delhi does not have the jurisdiction to legislate on the matter (Pandit 2015).[5] The bill largely followed the template of the Model Land Titling Bill, 2008, in terms of proposed institutional structures and processes, but the details were more contextualised to Delhi and the complexity of its urban property records. Extensive cadastral surveys were to be carried out assigning unique property IDs. The survey findings could be challenged and corrected up to seven to ten years, after which the record was supposed to turn into a conclusive record.

Rajasthan Urban Land (certification of titles) Act, 2016

In April 2016, Rajasthan became the first state in India to have legislation on land titling. Subsequent rules under the Act have not been framed yet, and there are no reports of on-ground implementation as of date. The Act has a provision for surveys to be conducted by various urban local bodies or development authorities in their respective jurisdiction. A voluntary application by a titleholder would lead to an enquiry by the to-be-constituted Urban Land Certification Authority, and if the Authority is satisfied, a provisional certificate of title may be granted. If a provisional certificate is unchallenged for two years, a permanent certificate of title may be issued, for which the state government shall stand as a guarantor (Goswami and Jha 2016). Rajasthan has also had a change in political regime in 2018 and, therefore, given political economy realities, the new government's inclination to effect such change remains to be seen.

Maharashtra land revenue code (amendment) bill, 2018 (draft)

There is an attempt in Maharashtra to bring in titling legislation through amendment of the state Revenue Act. The draft bill has seen various rounds of discussions and amendments and has been cleared by the state Cabinet but is yet to be passed by the state legislative assembly.[6] The bill follows the Torrens system of creation of Register of Titles, Register of Disputes, and Register of Charges and Covenants, which would be termed conclusive after a three-year challenge period. It also proposes a new Land Titling Authority, but the composition of the proposed six-member Authority would be more contextualised to the local revenue administration system. It would include two divisional commissioners who are in charge of revenue functions, the state Inspector General of Registration and the Survey and Settlement Commissioner. The draft bill mentions a 'strata' title for urban areas, with special focus on newly created titles such as apartments and flats. Critically, it does not emphasise fresh cadastral surveys and instead seeks to enable use of existing records to be adapted for the purpose.

Andhra Pradesh (AP) Land Titling Bill, 2019

The Andhra Pradesh Legislative Assembly passed the AP Land Titling Bill on 29 July 2019. Since there are legislative competence issues between Centre and State (especially with regard to inconsistencies with the *Registration Act, 1908*; the *Stamp Act, 1899*; and other Central legislation), the AP Land Titling Bill, 2019, would require assent from the President of India, before it is notified in the *Gazette* as a new law. Similar to Maharashtra, the AP Bill also enables use of existing records, instead of *de novo* surveys, to create a Title Register, a Register of Disputes as well as a Register of Charges and Covenants. It states that draft land title records shall be termed conclusive if they remain unchallenged for a period of two years after the initial notification. It emphasises that all records must be in electronic format, consistent with the provisions of the *Information Technology Act, 2000,* and the *Evidence Act, 1872.* Powers of respective authorities under the *Registration Act, 1908;* the *Stamp Act, 1899;* and the *AP Survey and Boundaries Act, 1923,* would also vest with the newly created Land Titling Authority. However, the bill does not define what a conclusive title is. It also does not include provisions related to the 'guarantee' aspect of the Torrens system since that involves questions of State indemnity.

Achieving a conclusive titling system through legislation is not an easy panacea. So far, states have not been able to achieve much movement on such initiatives, as the legislation often does not offer a way to resolve the incremental difficulties that have arisen in land records modernisation efforts. In particular, there is a need for clarity on verification processes and relevant due diligence, which need to be followed by the new institutions, in order to implement and maintain the 'curtain' and the 'mirror' principles. Without clear and accurate processes, it is unlikely that the courts will accept the change from presumptive to conclusive since the courts have traditionally allocated to themselves the task of adjudicating land disputes.

Through technological initiatives

Technological initiatives across states also have seen variations and trajectories. Some of these have been in the nature of a pilot project, or a proof of concept, while some others have seen more extensive implementation. Three such initiatives are referred to here for a comparative overview.

Resurveys in Gujarat: Beginning in 2008–09, Gujarat was among the earliest states to start an extensive resurvey exercise under NLRMP. To date, it has also achieved the highest rate of finalisation of new records across the state.[7] A study by IIHS (Indian Institute for Human Settlements) (2017c) revealed that the objective in Gujarat has been to create a set of land records which are an accurate 'mirror' of the on-ground situation, including provisions for their subsequent updation. Following the due process of survey and settlement, new records have been promulgated for thousands of villages, but the state has not drawn a legal 'curtain' over the older records. The new records thus created remain presumptive in nature: open to objections and challenge.

UPOR in Karnataka: The Urban Property Ownership Record (UPOR) project in Karnataka was initially introduced in the cities of Mysuru, Shimoga, Hubli Dharwad, and Ballari in 2009. It aimed to create property records in urban areas, which were otherwise not covered in sufficient detail. While the project's ultimate aims were to reach conclusiveness of title, in the short run it instead aimed to reach 'clear presumptive title' alone based on a 'quasi legal' process of verification and review (IIHS 2017a: 84).

Chandigarh Land Titling Initiative: In 2016, an attempt was also made in Chandigarh, to introduce a conclusive land title certificate for urban and rural areas of the Union Territory, on a pilot basis. However, it was later shelved because of lack of a suitable legislative framework in the Union Territory, among other reasons.

It is largely recognised among states that if conclusive titling is the ultimate aim, then both legislation and technological implementation would be required. A law with limited/restricted implementation – for example, the *Rajasthan Certification of Urban Land Titles Act*, 2016 – may fail the purpose as it creates a duality of the de jure situation differing from the de facto, along with process ambiguities. In other words, while the ostensible goal of the Centre is conclusive titling, states seem to prefer muddling along the incremental path, acknowledging its own political realities and administrative systems.

Focus on urban areas

Urban areas have strongly emerged as priority areas when it comes to land titling in India. This is in marked contrast to the traditional focus on rural land records in land records modernisation programmes. NLRMP, and subsequently DILRMP, was placed under the Ministry of Rural Development of the Central Government. Even as late as 2017, the Department of Land Resources (DoLR), the nodal agency for implementation of DILRMP under the Ministry of Rural Development, has clarified that DILRMP funds may be used in urban areas but only to create or modernise 'land' records, and not 'property' records. The distinction is germane, keeping vertical apartments in mind, which DoLR keeps out of its ambit.

The focus on titling in urban areas was initially reflected in the optional reforms under JNNURM (2005–2014), the Rajasthan Urban Land Titling Ordinance, 2008, and the Delhi Land Titling Draft Bill, 2009 – which were all applicable only to urban areas. In policy discussions, newly developed urban areas, especially apartment complexes, are understood as initial measures to be undertaken from where systematic selective titling can be initiated (GOI Expert Committee 2014) – as they have a relatively clean slate, given that historically there are very few instances of land surveys in urban India. Among the recent technological initiatives, UPOR in Karnataka (2009–10 onwards) and the conclusive titling initiative in Chandigarh (2015–16) have also had an urban focus. Similarly, the Rajasthan legislation (2016 Act) has focused only on urban areas.

The reasons for focusing on urban areas are not difficult to understand. The land values in urban and peri-urban areas make them financially extremely valuable. They are also characterised by a higher frequency of transactions, as well as rapid development in real estate and other commercial ventures.

The capacity of urban areas in attracting investment and the potential for higher tax collection in terms of stamp duty and property taxes increase their relevance for the national as well as the state economy.

However, urban areas have their own complexities, which cannot be ignored while initiating such legislative changes, as discussed in the next section.

Challenges to achieve conclusive titling

Conclusive titling is often justified as a way to resolve a litigious environment, without adequate acknowledgement to the nature of structural challenges involved in this shift. The clarity and indemnity of a Torrens-like system may not be realised, especially in the short term, without addressing underlying systemic and structural causes of current legal and other disputes: the rent-seeking behaviour characterising current land and real estate transactions and the diverse transaction formats in use to meet requirements of various socio-economic groups. On-ground difficulties of sourcing and verifying property documentation are among the other practical difficulties of the proposed transition.

Ashokvardhan (2017) notes that the de facto implementation of titling systems would require associated systems such as planning, legislation, and financial-related regimes to be robust and updated. Issues such as surveying land and inter-linkages with other departments will also need to be addressed. According to Ganguly and Mishra (2017), of the four models of titling–Systematic, Incremental Compulsory, Incremental Optional, or the Systematic Selective Model – the best model would have to be determined for each state, depending on specific conditions prevalent in the state.

The challenges to achieving a conclusive titling system in India can be classified into the following six categories.

Legal challenges

'Land records and Records of Rights' fall under the 'State List' of the Constitution of India. As per Entry 45, List II, Seventh Schedule of the Constitution, matters pertaining to 'land revenue, including the assessment and collection of revenue, the maintenance of land records, survey for revenue purposes, and Records of rights, and 'alienation of revenues' are the domain of respective states.[8]

Land Revenue Acts (under which the land records maintained by various states derive their basis), for example, are within the jurisdiction of states and not the Union Government. Similarly, varied post-independence era legislation on land reforms, consolidation of landholdings, land ceiling, and tenancy reform are also within the states. In addition, there are laws that provide a legitimate basis for development authorities (especially for expanding peri-urban areas), town and country planning authorities, and municipal and other urban local bodies (with taxation powers and records), the majority of which are also in the state government's domain.

The GOI can, through its various programmes and schemes, attempt to incentivise state action, but legislative authority on the most critical land records questions ultimately rests with the states. This means, without initiative from the respective state governments, within their own political and social contexts, there is little traction for any such measure.[9]

Litigation

As per some survey estimates, about 66 percent of the civil cases pending in Indian Courts pertain to land disputes (Daksh 2016: 7).[10] India follows an adversarial model of litigation (while there are new mechanisms on mediation, conciliation, and arbitration) in a Common Law system that is predominantly reliant on courts and the efficacy of judicial dispute resolution procedures. This makes the legality or otherwise of particular transactions the pivotal point, especially in light of the proposed titling efforts. The multiple causes for disputes, and the nature of the dispute resolution process, are serious impediments to an effective land administration system.

Since the Judiciary assumes an indispensable role in upholding claims in India, a shift from presumptive to conclusive titling needs to be understood in terms of legal processes, structures, and verification protocols involved in judicial determinations.

For ownership and other land rights to be conclusive beyond doubt, two sets of actions are critical. The first is the recording of disputes to ensure no disputed properties are granted 'conclusive title'. To date, the land records systems in most states do not have an easy way of incorporating information on pending disputes. Similarly, Courts also do not maintain a record of disputes identifiable by survey number or property identification number. This makes determining the dispute-free land parcels for conclusive titling a risky proposition, unless timely interventions are made in the format of recording disputes.

The second set of actions would be to ensure clearing the existing backlog of millions of disputes at various levels of the judicial system. For future disputes, most of the state-level titling initiatives suggest setting up land titling tribunals and barring title suits from civil courts. However, a legislative route for such transfer of cases may not be enough, and Courts will have to be convinced of this, with a well-defined procedure for due diligence, use of reliable technology, and suitable legislative support.

Institutional complexity

A common feature across most titling legislation is the proposal for formation of a new authority for land titling – it is recommended by the Draft Model Land Titling Bill, 2011, and the AP Land Titling Bill, 2019, and is also seen in the draft Bill of the National Capital Territory of Delhi. Rajasthan also proposes creation of an urban land certification authority. The latest draft of the proposed land titling legislation in Maharashtra also recommends creation of a new authority, even though the earlier versions of the draft recommended land titling within the domain of the state revenue department.

However, despite this uniformity of approach across states, the idea of creating a new authority for land titling faces its own share of roadblocks. The most significant among these is likely to be the perceived loss of authority on part of revenue, registration, and survey departments. These departments have traditionally been the custodians of land records and are also dependent on such power for their revenue sources. Replacing the revenue department as the primary custodian, or creating a *sui generis* authority supervising its functions, directly impacts existing institutional systems. The recent draft land titling legislation in Maharashtra recommends that the heads of the three wings within the Revenue department – revenue, registration, survey and settlement – would all be part of the land titling authority – thus, attempting better cooperation and coordination. This, however, does not take away from the fact that a new authority is being envisaged on titling issues.

The early experiences of modernising land records in Karnataka (Benjamin et al. 2007), Himachal Pradesh, Haryana, and Bihar (IIHS 2017b, 2017d, 2017e) have highlighted that there is often a resistance to change, especially in the early years. Acclimatising to new systems requires coordination and cooperation across a range of stakeholders, and the incentive of each plays a critical role. There is a need to define functional jurisdictions of each of the existing and new institutions, as well as crucially, the sharing of revenue streams among them. Personnel and resource constraints, particularly to manage technological transitions, would also be one of the deciding factors.

When it comes to urban and peri-urban areas, there is a manifold increase in the complexity of regulations and multiplicity of urban authorities and their changing jurisdictions. While rural areas have the Revenue department as the single authority in charge of land records, the same is not be true for urban areas. Cities also have urban local bodies, planning authorities, development authorities, housing authorities, slum development agencies, industrial area authorities, and other special authorities – each of which performs a distinct function within urban land governance and maintains its own set of records. For a conclusive title regime to understand these institutional roles, and the political economy around them, and to incorporate various existing databases –to draw a curtain over previous transactions and ensure guarantee – there would be a need for comprehensive customisation at the state, if not city level. For example, under the *Rajasthan Urban Land (Certification of Titles) Act*, 2016, respective urban authorities oversee the surveys and dispute settlement processes in their areas, while the state-level

Urban Land Title Certification Authority would carry out verification of the applications for certificate of titles. The legislation does not address the lack of incentives for the urban local bodies to maintain an up-to-date record, and how their functioning could be linked to the certification authority.

Political economy and land tenure

The emergence of the Torrens system in Australia, or its adaptation in other countries such as the United Kingdom (UK), represents a distinctly different political economy. These are countries which have either managed to nullify previous historical claims on land and property (Wensing 1999; Secher 2000) or have had well-documented histories and record-keeping structures (Mayer and Pemberton 2000), thus making it possible to draw a curtain. Despite this, the shift from deed registration to title registration in the UK took more than 100 years (ibid).[11]

However, the political economy in India, and its rapidly urbanising status, presents a very different set of challenges. India has a relatively nascent, recent, and incomplete post-colonial history of land reforms. The largely failed land redistribution efforts in independent India, and the inability to ensure tenancy reform in practice, has resulted in a failure to address the multiple issues relating to land, of diverse sections of the population. The country continues to have a large section of the population experiencing poverty, and as such, economic considerations regarding the link among land, land tenure, and economic growth is a recurring question in national and state-level policy. Empirical studies in India have shown that property titles via computerisation of registration system did not improve access to credit in rural areas (Deininger and Goyal 2009). Such attempts are also read in light of the context of the vexed issue of urban irregular and informal settlements for which traditional titling regimes are inadequate and counterproductive. These larger questions regarding the relationship between land and people need to be recognised before adopting a Torrens-like approach.

More recently, implementation of land records modernisation programmes has highlighted that it is difficult to capture the on-ground diversity of property transactions within a standardised technological approach. A variety of documentation and arrangements are used in land transactions – both formally and informally – and several of them are yet to be captured by the formal system of land records. In addition, the tenure spectrum in urban areas is equally diverse, if not more, than rural areas. There are a range of tenure options, a result of various urban development processes as well as the gaps created by them.

Apart from ownership, properties in urban areas are often characterised by their adherence (or lack of it) with respect to building byelaws, planning processes, and municipal byelaws. For example, a particular property in the city may well have an undisputed owner of the land and building. However, that plot may be a part of an unauthorised colony and unable to access water and sanitation services. The plot could have unauthorised land use, which does not follow the city's master plan, and could further be under threat of relocation outside the city. Alternatively, the building on that plot may have an additional floor as unauthorised construction, which is under threat of demolition by the municipal authority. In addition, while the ownership is not under question, the actual possession may be with other parties. Under a simplistic conclusive titling regime focused on ownership, the property record is likely to note only the land/building ownership and not the other characteristics, which are also significant. Critically, none of these would convey an adequate sense of the de facto situation on the ground, especially where the de jure position also remains to be clarified.

Bhan (2013) defines such a comprehensive spectrum in Delhi using legality, formality, planning status, and legitimacy of the settlement as the indicators. A conclusive titling system in urban areas is by definition unable to define and acknowledge the comprehensiveness and complexity of such tenure. It is also unable to recognise or deal with the likely legal and political implications of these issues. None of the titling legislation reviewed under this study seem to demonstrate adequate cognisance of, and sensitivity to, such factors.

Status of land records

The digitisation of land records since the first GOI schemes of CoLR and SRA&ULR were introduced in 1988–89 has helped to better manage land records. As per statistics from DoLR (dated December 2018), out of a total of 36 states /Union Territories (UTs), 15 have computerised their Records of Rights to an extent of 95 percent and above, while another 17 states/ UTs have on-going initiatives. Similarly, 19 states/ UTs have computerised their registration process, while 12 are in the process of doing so. However, there is relatively slower progress in the other indicators.

One of the most crucial aspects to move towards conclusive titling is the integration of registration and land records systems. Transitioning to conclusive titling would require the registration process to verify the landownership data, and to automatically mutate the record of right subsequent to registration. However, only 11 states/UTs have been able to achieve such inter-linking, and another ten are in the process.

Similarly, linking the spatial records and the textual records is critical, but only three states have managed to do so, with ongoing initiatives in another 15 states/UTs. One of the reasons for the slow progress is because the details in textual records often do not match the spatial records, and the revenue administration needs to resolve these issues through a set of protocols, which need further implementation based on ground realities.

While these statistics reveal that not all states have made equal progress in computerisation of land records, there are certain states that have been able to achieve all four of the aforementioned steps. However, details are still awaited as to the quality and extent of such efforts, thus restricting their transition to a conclusive title regime. Other factors also play a critical role, including unrecorded encumbrances (land acquisition, partition, pending disputes, and mortgage), inadequate infrastructure, as well as recording of legacy information.

The disconnect between recent technological initiatives and the legal position is also important. Some statutory developments at the Centre have enabled the status of 'electronic records' for some computerised land records. The *Information Technology Act, 2000*, and the amended *Indian Evidence Act, 1882*, confers evidentiary value on electronic records. However, procedural aspects such as the necessary legal due diligence required, as well as issues pertaining to public access of records, remain to be addressed. In most states, technological initiatives may not be backed by sufficient legislative endorsement, thus stopping short of providing these initiatives with complete legal protection. For example, computerisation of registration process and its inter-linking with land records has enabled the sub-registrar to verify whether the seller is indeed the owner of the land, as a way to ensuring a more transparent system and fewer fraudulent transactions. However, under the deeds-registration system, the sub-registrar is not required to verify such chain of ownership, and further, the technological link between registration and revenue records may well not be taken into account. There is, therefore, a need to ensure adequate statutory foundations for such technological initiatives. This may also help in bringing greater clarity with respect to various procedural protocols that revenue departments in different states undertake for their departmental operations.

Urban and peri-urban areas face particular challenges of maintaining up-to-date land records, especially regarding the areas covered under the records, relevant details being captured, comprehensiveness of the record format, and status of updation (IIHS 2017a). Some of these are as follows:

Urban/abadi areas not covered: North Indian states such as Delhi, Punjab, and Haryana do not have land records for abadi areas, and the rural records typically stop getting maintained as soon as urbanisation processes start.

Inadequate level of detail; records not comprehensive: Maharashtra and Gujarat have a system of city surveys in which records of urban areas are maintained in a format different than rural areas, and by a different agency. However, these too typically tend to omit/overlook record keeping in apartments. The details captured in these formats are also reflective of the local landholding pattern and are not typically standardised – for example, in Maharashtra, city survey records of most apartment complexes reflect the name of the cooperative housing society, and not of individual apartment owners. This is because the ownership of the flat is typically vested by way of their membership of the cooperative housing society – which may not be congruent to the idea of property ownership under the conclusive titling regime.

Urban records not up-to-date: Some other states in eastern and southern India maintain records of urban areas in the same format as rural areas – however, the frequency of transactions (including changing spatial demarcation) in urban and peri-urban areas is often so high that the records may not reflect the on-ground situation in adequate detail or an updated state.

As a result, across India, even if some urban land records exist, they are often not updated (in terms of spatial or textual information) and do not have information adequate to represent the complexities of urban property.

In this context, it is important to note that among the legislative documents analysed for this chapter, only Maharashtra talks about a 'strata' title – or a title for vertical properties. The Rajasthan Act, despite being meant only for urban areas, does not address the question of whether vertical properties would be recorded. Beginning in 2014, Gujarat now attempts to capture vertical properties in its city survey records, but the initiative is restricted to newer areas under city survey jurisdiction (IIHS 2017b).

Status of resurveys and spatial records

Survey is a very distinct and important part in most of the proposed titling legislations and the state-level technological initiatives. Assigning a unique property ID is also a common feature among them. The link between conclusive titling and resurvey was first instituted in the policy domain by NLRMP, which introduced funding sources for mass-scale resurvey exercises in various states. The GOI Expert Committee, in its 2014 report on roadmap to land titling, had recognised that an essential prerequisite for the systematic model of land titling was the existence of a 'proper cadastral survey record', and also noted 'definite advantages in terms of time, cost and resources if the resurvey exercise and titling are done simultaneously'. The Delhi Land Titling Bill, 2009; the Draft Model Land Titling Bill, 2011; and the *Rajasthan Urban Land Titling Act, 2016*, recommend surveys to create the initial set of records for the title register.[12] The Maharashtra draft legislation (2018) and the AP Land Titling Bill, 2019, also recommend creation of an initial record of accurate or approximate boundaries with distinct property identity numbers but enable use of existing records to be adapted for the purpose, instead of a focus on cadastral surveys.[13]

When the NLRMP began in 2008, 50 percent of the funds under the programme were targeted towards resurvey (DoLR 2008–09: 41). This led to massive resurvey exercises being initiated in several states. However, the survey results could be finalised in only a handful of villages across the country, except for Gujarat (IIHS 2017a). The resurvey experiences revealed that often there is divergence between new geo-referenced spatial databases (which are more accurate because of the use of the latest technology but do not have immediate legal validity) when compared with physical existing spatial records (which are less accurate but are legally valid documents).

Increased spatial accuracy as a result of resurveys may increase disputes in the short and medium term, as the survey findings are often challenged by people whose landholding size mentioned in the record of right decreases. For example, according to some settlement officials from Himachal Pradesh, in some areas the number of objections received after a resurvey exercise may be around 20,000–30,000 per tehsil, or filed by 10 to 20 percent of all landowners (IIHS 2017e: 30, 61). As per recent news reports ('Gujarat government receives' 2018), it appears that the Gujarat state government received around 18,000 complaints regarding the resurvey. These objections often lead to new spatial records being shelved by the state government, thus not creating an accurate up-to-date spatial mirror. For example, as per recent news reports ('Guj govt halts process' 2018), finalisation of resurvey records in the remaining 6,000 villages of Gujarat was recently put on hold, apparently because of issues pertaining to reduction in plot sizes, disappearance of grazing land, and other procedural issues ('Govt halts process of' 2018, 'Gujarat halts agricultural land' 2018).

By the end of 2016, the DoLR issued policy circular no. 1 of 2016 (DoLR 8 December 2016), which restricted any Central fund allocation for resurvey and limited availability of funds to only new surveys of unsurveyed areas.[14] Some countries have implemented the Torrens system or have title guarantee systems in place but do not assure accuracy of boundaries.[15] In India, the years 2017 and 2018 have witnessed an increasing number of conversations on title insurance for real estate projects (refer to IRDAI Working Group 2016), and the position of insurance policies on accuracy of boundary details would become increasingly relevant.

A review of the existing status of land records management in India brings out challenges in each of the four principles of conclusive titling advocated by NLRMP/ DILRMP. The current land records are not a mirror of the on-ground situation – they are either not reliable, or not up-to-date, and the textual records often do not match the spatial records. Some states have made significant technological progress, but a lot remains to be done in terms of ensuring access to the common citizen. The latest attempt to create a mirror of the on-ground situation – through the resurvey initiatives under NLRMP – has not seen any major success and may have inadvertently led to an increased number of disputes in the short term. These existing disputes form a major roadblock to drawing a curtain over the older chain of titles, again, demonstrated through the resurvey experience.

Maintaining a record of land-related disputes is itself fraught with issues, and clearing the current backlog or transferring it to special tribunals would need strong judicial support at various levels. The efficacy of evidence and verification protocols would determine whether or not the Judiciary recognises the legal curtain over historical land and property rights. The third principle of indemnifying against any defect in title is related to the mirror and curtain aspects, and it would need a much-strengthened land record system for the state guarantee to be a viable option. The private sector may be considering the prospect of title insurance, but its limited application to real estate projects and restrictive affordability may prevent it from making a substantial difference in the conclusive titling prospects. The fourth principle of having a single authority, often de novo, is one of the more complex institutional questions, and the implications would vary substantially from one state to another.

Crucially, land records fulfil more than just economic functions. In the states of Punjab and Haryana, land records include *shajra-nasb* (the genealogy tree of each landowning family in a village). In Himachal Pradesh, *wajib-ul-arj* (a part of the record of right) denotes the customary rights in a village, including sharing of water sources, grazing rights, and the right to timber. In Maharashtra, they are used to record areas under cultivation every year, including crop type and irrigation. In several other states, land records are used to record and determine caste structures, and accordingly provide legal certificates. These records also serve as archives to historical tenure systems, distinguishing freehold ownership from *inam* land, *shamlat* land, *poramboke* land, *khas mahal* land,[16] etc., each of which has a distinct meaning and legal connotation in the local context. Reducing these land records to simply their economic function – largely of ownership rights – under conclusive titling requires structural changes for which many states may not be ready.

The neoliberal impulse is manifest in the tendency to reduce land records to the purely economic and transactional, ignoring other socio-historical aspects. Ensuring accurate records is a measure that the state can use to harness other distributive ends, but the narrow focus on titling and ownership, through the adoption of the Torrens system, to the exclusion of other tenure aspects, directs all attention to the areas with maximum economic activity and neglect of other areas. This creates disincentives for the difficult task of improving the larger system. Further, the lack of accurate survey details in such titling efforts makes the title itself fraught with the threat of litigation. Therefore, there is need to distinguish the State's modernising impulse of computerising and digitising land records from the neoliberal impulse of focusing on title legislation based on the Torrens model, to the exclusion of other systemic issues.

There appears to be a tendency of reducing records to transactional frequency, especially focusing on registration. This would imply that other considerations which impact political economy, such as social aspects of gender and caste; informal settlements with insecure property rights; acquisition, rehabilitation, and resettlement issues; questions of land use, including commons in urban and rural areas; and land in the context of fragile ecosystems (especially where more community-based maintenance of such systems are involved), do not receive adequate attention. The ostensible objective seems to be the need to make records clear and accurate in terms of title and extend such information to questions of litigation and charges on such records, in order to make buyer-seller transactions more transparent and accurate. This focus on transactions alone takes away from other realities around land use, in rural as well as urban areas.

State governments remain the primary institutional actors when it comes to land administration. Most of the states are cognisant of their respective positions with respect to status of land records and the significance of land systems in their overall social, political, economic, financial, and institutional structures. The key challenge remains one of ensuring real-time accuracy, that is, up-to-date land records, accessible to the common citizen, beyond mere formalities of computerisation and digitisation. Given the systemic nature of the issues highlighted, incremental measures to ensure an updated, more comprehensive real-time land record system appear more pragmatic than instant top-down measures such as titling legislation, which do not seem to adequately account for the complexities within land tenure and land administration systems in India.

Notes

1 The authors work with the Indian Institute for Human Settlements (IIHS). Views expressed are personal.
2 Record of Right (RoR) in the states of Punjab and Haryana. It is the revenue record in which various rights and liabilities in respect of every piece of land are noted.
3 With revenue records in a state of disrepair, the earliest Central Government schemes to computerise land records began with the Computerisation of Land Records (CoLR) Scheme in 1988–89 and the Strengthening of Revenue Administration and Updating of Land Records (SRA&ULR) Scheme in 1989–90.
4 For the purpose of this chapter, the 2011 version of the Draft Model Land Titling Bill (from the DoLR website) has been referred to. However, this document is no longer available on the website.
5 An official copy of the bill was put up on the Delhi government website for public consultation (Nov 2009) but is currently not available on the website.
6 An interim draft (dated July 2018) has been referred for the purpose of this chapter. An earlier draft (dated 2015) was accessible on the Chandrapur district website but is not currently available.
7 Resurvey records of approximately 11,000 villages (out of a total 18,000 villages) in Gujarat have been finalised ('Gujarat: Brakes on fixing' 2018).
8 At the same time, the 'transfer of property other than agricultural land; registration of deeds and documents' fall within the Concurrent List (List III, Seventh Schedule) powers (to both Union and states). A number of central laws exist on matters that have a direct relationship with land records: the *Registration Act, 1908*; the *Stamp Act, 1899*; the *Transfer of Property Act, 1882*; the *Evidence Act, 1872*; and so on. It is important to note that the Constitution of India does not expressly refer to 'title' in relation to land and land-related transactions.
9 At the same time, certain amendments will also be required in the *Indian Registration Act*, 1908, to move from deed-based registration to title-based registration,

as recommended by the Model Land Titling Bill, 2011; the Maharashtra Draft Bill, 2018; and the AP Land Titling Bill, 2019.

10 Estimated by Daksh (2016: 7) from a survey of 9,329 litigants across 305 locations in 170 districts of 24 states. According to the National Judicial Data Grid, as of January 2019, a total of 8.5 million civil cases are pending in the district and taluka courts of India, and another 2.3 million civil cases are pending in the High Courts.

11 According to Mayer and Pemberton (2000), deed registration in the UK began as early as 1535. Title registration was introduced via a Statute in 1862, and then made compulsory for the first time in 1897. The last areas in the UK to opt for compulsory title registration were brought in by 1990. New legislation in 1998 widened the scope for compulsory registration, but the system is yet to include all the properties in England and Wales.

12 Following a systematic model, the Delhi Land Titling Bill, 2009, and the Draft Model Land Titling Bill, 2011, propose notification of survey results, and use of these to create a provisional title register, unless challenged. The *Rajasthan Act of 2016* proposes a mix of systematic model and incremental-optional model wherein a survey is to be conducted in the notified urban areas, but the title registration would take place only upon voluntary application by the landholder, with no distinct link to the survey proceedings within the Act.

13 In the case of Maharashtra, this is more likely in view of a systematic selective titling, targeted at apartment complexes and other clean titles in urban areas.

14 NLRMP Guidelines 2008–09 allocated INR 31.48 billion over an estimated five-year period. Of this, INR 16 billion was earmarked for resurvey exercises (DoLR 2008–09: 41). At the end of eight years, by December 2015, only INR 11.7 billion of the sanctioned 31 billion had been released (DoLR 2016: 26). The revised DILRMP guidelines 2018–19 have reduced the total outlay to INR 9.5 billion over a three-year period and do not have any amount earmarked for resurvey exercises (DoLR 2018: 38–39).

15 As noted by Sinha (2017), the Torrens system in Queensland, Australia, 'guarantees only the correctness of the title and of the recorded land rights and; it neither guarantees, nor pays compensation for errors in measurements of the land and in the delineation of boundaries.' Similarly, Her Majesty's Land Registry (HMLR) in the United Kingdom also does not guarantee the correctness of land parcel boundaries and instead relies on 'general boundaries' (Ordnance Survey 2018).

16 These are different categories of lands which are not under freehold private ownership, and their legal status and characteristics vary based on the prevalent revenue system. For example, *inam* lands in Gujarat are rent-free lands received as grants, which can be inherited. *Shamlat* lands in Punjab are areas which are under community ownership of all landowners in a village, while *poramboke* lands are typically uncultivable lands which are outside the revenue records. *Khas mahal* land in West Bengal is government-owned land historically given out on lease for particular purposes.

References

Ashokvardhan, C. 2017. 'Critique of the land titling bill, 2011: Bihar experience', in Varsha Ganguly and Snehasis Mishra (eds.), *Journey towards land titling in India* (pp. 18–29). Mussoorie: LBSNAA.

Benjamin, S., R. Bhuvaneswari and P. Rajan Manjunatha. 2007. *Bhoomi: "E-Governance", or, an anti-politics machine necessary to globalize Bangalore?*

CASUM-m Working paper. Retrieved from https://casumm.files.wordpress. com/2008/09/bhoomi-e-governance.pdf accessed on 13 October 2018.

Bhan, G. 2013. 'Planned illegalities: housing and the "Failure" of planning in Delhi: 1947–2010', *Economic and Political Weekly*, 48(24): 58–70.

Constitution of India, Seventh Schedule.

Daksh. 2016. *Access to justice survey 2015–16*. Bengaluru: Daksh. Retrieved from http://dakshindia.org/wp-content/uploads/2016/05/Daksh-access-to-justice-sur vey.pdf accessed on 11 January 2019.

Deininger, K. and A. Goyal. 2009. *Going digital: credit effects of land registry computerization in India (English)*. Washington, DC: World Bank.

Delhi Survey, Registration and Recordal of Title of Immovable Properties in Urban Areas Bill (Draft). 2009. *Digital India land record modernization programme (DILRMP)*. New Delhi: Department of Land Resources, Ministry of Rural Development, Government of India. Retrieved from http://dolr.gov.in/sites/default/ files/Review%20of%20Physical%20Progress%20in%20respect%20of%20DIL RMP-%2028-12-2018.pdf accessed on 17 January 2019.

DoLR. 2008–2009. *The national land records modernization programme (NLRMP), guidelines, technical manuals and MIS, 2008–09*. New Delhi: Department of Land Resources, Ministry of Rural Development, Government of India.

DoLR. 2016. *Outcome budget 2016–17 of Ministry of Rural Development, Department of Land Resources*. New Delhi: Department of Land Resources, Ministry of Rural Development, Government of India.

DoLR. 2016, 8 December. *Survey/Resurvey under digital India land records modernization programme (DILRMP) – policy circular no. 1 of 2016*. New Delhi: Department of Land Resources, Ministry of Rural Development, Government of India.

DoLR. 2016, 22 September. *Rationalization of centrally sponsored scheme DILRMP as central sector scheme – clarification thereof and progress till date*. New Delhi: Department of Land Resources, Ministry of Rural Development, Government of India.

DoLR. 2017, 21 February. *Digital India land records modernisation programme (DILRMP) – implementation in urban areas – regarding [Policy circular no. 2 of 2017]*. New Delhi: Department of Land Resources, Ministry of Rural Development, Government of India.

DoLR. 2018, 26 December. *Review of physical progress in respect of digital India land records*. New Delhi: Department of Land Resources, Ministry of Rural Development, Government of India.

DoLR. 2018–2019. *The digital India land records modernization programme (DILRMP) guidelines, technical manuals and MIS, 2018–19*. New Delhi: Department of Land Resources, Ministry of Rural Development, Government of India.

DoLR and NIC. 2012. *Success stories on national land records modernisation programme (NLRMP)*. New Delhi: Department of Land Resources, Ministry of Rural Development, Government of India.

Draft Model Land Titling Bill. 2011. Retrieved from http://dolr.nic.in/dolr/down loads/docs/Revised Draft Land Titling Bill 2011 13-05-2011.doc accessed on 24 July 2016.

Ganguly, Varsha and Snehasis Mishra. 2017. 'Introduction: journey towards land titling in India', in Varsha Ganguly and Snehasis Mishra (eds.), *Journey towards land titling in India* (pp. 1–17). Mussoorie: LBSNAA.

GOI Expert Committee. 2014. *Land titling – a road map*. Retrieved from https://landportal.org/pt/file/36816/download?token=0QFtR3F1 accessed on 28 December 2018.

Goswami, Amlanjyoti and Deepika Jha. 2016. 'Your title is not ready yet: Rajasthan's land titling legislation', *Economic and Political Weekly*, 51(34): 26–19.

'Govt halts process of finalising land records'. 2018, 22 August. *The Indian Express*. Retrieved from https://indianexpress.com/article/cities/ahmedabad/govt-halts-process-of-finalising-land-records-5318379/ accessed on 15 January 2019.

'Gujarat: Brakes on fixing land records of 6,000 villages'. 2018, 22 August. *The Times of India*. Retrieved from https://timesofindia.indiatimes.com/city/ahmedabad/brakes-on-fixing-land-records-of-6k-villages/articleshow/65494436.cms accessed on 15 January 2019.

'Gujarat government halts process of finalising land records'. 2018, 21 August. *Business Standard*. Retrieved from www.business-standard.com/article/pti-stories/guj-govt-halts-process-of-finalising-land-records-118082100812_1.html accessed on 15 January 2019.

'Gujarat government receives 18,000 objection applications against land survey'. 2018, 2 August. *DNA*. Retrieved from www.dnaindia.com/ahmedabad/report-gujarat-government-receives-18000-objection-applications-against-land-survey-2644607 accessed on 15 January 2019.

'Gujarat halts agricultural land resurvey process due to errors and irregularities'. 2018, 22 August. *The Pioneer*. Retrieved from www.dailypioneer.com/2018/india/gujarat-halts-agricultural-land-resurvey-process-due-to-errors-and-irregularities.html accessed on 15 January 2019.

IIHS. 2017a. *Land records modernisation in India: an institutional legal and policy review*. Bangalore: Indian Institute for Human Settlements.

IIHS. 2017b. *Land records modernisation: Bihar*. Bangalore: Indian Institute for Human Settlements.

IIHS. 2017c. *Land records modernisation: Gujarat*. Bangalore: Indian Institute for Human Settlements.

IIHS. 2017d. *Land records modernisation: Haryana*. Bangalore: Indian Institute for Human Settlements.

IIHS. 2017e. *Land records modernisation: Himachal Pradesh*. Bangalore: Indian Institute for Human Settlements.

Indian Evidence Act. 1882.

Indian Registration Act. 1908.

Indian Stamp Act. 1899.

Information Technology Act. 2000.

IRDAI Working Group. 2016. *Title insurance in India*. Retrieved from www.irdai.gov.in/ADMINCMS/cms/frmGeneral_NoYearList.aspx?DF=Creport&mid=12 accessed on 21 November 2018.

Maharashtra Land Revenue Code (Amendment) Bill (Draft). 2018.

Mayer, P. and A. Pemberton. 2000. *A short history of land registration in England and wales*. London: Her Majesty's Land Registry.

McKinsey Global Institute. 2001. *India: the growth imperative: understanding the barriers to rapid growth and employment creation*. New Delhi: McKinsey Global Institute.

National Judicial Data Grid. 2019. *Statistics on number of pending civil cases*. Retrieved from http://njdg.ecourts.gov.in/hcnjdg_public/main.php accessed on

11 January 2019; https://njdg.ecourts.gov.in/njdgnew/index.php accessed on 11 January 2019.

Nayak, P. 2013. 'Policy shifts in land records management', *Economic and Political Weekly*, 48(24): 71–75.

Ordnance Survey. 2018. *Property boundaries and who records them.* Retrieved from www.ordnancesurvey.co.uk/resources/property-boundaries-owners.html accessed on 21 November 2018.

Pandit, Ambika. 2015, 11 July. '7 years after land titling bill drafted, state govt told it has no jurisdiction', *The Times of India.* Retrieved from https://timesofindia. indiatimes.com/city/delhi/7yrs-after-land-titling-bill-drafted-state-govt-told-it-has-no-jurisdiction/articleshow/48026473.cms accessed on 15 January 2019.

Rajasthan Urban Land (Certification of Titles) Act. 2016.

Ramanathan, S. 2009. *Introduction of land title certification system: state level reform.* Retrieved from http://jnnurm.nic.in/nurmudweb/Reforms/Primers/Optional/primer_LTCS.pdf accessed on 5 February 2011.

Secher, U. 2000. 'Native title: an exception to indefeasibility and a ground for invoking the deferred indefeasibility theory', *James Cook University Law Review*, 7: 17–73.

Sinha, R. 2017. 'Adapting the Torrens conclusive titling system in India: debatable issues and way forward', in Varsha Ganguly and Snehasis Mishra (eds.), *Journey towards land titling in India* (pp. 66–85). Mussoorie: LBSNAA.

Suraj Bhan vs. Financial Commissioner and Others. 2007 (6) SCC 186.

The Constitution of India. 1950. Schedule VII.

Transfer of Property Act. 1882.

Wadhwa, D.C. 1989. 'Guaranteeing title to land – a preliminary study', *Economic and Political Weekly*, 24(41): 2323–2334.

Wensing, E. 1999. *Comparing native title and Anglo-Australian land law: two different timelines, two different cultures and two different laws.* Australia: The Australia Institute. Retrieved from www.tai.org.au/sites/defualt/files/DP25_8.pdf accessed on 19 January 2019.

Williamson, I., S. Enemark, J. Wallace and A. Rajabifard. 2010. *Land administration for sustainable development.* Redlands: ESRI Press Academic.

Zasloff, J. 2011. 'India's land title crisis: the unanswered questions', *Jindal Global Law Review*, 3(1): 1–34.

3 Critical assessment of recent real estate regulatory reforms in urban spaces

Whether trickle-down effect is for all?

Ray Sharat Prasad

Introduction: manifestations of neoliberalism in India

Fresh with the memories of exploitative colonial experience and Fabian socialism being in vogue among decision makers, India, after independence, adopted a model of governance which was based on the tenets of a 'welfare state' and which was inclined towards State monopolisation of resources and redistribution, protectionism, and intervention – both at macro and micro levels of governance – through central planning.

In 1992, a paradigm shift from a pre-1992 model of governance towards a new model of governance occurred in India. The new model adopted is one of the variations of the neoliberal model of governance[1] (Steger and Roy 2010), which believes in establishment of a robust market as the driving force for socio-economic growth, with minimal State intervention at the micro level of governance but with greater State intervention at the macro level of governance (Peck 2001) as a market regulator and facilitator of demand, supply, and value creation in commodities. It does not entail the 'rolling back' of State regulations and the 'rolling forward' of the market; instead, it advocates a complex reconstitution of State-economy relations in which State institutions are actively mobilised to promote market-based regulatory arrangements (Brenner and Theodore 2005).

The new economic model – structural adjustment programme – carries the elements of neoliberalism advocated by the International Monetary Fund and the World Bank and backs liberalisation, privatization, and globalisation as the tools for driving economic growth in India. The reasons for this paradigm shift could be both external and internal. External reasons could be to bail India out of the balance of payment crisis that was accelerated by the first Gulf War and sudden decline in remittances from Indian expatriates in the Middle East (Ahmed, 2007), and a decline in India's foreign trade because of the collapse of the Soviet Union and the growing availability of investible resources in foreign exchange (Kohli 2006). Internal reasons could be that Indian capital had split politically – being fed up with the license raj, red-tapism, and corruption – with significant factions at least willing to experiment with a more open economy.

This paradigm shift from a pre-1992 'welfare state' model of governance towards the neoliberal model of governance can also be witnessed in a series of post-1991 legislative and policy reforms regulating the urban real estate sector in India. The neoliberal approach adopted by the State (henceforth neoliberal India) in regulating the urban real estate sector envisages a systematic, rather proactive, intervention of the State as a regulator and the facilitator in creating sustainable demand, supply, and value in urban land parcels and urban real estate commodities.[2] The State, by acting as a facilitator and regulator of the urban real estate market, aims to create better opportunities and possibilities for all the actors in the urban real estate sphere – landowners, investors, developers, and consumers – involved in the creation of supply and demand in urban real estate commodities. The State expects that this approach will assist in achieving the twin objectives of sustainable economic growth and fulfilment of the socio-economic aspirations of all such actors, including those of the urban poor, through the trickle-down effect.

The new land acquisition act[3] – *Right to Fair Compensation and Transparency in Land Acquisition, Rehabilitation & Resettlement Act, 2013* (RFCTLARRA), which replaces the old act (*Land Acquisition Act, 1984 –* LAA) made the land acquisition process difficult and stringent. Under RFCTLARRA, in cases in which the government intends to acquire land for public-private partnership (PPP) projects or for private companies, a prior consent of at least 70 percent and 80 percent of the affected landowners, respectively, is required to be obtained. Further, in addition to one-time cash payments, a payment of compensation of up to four times the market value of the land in rural areas and up to twice the market value in urban areas is required to be made by the State to the landowner whose land is acquired. Additionally, the government is also obligated to resettle and rehabilitate all project-affected persons, including the landless, and to provide socio-economic benefits such as land for land, housing, employment, and annuities to such persons. In case the land is acquired for urbanisation purposes, 20 percent of the developed land is required to be reserved and offered to the landowners, in proportion to the area of the land acquired, keeping into consideration the cost of its acquisition and development.

Given the stringent provisions of RFCTLARRA as well as that it is a time-consuming process, with huge upfront costs and long, drawn-out litigations involved in acquiring land parcels for various projects, the State is consciously giving up its pre-1992 era role of an acquirer and accumulator of land for projects and is looking for alternative modes of land aggregation.

Specifically in the urban context, the State has taken up the new role of a broker to facilitate land aggregation in urban areas by private real estate developers for the development of urban real estate commodities 'because in a market economy private companies are the main agents of economic growth, [and][4] they too must be assisted in overcoming this obstacle' (Levien

2018: 11). In other words, in the context of a market economy, the State has become an agent for generating the supply of urban land parcels (a scarce commodity) to be exploited by real estate investors and private developers to produce the urban real estate commodities to be sold in an open market to maximise their returns on investments (RoIs).

The State is also taking up the role of a value creator in urban and urbanisable land parcels through integrated development of large-scale, city-level infrastructure in urban areas, more often on a PPP model. Recent policies such as the Smart City Mission, Atal Mission for Rejuvenation and Urban Transformation (AMRUT), and National Heritage City Development and Augmentation Yojana (HRIDAY), to name a few, which are discussed later in this chapter, stand as a testimony for the same. Development of urban real estate commodities on such value-added urban and urbanisable land parcels promises creation of a healthy market for such products to fetch exponential RoIs.

Further, in a market economy, creating a healthy demand in urban real estate commodities is imperative. It requires a robust regulatory framework for regulating the real estate sector. Keeping this in mind, the State is proactively making legislative and policy interventions to regulate real estate deals and bring legal certainty to title and ownership in urban land parcels and urban real estate commodities.

In the given background, this chapter first presents how, through its recent legislative actions and policies, the State aims at creating innovative means for generating a supply of developable urban land parcels, both horizontally and vertically, for development of urban real estate commodities. Through systematic and proactive intervention as a regulator and facilitator, the State attempts to attract investments from real estate investors and private developers for the development of urban real estate commodities. By doing so, the State also facilitates creation of the city-level infrastructure in and around urban areas and urbanisable land, resulting in value creation therein and thereby attracting investments for their development. By revealing the role played by the State in bringing legal certainty to title and ownership in urban land parcels and urban real estate commodities, the chapter discusses the State's creating a conducive environment for stimulating demand in urban real estate commodities among the consumers and investors. The chapter concludes with discussion on whether recent legislative trends and policies regulating the real estate sector would lead to balanced economic growth, which would have a trickle-down effect of such nature that the socio-economic benefits and prosperity – as claimed by neoliberalists to be associated with the economic growth generated based on the operation of market forces – would permeate to all sections of the urban population, especially the urban poor who are historically prone to dispossession, displacement, and marginalisation during the whole land-grab process.

Generating land supply

In the 1960s economy, as the private sector was not sturdy enough to shoulder the responsibility of urbanisation and housing, the State used land acquisition as the tool for generating a supply of urbanisable land. However, the increasing cost of land acquisition and protracted litigations involved in the whole process made such land acquisitions unviable for the State during the 1980s. Further, the surge in consumer demand for urban real estate commodities because of their increased spending appetite had made the supply of urban real estate commodities from the government stable inadequate. The private sector, now with surplus capital at their disposal, started seeking a larger role in the development of urban real estate commodities. The neoliberal state started exploring alternatives to the land acquisition method for creating a pool of urbanisable land to be exploited by real estate investors and private developers, which culminated in the framing of new State policies for creating an urbanisable land bank such as land pooling, transferable development rights, transit-oriented development, reclassification of zones and land use, and liquidation of public landholdings.

Land pooling policy

Land pooling policy (LPP) is a land aggregation policy being taken up by various state governments in India, which aims at pooling of land parcels owned by private landowners in urban villages, urbanisable areas, and urban extensions for the development of urban sectors. With the State acting as a facilitator and regulator of such land-pooling schemes on the PPP model, LPP works as an alternative to the land acquisition method and supplies large, contiguous, urbanisable land parcels for the development of urban real estate commodities and city-level infrastructure. Depending on the purpose, different models of LPP have been adopted by different states. The cases of Delhi and Andhra Pradesh are discussed here.

Case study I – Delhi

The Ministry of Urban Development (Delhi Division) has recently notified an amendment in the Master Plan for Delhi-2021 (MPD-2021) to adopt the LPP for Delhi (Delhi LPP).[5] The Delhi Development Authority (DDA), the nodal agency for implementation of Delhi LPP, has also notified the regulations for operationalisation of Delhi LPP.[6]

Under Delhi LPP, the private sector has been entrusted with the role of pooling contiguous land parcels from private landowners in urbanisable areas of Delhi's 95 urban villages lying in its urban peripheries and developing physical and social infrastructure thereon. Under this concept, landowners or groups of landowners pool land parcels free of cost for the development of urban sectors. Once a minimum of 70 contiguous land parcels have been pooled, free of encumbrances, such pooled land becomes eligible for development under the LPP. For an integrated planning of a sector, 40 percent of the pooled land will be made available to DDA and service-providing agencies for the development of the city-level infrastructure (external development) as per zonal development plan (ZDP) and sector layout plans approved by DDA. The remaining 60 percent of the pooled land will be handed over by DDA post development of the city-level infrastructure to the consortium[7] of the participating landowners or the developer entity[8] for the development of residential (53 percent), commercial (5 percent), and public/semi-public (PSP) facilities (internal development) as per the sector plans and ZDP approved by DDA. The external and internal development charges will be borne by the participant landowners. Only the consortium or developer entities registered under RERA[9] will be eligible for return of separate land parcels by DDA, for the final development. However, there is no minimum land size prescribed for being eligible to participate in the land pooling scheme.

A maximum of 200 floor area ratio (FAR)[10] on the returned land has been permitted for development by the consortium or developer entity. They are, however, required to utilise a mandatory FAR of 15 percent over and above the maximum permissible residential FAR for the development of housing for economically weaker sections (EWS). Delhi LPP, however, does not provide for the interim rehabilitation and resettlement of small landowners who pool their land parcel under the scheme.

Case Study II – Andhra Pradesh

The *Andhra Pradesh Reorganization Act, 2014*, laid the foundation for reorganisation of the existing state of Andhra Pradesh which prioritised the formation of a new capital city for the state. The Government of Andhra Pradesh (AP Government) enacted the *Andhra Pradesh Capital Region Development Authority Act, 2014* (APCRDA Act) for the declaration of the new capital area for the state and establishment of the Andhra Pradesh Capital Region Development Authority (APCRDA) for the planned development of the greenfield capital region and capital city area for the state known as 'Amaravati'. The APCRDA Act provides for the development of Amaravati based on two modes of land aggregation – voluntary land pooling scheme (LPS) and land acquisition under RFCTLARRA.

The LPS aims at facilitating the AP Government to consolidate the land parcels owned by individuals or group of owners (mostly farmers) in the city capital area, identified between the cities of Vijayawada and Guntur on the banks of the river Krishna covering an area of 122 square kilometres,[11] through voluntary transfer of their ownership rights therein to CRDA. The CRDA takes responsibility for developing the city-level infrastructure on the pooled land and allotting residential or commercial plots developed on the pooled land through a draw of lots to the original landowners proportional to their surrendered land parcels along with land-pooling ownership certificates and other benefits as provided in Table 3.1. Ownership of the

Table 3.1 Returnable land and benefits to landowners per 0.4 hectares of land pooled

Returnable land	Category		Social benefits
	Dry land	Jareebu land (wetland)	AP Government to provide:
Patta (leasehold)			
Residential	1,000 sq. yds.	1,000 sq. yds.	1 Pension of INR
Commercial	200 sq. yds.	300 sq. yds.	2,500
Assigned			a month per family
Residential	800 sq. yds.	800 sq. yds.	for a period of
Commercial	100 sq. yds.	200 sq. yds.	ten years to all
Yearly payment	30,000	50,000	landless
for ten years			families through
(INR)			a capital region
Yearly increase	3,000	5,000	social security
(INR)			fund
One-time	50,000		2 One-time
additional			agricultural loan
payment for			waiver of up to
gardens like			INR 0.15 million
lime/sapot/			per family to
guava (INR)			farmers
			3 Interest-free loan of up to INR 2.5 million to all poor families for self-employment
			4 Housing to houseless people as well as those losing houses in the course of development
			5 Free education and medical facilities to all those residing as on8 December 2014
			6 Old-age homes
			7 Enhancement in the limit under NREGA up to 365 days a year per family

Source: G.O.MS.No.1, MA & UD (M2) Department dated 01.01.2015, Government of Andhra Pradesh

excess land, remaining after the allotment of the developed plots to such landowners, vests with CRDA. Development of the residential or commercial plots allotted to the original landowners under LPS is to be carried out by the landowners themselves at their own cost.

The AP Government has empowered itself under the APCRDA Act to acquire the land parcels of landowners – who fail to give consent for pooling their land parcels – under RFCTLARRA. The APCRDA Act also contains penal provisions, including imprisonment of any person who obstructs the implementation of LPS or such land acquisition.

Transferable development rights

Transferable development rights, or tradable development rights (TDR), is a zoning tool used by the State as an alternative to land acquisition, to increase the vertical and horizontal densities in planned areas of a city and its suburbs. It is a mechanism used by urban local bodies (ULBs) in India for making available additional FAR, tradable in market, in the form of TDR certificates to owners who have surrendered their land to ULBs. TDRs can be used at some other planned areas of a city or its suburbs for construction of built-up space over and above the normally available FAR in such areas. TDR, in other words, enables the transfer of development potential, partly or fully, from one plot to another. By issuing TDRs, the government aims at implementing planned development of urban spaces. Such planned development may, *inter alia*, include development of housing (including affordable housing and slum rehabilitation), commercial spaces, and city-level infrastructure.

Transit-oriented development

Transit-oriented development (TOD) is a zoning tool used by the state governments in India which creates opportunities for restructuring of urban spaces in a city by incentivising optimum utilisation of available developed, semi-developed, or developable urban spaces along transit corridors such as the mass rapid transit system (MRTS), metro rail corridors, and bus rapid transit system (BRTS). TOD aims at integrating land use and transport planning to develop planned urban growth centres by generating a supply of vertical urban spaces with additional FAR over and above what is generally available along transit corridors. TOD helps in achieving high-density, mixed land use by generating a supply of additional vertically developable urban spaces, further opening up opportunities for development of urban real estate commodities by private developers.

Reclassifying zones and land use

The policy of carrying out strategic amendment in the city master plans by the state governments for re-classification of existing zones and land use – from agricultural to residential or from residential to commercial or from industrial to residential/commercial (mixed use) – facilitates the generation of supply of urban land parcels for development by bringing peripheral urban villages within urbanisable zones and also allows for the redevelopment of land (e.g., falling under industrial zone) within urban areas for residential or commercial use. It complements the objectives of the TDR policy, the TOD policy, the policy for development of low-density residential plots[12] (in Delhi), and the policy for development of low-density residential country homes[13] (in the state of Punjab).

Liquidation of public landholdings

Another method adopted by the central and state governments for generating a supply of urban land parcels is liquidating urban land parcels held by various government and quasi-government departments and loss-making public sector undertakings (PSUs) for development of urban real estate commodities under the PPP model.

Attracting investments in the urban real estate sector

Given the limited resources of the state, attracting private investments for development of urban real estate commodities becomes imperative for a state adopting a neoliberal approach of governance. Such investments are required at two stages – at the stage of land aggregation or acquisition and at the stage of construction and development of the urban real estate commodities. The state is playing a vital role in generating a supply of urbanised land and urban real estate commodities by creating an ecosystem for attracting investments from private investors and developers through systematic liberalisation of foreign direct investment (FDI) policy, single window clearance system, creation of Real Estate Investment Trusts (REITs), modification of city master plan and zoning policy, conversion of land use, and strategic development of urban infrastructure.

FDI policy

FDI is, *inter alia*, a source of non-debt financing for greenfield or brownfield projects across various sectors, including the real estate sector. It is one of the major sources for attracting private capital for generating a supply of urbanized land and development of urban real estate commodities. During the years 2010, 2011, and 2017–18, a trend towards systematic liberalisation of the FDI policy in the real estate construction and development sector occurred.

In 2010, 100 percent FDI in an Indian developer company (Investee Company) under the automatic route was permitted, subject to minimum capitalisation norms. However, a foreign investor was required to meet stricter exit conditions from a real estate project. Without prior government approval, foreign investors were not permitted to leave a real estate project for three years from the date of completion of minimum capitalisation by an investee company. Additionally, at least 50 percent of a real estate project was required to be developed by the investee company within a period of five years from the date of obtaining all statutory clearances to allow a foreign investor to exit from such a project. In 2011, the conditions of exit for a foreign investor from such FDI projects were relaxed to some extent. A foreign investor was now also permitted to make a tranche-wise exit from such a project, subject to its completion.

In 2017–18, the norms for making FDI in such projects were further relaxed, which has made the infusion of FDI by foreign investors in real estate projects even more attractive. Under the new FDI policy, the criteria of minimum area development by the investee company and the norm of minimum capitalisation of the investee company with FDI have been done away with. A foreign investor is now permitted to make a tranche-wise exit from a real estate project even before it is completed, provided that a lock-in-period of three years, calculated with reference to each tranche of foreign investment, has been completed. Further, transfer of stake by a foreign investor to another non-resident without repatriation of FDI investments, has also been permitted, without there being requirements of meeting any investment lock-in period or obtaining prior government approval.

With the FDI norms being liberalised to a great extent, capitalisation of large real estate projects in India through private investments has become easier. The FDI equity inflows in the real estate construction and development sector have increased from INR 7.03 billion in 2016–17 to INR 34.72 billion in 2017–18 (Ministry of Commerce and Industry 2018: 2), which is among the highest FDI equity inflows in a particular sector in India.

Single window clearance system

For development of a real estate project in India, a number of time-consuming pre-construction, construction-stage, and post-construction approvals are required to be obtained by a developer from the central as well as from various state government authorities.[14] This is one of the main reasons for corruption and delays in completion of real estate projects in India that result in exponential cost escalation, which eventually gets passed on to consumers. The number of such approvals can be as high as 40 (Rohokale 2017), depending upon in which state a real estate project is being developed. Under the 'ease of doing business' policy adopted by the Government of India, the Central Government, and the state governments, in coordination with each other, have started implementing the policy of a 'single widow clearance system', which enables a developer to obtain approvals through a single window and through a common application. Many states have passed their own single window clearance acts. By doing this, the state aims to make investments in the real estate sector more attractive for private investors and developers.

Real Estate Investment Trusts

The Finance Minister in his budget speech for the financial year 2014–15 proposed the introduction of real estate investment trusts (REITs), which have been successfully used as an instrument for pooling of investments by several countries for the development of real estate projects. To implement REITs, the Securities and Exchange Board of India (SEBI) has framed the SEBI (Real Estate Investment Trusts) Regulations, 2014 (SEBI REITs Regulations). SEBI REITs Regulations were subsequently amended in 2016, 2017, and 2018[15] to make them more investor friendly.

REITs, in India, are trusts registered under the SEBI REITs Regulations, which own real estate assets and other permitted assets (REIT assets), whether directly or through a holding company[16] (holdco) or special purpose vehicle (SPV).[17] REITs issue units[18] against REIT assets to the investors. The main actors involved in the creation and management of REITs and issuance of REIT units to investors are the sponsors,[19] REIT, trustees,[20] holdco and/or SPV, valuer,[21] and manager.[22] To explain a typical structure involved in setting up REIT, the case of 'Embassy Office Parks REIT' is shown in Figure 3.1.

SEBI has also issued guidelines for the public issue of the units of REITs (SEBI, 2016).[23] REIT units are tradable on a recognised stock exchange on which they are registered, which enables a quick exit for the investors in the secondary market, thereby making investments in these units attractive for investors.

REITs are permitted to invest, *inter alia*, not only in the completed real estate projects but also in the under-construction projects. Recent amendments in the FDI policy have also permitted REITs to be investment vehicles for attracting FDI in real estate projects (Ministry of Commerce and Industry 2017).

Creating urban infrastructure

The Ministry of Housing and Urban Affairs (MoHUA), Government of India, has recently launched the Smart City Mission (SCM),[24] which aims at developing an entire urban eco-system, which is represented by the four pillars of comprehensive development – institutional, physical, social, and economic infrastructure. SCM aims to promote cities that provide core infrastructure and give a decent quality of life to its citizens, a clean and sustainable environment, and application of smart solutions[25] to help them meet their socio-economic aspirations, and advocates creation of compact areas which can be a replicable model to other aspiring cities in various regions of the country. The convergence of various city-planning schemes of the government such as the AMRUT,[26] HRIDAY,[27] development of transit

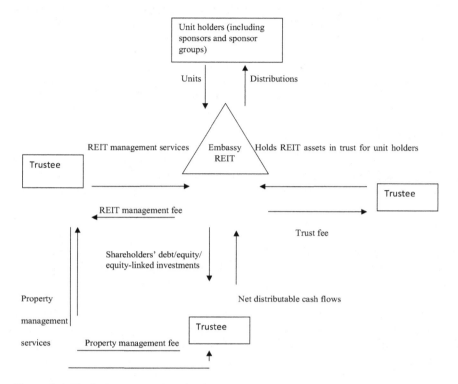

Figure 3.1 Typical structure involved in setting up REIT

Source: Draft offer document filed by 'Embassy Office Parks REIT' with SEBI on September 24, 2018, for listing of its units on the stock exchanges. See: *Embassy Office Parks REIT* (*2018, September 24*). Retrieved October 15, 2018, from the SEBI website www.sebi.gov.in/ sebiweb/home/HomeAction.do?doListing=yes&sid=3&ssid=74&smid=80

corridors and transit-oriented development, mixed land use, land pooling and reconstitution, zonal planning, conversion of land use, and the like are part of the SCM.

Strategic models for area-based development under the SCM involve city improvement (retrofitting), city renewal (redevelopment), city extension (greenfield development), and pan-city development (application of smart solutions).

Generating demand in urban real estate through regulatory reforms

The State has taken up the neoliberal role of a facilitator in creating a conducive environment for stimulating demand for urban real estate commodities among investors and consumers, in particular, among the sizeable urban middle-class population, who traditionally consider owning and investing in urban real estate commodities as a tool for creating opportunities and possibilities themselves to meet their socio-economic aspirations. Through a series of legislative actions and policies, the State not only aims to bring legal certainty around the title and ownership of land parcels and urban real estate commodities, but also aims to provide adequate protection to the investments made by such investors and consumers.

Pre-RERA and post-RERA regime

Before 1970, no specific legislation existed which could provide adequate protection for investments made by investors and consumers in urban real estate commodities and to their ownership rights therein. Citizens relied on generic legislations[28] to protect their investments and ownership rights.

The enactment of the *Maharashtra Apartment Ownership Act* in 1970 brought urban real estate commodities within its ambit for the first time, which provided a framework for the regulation of urban real estate commodities and protection of consumers' investments and the ownership rights therein. Subsequently, other states in India enacted their own apartment ownership acts, providing similar rights and protections to the consumers of urban real estate commodities. However, these acts lacked stringent liability and penalty provisions for erring developers and failed to establish a dedicated forum to adjudicate disputes between the consumers and developers. The aggrieved purchasers had no other option than to approach civil courts to seek remedies against such erring developers, which has historically been a time-consuming procedure in India.

With enactment of the *Consumer Protection Act, 1986*, and subsequent amendments made thereto in the years 1993 and 2002, the legal framework for the protection of the rights of consumers of urban real estate commodities took a major leap forward. This Act provided consumer dispute redressal forums at the district, state, and national levels for the settlement of disputes, and also provided better protection for end-consumers of residential urban real estate commodities by expanding the definition of 'services' to include 'housing construction'. However, the said being a general act fell short of proving to be a dedicated act protecting the rights of consumers of urban real estate commodities.

To address this concern, the Central Government enacted the *Real Estate (Regulation and Development) Act, 2016* (RERA), which aims to regulate and promote the real estate sector in India and ensure the sale of urban real estate commodities in an efficient and transparent manner to protect the interests of consumers thereof. It provides for the establishment of an adjudicating mechanism for speedy dispute redressal arising out of real estate sale transactions and matters connected therewith or incidental thereto.

All the states in India have adopted RERA through appropriate legislative action, except West Bengal.[29] Most of the state governments have constituted the real estate regulatory authority (Authority) and the real estate appellate tribunal (Appellate Tribunal) under their respective rules for adjudication of disputes between the consumers and developers of real estate projects. Appeals from the decisions of the Authority lie before the High Court having appropriate jurisdiction.

RERA restricts the promoter of a real estate project or any ongoing real estate project[30] where the area of land proposed to be developed is 500 square meters (598 square yards) or above, or the number of apartments proposed to be developed in such a real estate project is eight or above (inclusive of all phases), from advertising, marketing or offering for sale, or inviting persons to purchase any plot, apartment, or building without registering the real estate project with the Authority. Any violation of the said provision attracts a penalty up to 10 percent of the estimated cost of the real estate project.[31] Any non-compliance by the promoter with the said provision risks imprisonment for a term of up to three years or a fine up to a further 10 percent of the estimated cost of the real estate project, or both.

RERA obligates the promoter to submit details of the real estate project for registration along with a declaration regarding his/her legal title to the project land, timelines for project completion, and the deposit of 70 percent of the amounts realised from the allottees, from time to time, against the allotment of apartments or plots in a separate bank account to cover the cost of construction and the land cost.

In case of failure of the promoter to complete the project and handover the allotted apartment or plot to the allottee within agreed timelines, the allottee, at his/her option, has the right under RERA to withdraw from the project and seek a refund of the amount paid by her/him to the promoter along with interest and compensation, or to seek payment of interest as determined by the Authority on such amount paid by her/him to the promoter for every month of delay in handing over of the possession of such allotted apartment or plot to her/him by the promoter (section 18 of RERA).

In a plethora of cases decided by the Authorities, including in the states of Maharashtra and Haryana, the allottees of the apartment or plots in real estate projects which have not been completed within the agreed timelines have been awarded interest ranging from 10.15 to 10.45 percent per annum on the amounts paid by them to the promoter from the date of such allotment.[32] In cases in which allottees have demanded withdrawal from the projects on account of delay in completion, promoters have also been directed by the Authority to refund the allotment amounts to such allottees together with interest and compensation[33] (Ramnani 2018). However, in a few cases[34] decided by the Authority, where at least 40 percent of a real estate project has been completed, even though there has been a delay in completion of the project beyond the original proposed timelines, the Authority has, as a matter of policy, denied refund of the allotment amounts to the allottees even though they are legally entitled to seek refund at their option under RERA. In doing so, the Authority seems to have taken a neoliberalist approach to protect the private investments of the promoters by offering them another chance to complete the project, which is contrary to the strict interpretation of the provision contained in section 18 of RERA. The reason given by the Authority for this is that to protect the interest of one person, one cannot jeopardize the interests of scores of others (ibid.).

In the Simmi Sikka case[35] (Ramnani 2018; Sinha 2018), the Haryana Authority extended the scope of applicability of RERA (other than the registration provisions) to all real estate projects, whether registered under RERA or not, which have already been completed before enactment of RERA, thus bringing all delayed real estate projects and the structural defects therein within its ambit.

Other relevant legislations

Insolvency and Bankruptcy Code, 2016 (IBC) together with its first[36] and second amendments,[37] opened a new avenue for the allottees of apartments[38] or plots, other than RERA, to seek refund of the amount (with interest) paid by them to the real estate promoters towards allotment of apartments or plots. IBC has recognised such allottees[39] (as defined under RERA),[40] as the financial creditors, to whom the promoters are deemed to owe financial debt[41] until the title of the allotted apartments or plots is transferred to the allottees. This entitles such allottees, either individually or jointly, to file an application with the National Company Laws Tribunal (NCLT) for initiating a corporate insolvency resolution process against the defaulting promoter companies (section 7 of IBC). Further, they have been allowed representation and voting rights in the committee of creditors (COC) constituted by the interim resolution professional (which, *inter alia*, appoints a resolution professional and approves the resolution plan against a defaulting promoter company (corporate debtor) to be submitted with NCLT (section 30 of IBC). The NCLT may order the liquidation of the corporate debtor in case it is not approved by COC within the prescribed time or the COC-approved resolution plan is rejected by NCLT. Upon liquidation of the corporate debtor, the allottees (as financial creditors) get priority in the order of distribution of the proceeds from the sale of the liquidation assets of the corporate debtor over the operational creditors and other creditors (section 53 of IBC).

IBC, however, provides for the declaration of a moratorium by NCLT upon submission of application under IBC by a creditor against a corporate debtor till completion of the corporate insolvency resolution process (sections 13 and 14 of IBC), during which period the institution of suits or continuation of pending suits or proceedings against the corporate debtor, including complaints under RERA and execution of any judgment, decree, or order in any court of law, tribunal, arbitration panel, or other authority against the corporate debtor, remain suspended.

DLF case

The Competition Act, 2002 (Competition Act) also protects investments made by consumers in urban real estate commodities against developers who hold a dominant position in the market and impose unfair and discriminatory conditions in the sale agreements. In the DLF case,[42] the Competition Commission of India (CCI) held DLF guilty of contravening the provisions of the Competition Act,[43] directly and indirectly, as it was held to impose unfair or discriminatory conditions in the sale of services[44] by formulating and imposing unfair conditions in its agreement with buyers for sale of flats. CCI finding DLF guilty of abusing its dominant position in the market imposed a penalty of INR 6.3 billion on it and directed DLF to cease and desist from formulating and imposing such unfair conditions in its sale agreements.

Land titling

In India, the provision of land title certificates to landowners, which are guaranteed by the government as conclusive proof of their ownership in urban plots, is still a work in progress. At present, generally, title of a person to urban land is derived from the sale deed registered with the sub-registrar of assurances in accordance with the provisions of the *Registration Act, 1908*. Such sale deed merely grants a presumptive title to a person in the land.

However, in April 2016, the state of Rajasthan passed the *Rajasthan Urban Land (Certification of Titles) Act, 2016*, which provides for certification of urban land titles. Further, in Maharashtra, urban local bodies (ULBs) have started issuing *malmatta patrak*, or property registration card (property card), to landowners of plots in urban areas. The property registration card is a government-certified title document, *inter alia*, based on the city survey and the cadastral mapping exercise conducted by the state government. The state of Gujarat is also in the process of issuing property registration cards to owners of urban real estate commodities. Property cards and land title certificates bring legal certainty to the titles of landowners in urban real estate commodities.

Whether trickle-down effect is for all?

Post-1991, the neoliberal approach adopted by the State in the development of urban real estate can be clearly seen. This approach assumes that the economic growth generated by the establishment of a robust market in urban real estate commodities will allow all stakeholders – landowners, developers, investors, and consumers – to capitalise on the opportunities, socio-economic benefits, and prosperity associated with it. The moot question which needs to be analysed is how far this assumption is true.

Let us first examine the case of private developers, land aggregators, and investors. The neoliberal regulatory and policy reforms introduced by the State in the real estate sector, which, *inter alia*, aims at generating a supply of value-added developable, urbanisable land to be developed privately, will be beneficial for private developers, land aggregators, and investors with surplus capital. It will facilitate creation of opportunities and possibilities for them to maximise returns on their investments. It will lead to creation of wealth in fewer hands and 'restoration of class power and in particular, the restoration of class power to very privileged elite' (Harvey 2007: 12).

Further, such neoliberal reforms will also be beneficial for the urban upper- and middle- class population with means. With greater legal certainty around title and ownership in urban real estate commodities in place, they would be encouraged to make investments in value-added urban real estate commodities with better city-level infrastructure – both for their own consumption as well as for seeking returns on their investments, either through speculation or by capitalising on the rentals. The urban middle class, in particular, will see this as a prospect for improving their quality of life by treating this as an opportunity to own value-added urban real estate commodities in a city with high-class city-level infrastructure. Owning such urban real estate commodities would also help them to meet their aspirations of climbing up to the next level on the socio-economic ladder. Such reforms will also open up more employment opportunities in urban areas, particularly in the real estate sector and other related service sectors, for the urban middle-class population – both skilled and semi-skilled.

This may not be the case for the urban lower middle-class and the urban poor (mostly unskilled) without means, who, as a by-product of rapid urbanisation, will get further marginalised and impoverished (Pádraig and Owusu 2016). They will not only be dispossessed of their small landholdings and their dwelling place, but also become detached from the sources of their livelihood. Such dispossession and detachment will occur not only within the city limits but also in urban villages and urban extensions. Given the often dramatic effects of land loss on people's livelihood, combined with the difficulty in compensating for non-monetary values, the promise of material compensation by the State – politically important in eliciting compliance – if and when broken, will typically be too late for the disposed to get their land back (Levien 2018: 19). Further, recent regulatory reforms, such as RERA, IBC, and the Competition Act, which aim to bring legal certainty around ownership and title in urban real estate commodities, are relevant for those who own or who have the means to own urban real estate and certainly not for the urban poor who are deprived of such a luxury.

In this context, Delhi LPP, as discussed earlier in this chapter, is inherently biased towards cash-rich private land aggregators, developers, and investors and promises them high returns on their investments at the cost of small landowners and farmers. Even before Delhi LPP was notified, developer entities have managed to lure landowners (mostly farmers and unskilled workers) living in the villages situated in Delhi's urban peripheries to part with their small landholdings at a much lower price than such land would have fetched post-development under the land pooling scheme (Baruah 2018). Further, many farmers have also sold their small landholdings to developer entities as it has become difficult for them to carry out agricultural activities thereon because of an acute water shortage and a change in crop patterns, with the State being unsupportive (Akram 2012). The policy, by imposing external and internal development charges on participating landowners for the development of urban sectors in such pooled land, has made it impossible for poor landowners to participate individually in such a scheme. Delhi LPP in its present form, it seems, may leave small landowners and farmers dispossessed of their small landholdings and displaced, leading to impoverishment and marginalisation because they are detached from their sources of livelihood.

Although AP Government's LPS for the development of Amaravati purports to be a 'voluntary' land consolidation scheme, in reality landowners have no choice but to participate in the scheme and surrender their landholdings, as those who refuse to consent to pooling face compulsory acquisition of their land parcels under RFCTLARRA. Any resistance by them attracts penal provisions under the APCRDA Act, including imprisonment. Further, for their dispossession and displacement, they are promised (more as an inducement and to legitimise dispossession) a paltry monetary compensation and other socio-economic benefits (promissory in nature); it is doubtful these inducements would ever see the light of day (Jitendra 2017).

The in-situ slum redevelopment and rehabilitation project at Kathputli Colony in West Delhi undertaken by DDA in 2009 as a pilot project based on the PPP model, is an illustration of how such an unplanned city renewal model has led to dispossession and displacement of urban slum dwellers. The colony was one of the oldest slums, housing puppeteers, acrobats, storytellers, folk dancers, and painters for nearly 40 years. In October 2017, approximately 4,000 houses in the Kathputli colony were demolished to give way to a slum redevelopment project by a private developer. In all, 2,800 EWS (economically weaker sections) flats were proposed to be allotted to families in the slum redevelopment project within two years of their eviction, provided they met the prescribed 'eligibility' criteria. In consideration for constructing the EWS flats and to enable him to maximise the return on his investments, the private developer was permitted (rather, incentivised) to build and sell 170 HIG (high income group) flats on an ownership basis at a price determined by him and to lease the commercial built-up area in the project equivalent to 10 percent of the total available EWS FAR at market rates. The DDA never initiated any consultation process with or sought consent from the affected slum dwellers before announcing the slum redevelopment project, assuming that the slum dwellers would move out of the Kathputli colony of their own volition on the inducement of allotment of EWS flats in the project. Approximately 10 years have elapsed since the project was announced, and the slum dwellers who have been dispossessed, displaced, and detached from their place of livelihood have yet to be allotted dwelling units in the still-unbuilt slum redevelopment project. This aspect has also been analysed in great detail by Raman's study of the Kathputli Colony case where she highlights how high-end residential and commercial real estate projects are expanded in a city by use of the established tools of urban planning at the cost of systematic undermining of the property rights of squatters in land and access to housing in urban areas (Raman 2015).

Thus, the questions which require our attention are: Whether the State-induced urban real estate regulatory reforms and policies, which aim to achieve the neoliberal agenda of sustainable economic growth through operation of market forces, will create possibilities and opportunities for all? Whether they are merely aimed at protecting investments in urban real estate as against guaranteeing housing for all? Whether they will help in meeting the socio-economic aspirations of all? Has the State succeeded in creating a mechanism through which the trickle-down effect will take place? What are the opportunities created for the individual landowners and farmers who are made to part with their small landholdings for urban development and city renewal projects in Delhi and Andhra Pradesh? What are the safeguards for small landowners and slum dwellers against rampant dispossession, wherein a private developer prospers and State agencies remain unaccountable? These issues may be debated at length. However, the fact that such State-induced urban real estate regulatory reforms and policies have created opportunities, possibilities, and prosperity for private developers, investors, and the urban upper- and middle-class population, is not debatable.

This new land-grab mechanism in neoliberal India represents the emergence of a new regime of redistributing landed wealth upwards (Levien 2015). What it will result in is creation of 'divided cities; gated communities here, impoverished communities there' (Harvey 2007: 12), and the cities may get 'dissolved into micro-states of rich and poor' (*op. cit.*). The urban rich would get richer, and the urban poor will get poorer. The trickle-down effect and fulfilment of the socio-economic aspirations of all, in the complete absence of the State's redistributive role or its social welfare–oriented managerial role (Searle 2016), will remain a myth.

Notes

1 Neoliberalism comes in many variations which attempt to be adaptive to specific socio-political context.
2 Urban real estate commodities comprise residential and commercial projects and include developed plots, apartments, office spaces, shops, buildings, and houses in urban areas.
3 *The Right to Fair Compensation and Transparency in Land Acquisition, Rehabilitation & Resettlement Act*, 2013, No. 30 of 2013.
4 Emphasis added.

5 See: Notification on modification of Chapter – 19 (Land Policy) of MPD – 2021, bearing S.O. No – 5220 (E) issued by the Ministry of Urban Development (Delhi Division) on October 11, 2018.

6 See: Regulations for Operationalisation of Land Pooling Policy, 2018, notified by DDA vide notification bearing S.O.No – 5384(E) dated October 24, 2018.

7 'Consortium' means a duly registered association having rights, duties, and obligations in accordance with law, consisting of multiple landowners/developer entities who have come together to pool land for unified planning, servicing, and subdivision/share of the land or any other defined action for the development of sectors under Delhi LPP as per prescribed norms and guidelines.

8 'Developer Entity' means:

    a An individual landowner who has pooled one or more parcels of land in the sector, adding up to a minimum of 2 hectares.

    b A group of landowners who have collectively pooled one or more land parcels adding up to a minimum of 2 hectares and who have voluntarily grouped together, through a valid, legally enforceable agreement, for taking up development.

    c An entity (developer/business/corporate entity) which represents a group of landowners who have pooled one or more land parcels adding up to a minimum of 2 hectares, through a legally binding agreement.

9 The *Real Estate (Regulation and Development) Act, 2016*

10 Floor area ratio (FAR) is the ratio of a building's total floor area (gross floor area) to the size of the piece of land upon which it is built.

11 See: G.O.MS.No.254, MA & UD (M2) Department dated December 30, 2015, Government of Andhra Pradesh.

12 In the state of Delhi, vide notification no. K-12016/3/2008-DD-1-I dated May 10, 2013, issued by the Ministry of Urban Development (Delhi Division) published in the *Extra Ordinary Gazette* no. S.O. 1199(E) dated May 10, 2013, as public notice, which amended the Master Plan for Delhi-2021 (MPD-2021), low-density residential plots have been included in MPD-2021 as use premises in the areas falling in urban extension (23 villages) and green belt (47 villages) identified in the urban periphery of Delhi as low-density residential areas (which earlier were categorised for agricultural/farm land use for development of farm houses) vide notification issued by the Ministry of Urban Development (Delhi Division) published in *Extra Ordinary Gazette* no. S.O. 1199(E) dated June 18, 2013. In such low-density residential areas, development of low-density residential plots with up to two dwelling units with a maximum FAR of 30 has been allowed provided that the minimum plot size is 0.40 hectare.

13 In the state of Punjab, vide notification no. 17/09/2016–5hg2/2315 dated August 26, 2013, issued by the Department of Housing and Urban Development, Government of Punjab, development of low-density country homes residential development projects in Punjab have been permitted in the residential/agricultural zone within master plan or within agricultural zone outside master plan, The minimum land area requirement for such project shall be 12 hectares which must be contiguous. The plot size permitted in the colony developed on such land parcel shall range from 0.40 hectare to 1 hectare.

14 These approvals and no objection certificates (NOCs) include environmental clearances, forest clearances, clearances from Airports Authority of India, Archaeological Survey of India, State Urban Art Commission, traffic and coordination department, fire department, municipal authorities, panchayats, urban local bodies, town and country planning department, national and state highways authorities, utilities agencies, etc.

15 SEBI (Real Estate Investment Trusts) (Amendment) Regulations, 2017 and SEBI (Real Estate Investment Trusts) (Amendment) Regulations, 2018.
16 The term 'holdco', or 'holding company', means a company or LLP (limited liability partnership) registered under the *Limited Liability Partnership Act, 2008*:

   (i) in which REIT holds or proposes to hold controlling interest and not less than 51 percent of the equity share capital or interest and which it in turn has made investments in other SPV(s), which ultimately hold the property(ies);
   (ii) which is not engaged in any other activity other than holding of the underlying SPV(s), holding of real estate/properties and any other activities pertaining to and incidental to such holdings.

17 The term 'special purpose vehicle', or 'SPV', means any company or LLP:

   (i)   in which 21[either the REIT or the holdco] holds or proposes to hold controlling interest and not less than 51 percent of the equity share capital or interest;
   (ii) which holds not less than 80 percent of its assets directly in properties and does not invest in other special purpose vehicles; and
   (iii) which is not engaged in any activity other than holding and developing property and any other activity incidental to such holding or development.

18 The term 'unit' means a beneficial interest of REIT.
19 The term 'sponsor' means any person(s) who set(s) up the REIT and is designated as such at the time of application made to SEBI.
20 The term 'trustee' means a person who holds REIT assets in trust for the benefit of the unit holders, in accordance with SEBI REIT regulations.
21 The term 'valuer' means any person who is a 'registered valuer' under section 247 of the *Companies Act, 2013* 24[or as defined hereunder] and who has/have been appointed by the manager to undertake both the financial and technical valuations of the REIT assets.
22 The term 'manager' means a company or LLP or body corporate incorporated in India which manages assets and investments of the REIT and undertakes operational activities of REIT.
23 Vide circular bearing no. CIR/IMD/DF/136/2016 dated December 19, 2016 issued by SEBI, from SEBI website https://www.sebi.gov.in/sebi_data/attach docs/1482144526306.pdf (Accessed on 25 March, 2020).
24 See: *Smart Cities Mission (n.d.).* Retrieved October 17, 2018, from the Smart Cities Mission website http://smartcities.gov.in/content/
25 Examples of smart solutions are e-governance and citizen services (public information grievance redressal electronic service delivery, video crime monitoring, etc.), waste management (waste to energy and fuel, waste to compost, etc.), water management (smart meters and management, leakage identification and preventive maintenance, water quality monitoring, etc.), energy management (smart meters and management, renewable sources of energy, energy efficient and green buildings, etc.), urban mobility (smart parking, intelligent traffic management, integrated multi-modal transport, etc.), tele-medicine, tele-education, incubation/ trade facilitation centers, skill development centers, etc.
26 AMRUT is a mission launched by the Government of India which aims to provide basic civic amenities and infrastructure in identified cities and towns such as the water supply system, sewerage, septage, storm water drainage, urban transport, green space, and parks to improve the quality of life for all. See: *Atal Mission for Rejuvenation and Urban Transformation–AMRUT(2018, November 03).* Retrieved November 3, 2018, from the Ministry of Housing and Urban Affairs website http://mohua.gov.in/cms/amrut.php

27 HRIDAY is a mission launched by the Government of India which aims at the development of core heritage infrastructure projects which include revitalisation of urban infrastructure for areas around heritage assets identified /approved by the Ministry of Culture, Government of India, and state governments. These initiatives include the development of water supply, sanitation, drainage, waste management, approach roads, footpaths, street lights, tourist conveniences, electricity wiring, landscaping, and other such citizen services. See: *HRIDAY (2018, November 03)*. Retrieved November 0, 2018, from the Ministry of Housing and Urban Affairs website http://mohua.gov.in/cms/hariday.php

28 The *Indian Contract Act, 1872*; the *Code of Civil Procedure, 1908*; the *Specific Relief Act, 1963*; the *Indian Penal Code, 1860*, and the law of torts (based on common law principles evolved through judicial precedents)

29 West Bengal has its own real estate regulation and development act known as the *West Bengal Housing Industry Regulation Act, 2017*.

30 Ongoing real estate projects are projects which have not received a completion certificate from the competent local authority until May 1, 2017.

31 See: *Himanshu Goyal and another vs. M/s LID Millennium Pvt. Ltd. and others, Complaint No. RERA-GRG-299–2018*. Retrieved October 19, 2018, from https://haryanarera.gov.in/admincontrol/judgements/2

   Shobhit Mehrotra vs. M/s LID Millennium Pvt. Ltd. and others, Complaint No. RERA-GRG-422–2018. Retrieved October 19, 2018, from https://haryanarera.gov.in/admincontrol/judgements/2

32 See: *Shobhit Gupta vs. M/s North Star Apartment Pvt. Ltd., Complaint No. RERA-GRG-179–2018*. Retrieved October 19, 2018, from https://haryanarera.gov.in/admincontrol/judgements/2

   Navita Srinet and another vs. M/s Supertech Ltd., Complaint No. RERA-GRG-291–2018. Retrieved October 19, 2018, from https://haryanarera.gov.in/admincontrol/judgements/2

   Devender Singh vs. M/s Apex Buildwell Pvt. Ltd., Complaint No. RERA-GRG-386–2018. Retrieved October 19, 2018, from https://haryanarera.gov.in/admincontrol/judgements/2

   Vinod Kumar Sehgal vs. Shree Prakash Creative Buildcon jv, Complaint No. CC001000000000058. Retrieved November 04, 2018, from https://maharerait.mahaonline.gov.in/searchlist/SearchJudgements?MenuID=1072

   Pratik Kansara vs. Adani Estates Pvt. Ltd., Complaint No. CC006000000000262. Retrieved November 4, 2018, from https://maharerait.mahaonline.gov.in/searchlist/SearchJudgements?MenuID=1072

33 See: *Goodtime Real Estate Development Pvt. Ltd. vs. Gautamchand Salecha, Appeal No. AT006000000010332*. Retrieved November 4, 2018, from https://maharera.mahaonline.gov.in/Site/ViewPDFList?doctype=97tq_O7q PXrjozI3HJW8ym4H/94flAFVK02cR7fFwEap28L1ekDyiJUi0MgB_cLD BdaMt8qf2uTEc61idcTmAjlyT8nUZ/HEGjVWwuJz7qI=

   Ashok Kumar Yadav vs. M/s KST Infrastructure Ltd., Complaint No. RERA-GRG-17–2018. Retrieved November 4, 2018, from https://haryanarera.gov.in/admincontrol/judgements/2

34 See: *Ranjana Goyal & another vs. M/s Emaar MGF Land Ltd., Complaint No. RERA-GRG-360–2018*. Retrieved October 19, 2018, from https://haryanarera.gov.in/admincontrol/judgements/2

   Arijit Chakarbarti vs. Ramprastha Sare Realty Pvt. Ltd., Complaint No. RERA-GRG-31–2018. Retrieved October 19, 2018, from https://haryanarera.gov.in/admincontrol/judgements/2

   Anil Kumar Tyagi & another vs. M/s Sidhartha Buildhome Pvt. Ltd., Complaint No. RERA-GRG-28–2018. Retrieved October 19, 2018, from https://haryanarera.gov.in/admincontrol/judgements/2

   Sunil Paul vs. M/s Parsvnath Hessa Developers Pvt. Ltd., Complaint No. RERA-GRG-29–2018. Retrieved October 19, 2018, from https://haryanarera. gov.in/admincontrol/judgements/2
35 See: *Simmi Sikka vs. M/s Emaar MGF Land Ltd., Complaint No. RERA-GRG-7–2018.* Retrieved October 19, 2018, from https://haryanarera.gov.in/ admincontrol/judgements/2
36 *Insolvency and Bankruptcy Code, 2016(Amendment) Act*, No. 8 of 2018, which came into effect on November 23, 2017.
37 *Insolvency and Bankruptcy Code, 2016 (Second Amendment) Act*, No. 26 of 2018, which came into effect on June 6, 2018.
38 See: Section 2 (e) of RERA.
39 See: Section 2 (d) of RERA.
40 See: Explanation (ii) to section 5 (8)(f) of IBC and section 2 (zn) of RERA.
41 See: Section 5 (8)(f) of IBC. The term 'financial debt' means a debt along with interest, if any, which is disbursed against the consideration for the time value of money and includes any amount raised under any transaction, including any forward sale or purchase agreement having the commercial effect of a borrowing. Any amount raised from an allottee under a real estate project is also deemed to be an amount having the commercial effect of a borrowing. Explanation (ii) to section 5 (8)(f) of IBC provides that the expressions 'allottee' and 'real estate project' have the meanings respectively assigned to them in clauses (d) and (zn) of section 2 of the *Real Estate (Regulation and Development) Act, 2016* (16 of 2016).
42 See: *Belaire Owners' Association vs. DLF Limited, HUDA & Ors.* (Case No. 19/2010). Retrieved October 21, 2018, from the Competition Commission of India website, www.cci.gov.in/sites/default/files/192010S_0.pdf
43 4. 3 (1) No enterprise or group shall abuse its dominant position.
   (2) There shall be an abuse of dominant position under sub-section (1), if an enterprise or a group:
      (a) directly or indirectly, imposes unfair or discriminatory:
         (i) condition in purchase or sale of goods or service; or
         (ii) price in purchase or sale (including predatory price) of goods or service.
44 Definition of 'services' under section 2 (1)(o) of the *Consumer Protection Act, 1986*, as amended in 1993, includes 'housing construction'. The said definition of 'services' was considered by CCI while deciding the DLF case.

References

Ahmed, Waquar. 2007. 'Neoliberalism and the contested policies of the power industry in India', *The Industrial Geographer*, 5(1): 44–57. Retrieved from www. academia.edu/2654061/NEOLIBERALISM_AND_CONTESTED_POLICIES_ OF_THE_POWER_INDUSTRY_IN_INDIA accessed on 12 November 2018.
Akram, Maria. 2012, 18 June. 'Bend it like Najafgarh farmers', *The Times of India*. Retrieved from https://timesofindia.indiatimes.com/city/delhi/Bend-it-like-Najafgarh-farmers/articleshow/14218499.cms?from=mdr accessed on 9 June 2018.
Baruah, Sukrita. 2018, 4 July. 'Delhi: land pooling policy has farmers worried', *The Indian Express*. Retrieved from https://indianexpress.com/article/cities/ delhi/delhi-dda-land-pooling-policy-farmers-worried-5244775/ accessed on 9 June 2018.

Brenner, Neil and Nik Theodore. 2005. 'Neoliberalism and the urban condition', *City*, 9(1): 101–107. doi:10.1080/13604810500092106

Carmody, Pádraig and Francis Owusu. 2016. 'Neoliberalism, urbanization and change in Africa: the political economy of heterotopias', *Journal of African Development*, 18(1): 61–73. Retrieved from www.tara.tcd.ie/handle/2262/76229 accessed on 9 June 2018.

Harvey, David. 2007. 'Neoliberalism and the city', *Studies in Social Justice*, 1(1): 2–13.

Jitendra. 2017, 15 September. 'Andhra Pradesh farmers get a raw deal in exchange of land', *Down To Earth*. Retrieved from www.downtoearth.org.in/news/govern ance/capital-loss-58663 accessed on 9 June 2018.

Kohli, Atul. 2006. 'Politics of economic growth in India: part II: the 1990s and beyond', *Economic and Political Weekly*, 41(14):1361–1370. doi:10.2307/4418059

Levien, Michael. 2015. 'From primitive accumulation to regimes of dispossession: six theses on India's land question', *Economic and Political Weekly*, 50(22): 146–157.

Levien, Michael. 2018. *Dispossession without development: land grabs in neoliberal India*. New Delhi: Oxford University Press.

Ministry of Commerce and Industry. 2017. *Consolidated FDI policy circular of 2017*. Retrieved from the Department of Industrial Policy & Promotion, Ministry of Commerce and Industry website http://dipp.nic.in/policies-rules-and-acts/press-notes-fdi-circular accessed on 17 October 2018.

Ministry of Commerce and Industry. 2018. *Fact sheet on foreign direct investment (FDI) from April 2000 to June 2018*. Retrieved, from the Department of Industrial Policy &Promotion, website http://dipp.nic.in/publications/fdi-statistics accessed on 2 November 2018.

Peck, Jamie. 2001. 'Neoliberalizing states: thin policies/hard outcomes', *Progress in Human Geography*, 25(3): 445–455. Retrieved from https://spatialfix.files. wordpress.com/2010/08/peck-neoliberalizing-states-2001.pdf www.tara.tcd.ie/ handle/2262/76229 accessed on 2 November 2018.

Raman, Bhuvaneswari. 2015. 'The politics of property in land: new planning instruments, law and popular groups in Delhi', *Journal of South Asian Development*, 10(3): 369–395. doi:10.1177/0973174115610186

Ramnani, Vandana. 2018, 28 August. 'Refund may not be allowed if project is 40 percent complete: HARERA Gurugram chief', *moneycontrol*. Retrieved from www.moneycontrol.com/news/business/real-estate/refund-may-not-be-allowed-if-project-is-40-percent-complete-harera-gurugram-chief-2889041.html accessed on 19 October 2018.

Rohokale, Sunil. 2017, 15 November. 'View: Ease the "ease of doing business" in real estate', *The Economic Times*. Retrieved from https://economictimes.india times.com/markets/stocks/news/view-ease-the-ease-of-doing-business-in-real-estate/printarticle/61653274.cms accessed on 30 September 2018.

Searle, Llerena Guiu. 2016. *Landscapes of accumulation: real estate and the neoliberal imagination in contemporary India*. Chicago and London: The University of Chicago Press.

SEBI. 2016. *Circular bearing no. CIR/IMD/DF/136/2016 dated December 19, 2016*. Retrieved from Securities and Exchange Board of India website https://www.sebi. gov.in/sebi_data/attachdocs/1482144526306.pdf accessed on 17 October 2018.

Sinha, Prabhakar. 2018, 22 August. 'Unregistered projects come under Haryana RERA too: Gurugram bench', *Magicbricks*. Retrieved from https://content.mag icbricks.com/property-news/delhi-ncr-real-estate-news/unregistered-projects-come-under-haryana-rera-too-gurugram-bench/101163.html accessed on 19 October 2018.

Steger, Manfred B. and Ravi K. Roy. 2010. *Neoliberalism: a very short introduction*. Oxford: Oxford University Press.

4 The forest rights struggle and redefining the frontiers of governance

Dismantling hegemony, restructuring authority, and collectivising control

C.R. Bijoy

The forest in India has been a contested terrain, often violently, since the colonial period. The colonisation of the forests and her peoples continued into the post-independence period, and progressively intensified, threatening their expulsion en masse. That is when the struggle for democracy in the forest burst out, six decades after India becoming a 'democracy'. By then, India had adopted and come under the grip of neoliberalism, with an insatiable thirst for capital to secure forest and its resources for itself, coming into conflict and competing with forest dwellers' aspirations for survival with dignity. What follows is a narrative of how this is being played out in the governance arena against the backdrop of its brief history from the colonial era.

Of belonging to the land: a web of relationships

Historically, customary and traditional rights to land and natural resources expressed themselves as individual rights, use rights, and territorial rights in varied forms. In pre-colonial India, these were built upon the rigid, stratified caste system, entailing unequal power distribution that underpinned differential use of, access to, and control over natural resources. The economic dynamic of subjugation and exploitation through feudal rent was built over this caste edifice, with land being divided into *Jagirs*, a type of feudal land grant by rulers allotted to *Jagirdars*[1] who in turn allocated to subordinate *Zamindars*[2] who are hereditary, to extract the surplus from peasants as tax. The Adivasis stood outside the caste order and hence beyond the pale of the caste-based feudal order. The forested regions and the forest dwellers, again primarily the Adivasis, were, however, relatively distanced and free from this revenue-seeking regime, with the collection of revenue extended mostly to timber and non-timber forest products (Ghosal 2011: 107–116) that were extracted to be transported and traded.

The Adivasi-inhabited regions, for the most part the forested regions of the Indian sub-continent, were essentially self-governing realms – their ancestral domain,[3] even though nominally part of various kingdoms. The manner in which they related to the land – as belonging to the land – was through a complex mosaic of rights that were both material and relational, and temporal and spiritual. Some were temporary while others were long lasting. These rights spanned not just their historical terrain but also their political, social, emotional, sacred, and existential domains, spanning generations dating back to the time when they settled there. These were not merely their source of livelihood, but also the very source of their music, song, dance, legends, myths, and rituals. Their governance system was naturally non-centralised, non-hierarchical self-governing habitations with lateral shared rights; their functions and governance linkages based on clans, ethnicity, neighbourhood, and region to protect, conserve, and manage the land and its diverse resources. The manner in which this manifested also defined the relationship, whether convivial or contested, within and between habitations and communities that constituted their realm. These relationships effectively defined them as free people in sharp contrast to the 'others' distinguished by a graded system of subjugation through the caste structure.

The impact of and response by forest dwellers to colonisation of forest by the British, the internal colonialism that followed since independence, and the strategy of dispossession unleashed in the neoliberal era need to be understood from within the aforementioned complex web of relationship that they have with their habitats and homelands. It is important to note that most of these relationships cannot be commoditised in market terms and, therefore, faced with being dispossessed, these traditional forest dwellers affirmed and asserted this relationship, forcing the neoliberal state to accede to this political and material space, at least in law.

The frontiers of governance: perpetuating colonial control

British incursions into the forests since the mid-eighteenth century for extraction of timber and forest clearance for expanding cultivation soon widened to physically taking control and regulating the forests with the establishment of the Forest Department in 1864, the *Forest Act* in 1865, the Indian Forest Service in 1867, and the Provincial Forest Service in 1891 to manage the forests through scientific forest management that was introduced in 1871. Expansion of colonial control over forested regions led to persistent resistance and revolts by the tribals[4] right across the central Indian tribal belt from the east to the west coast and the northeast since the latter half of the 1700s. The British reconciled with these assertions for self-governance and autonomy by enacting specific governance regimes (Bijoy 2008) such as the *Scheduled District Act of 1874* and later the Excluded and Partially Excluded Areas under the *Government of India Act of 1935*, that excluded them from the purview of British laws while at the same time incorporating both the forests and the non-forest parts of their territories into the British empire. Regional laws too were enacted with similar intent in varying degrees as the *Wilkinson's Rule* (1837), the *Inner Line Permit under the Bengal Eastern Frontier Regulation* (1873),[5] the *Santhal Pargana Tenancy Act (1876)*, and the *Chotanagpur Tenancy Act (1908)*. These were the antecedents for the constitutional provisions of the Fifth[6] and Sixth[7] Schedule under Article 244, the special constitutional provisions such as Articles 371A and 371G for Nagaland and Mizoram, respectively,[8] and state laws to prevent alienation of land and their restoration when alienated (Bijoy et al. 2010).

Significantly the colonial response in the central Indian tribal belt was the takeover and tightening of grip over the resource-rich forests while providing for relative freedom by keeping the non-forest lands, mostly under subsistence agriculture with little scope of enhancing revenue collections, free from its rule, and therefore de facto autonomous. However, the postcolonial Indian State not only continued expanding its colonial control, from 59.8 million hectares in 1949 to 70.67 million hectares in 2019 under the forest regime, but also actually extended its administrative sway over all non-forest lands and its resources by ensuring that the Fifth Schedule provisions in the Constitution that empowered and mandated the office of the Governor to protect those notified as Scheduled Tribes (STs) and their lands, uniformly failing to fulfil the constitutional responsibility (Veeresha 2017).

The enactment of the Provisions of *The Panchayats (Extension to the Scheduled Areas) Act, 1996*[9] (PESA, 1996), the result of a nationwide struggle[10] (Akerkar 1996), came as a remarkable respite to this legal and governance vacuum. This law, popularly called village self-rule law, by essentially defining the powers of Gram Sabha (village assembly)[11] over community resources, land, and extending to the forests with ownership of minor forest produces, and control over development plans among others,[12] actually attempts to decolonize and democratize governance (a forerunner to legal reforms regarding forest and land acquisition) for the first time. The major burden of nation-building works, such as hydroelectric, thermal, and irrigation projects, and mines and industries, was felt in these tribal hinterlands through land acquisition and forest diversion for infrastructure, development, and industrial projects, resulting in disastrous consequences through large-scale displacement,[13] environmental destruction, and pollution on the one hand and enclosure conservation of forests on the other, disrupting lives and livelihood. This maladministration and mis-governance (Government of India 2008: 74–76) primarily around land-related issues, such as absentee landlordism amidst widespread landlessness, non-recognition of tenancy, land and forest rights; predatory development aggression resulting in displacement and forced evictions by irrigation, hydroelectric, mining, and industrial projects; livelihood issues such as non-enforcement of minimum wages, denial of access to land and natural resources by dominant sections; caste, class, and gender-based social oppression; the oppressive forest, revenue, and police departments; and the inaccessible and unresponsive justice system combined with development deficit and extensive deprivation, led to the spread of left wing extremism that promised quick justice. PESA, 1996, was identified as the much-needed critical governance reform that could effectively transform the region (Government of India 2008: 74–76). This Expert Group to Planning Commission, Government of India, even recommended that:

> A comprehensive regulation should be made to the effect that no law having a bearing on the provisions of PESA, read with the Fifth Schedule and other provisions of the Constitution concerning tribal people, shall extend to the Scheduled Area(s), until it is approved for extension there in full or with such exceptions and modifications as may be notified by the Governor, in consultation with the Tribes Advisory Council of the State.
>
> (*op. cit.*, 74)

PESA, however, remains a dead letter to date by design, effectively subverted through acts of omission and commission by the central and state governments (Menon and Bijoy 2014: 9–12) such as non-compliance of state laws with PESA, especially the non-adoption of the Sixth Schedule pattern; delayed notification and in some states, non-notification of rules to operationalise the law; not harmonising the state subject laws with PESA; and no meaningful consultation with the Gram Sabhas in cases of land acquisition which is mandated by the law.

Significantly, the nation had by then embarked on liberalisation of its economy with its *New Economic Policy* in 1991 that was market oriented, with primacy of investment by private capital, both domestic and foreign. The central Indian tribal belt, rich in natural wealth, was a prime target for investment. This can be gauged from the unrests and resistance to displacement that is perceived to have increased since 1991. While there is no precise data on displacement, yet available data indicates a sharp increase in, for instance, the number of displaced persons which rose from 21.3 million between 1951 and 1990 (Government of India 2002: 458) to almost 60 million by 2008 (Mathur 2008: 3). Accumulation by dispossession that held sway through expropriation of natural resources by non-recognition of rights of communities over government-held lands and forests, and their diversion, as well as by acquisition of titled lands and easing access to these resources through licensing and leasing simply got further institutionalised and legitimised with the call to meet the nation's high-growth agenda. The region transformed into a conflict zone, relegating democracy to the periphery. From just nine states and 53 districts in 2001, the number of Left Wing Extremism–affected districts are estimated to have increased to 180 in 2008, to as much as 232 in 18 states out of 601[14] districts then (Bakshi 2009).

In stark contrast, the northeast region has remained continuously autonomous since the pre-British period, with community control (STs numbering

12,415,054 or 27.3 percent of the total population of the region as per the 2011 census) over their territories and their resources, including the forested regions. This is because most of the northeast was tribal dominated unlike the central belt which had large tribal enclaves amidst a sea of non-tribals, difficult-to-access terrain, and the stiff resistance of tribal communities to external incursions of any kind. The dawn of independence saw militant uprisings, with demands ranging from total freedom to various degrees of autonomy over specific territories and their resources, and their governance, from statehood to autonomy under the Sixth Schedule[15] of the Constitution to other arrangements through state legislations.[16] The region, except Sikkim, remained restive and militarised all along. The traditional self-governing structures of the tribal peoples in the Northeast have been robust, with substantial control over their traditional or customary communal territories and resources, generally recognised by the formal governance structure through the special constitutional provisions for Nagaland and Mizoram, the Sixth Schedule, and the State enactments recognising various forms of autonomy.[17]

The *Look East Policy of the Government of India* was launched in 1991, the year that India began its neoliberal stride with the launch of the New Economic Policy, for economic and strategic ties with Southeast Asia. This was upgraded to the *Act East Asia* policy and expanded to the larger East Asia in 2014. During this period, a slew of ceasefire and peace accords were signed with numerous militant groups in an attempt to create a conducive political atmosphere for enhanced connectivity of all kinds and investment to exploit its as such unexploited rich natural resources, and to carve out land routes for ease of trade into the East Asian region. The region, with its unique history of community control over land, resources, and governance rooted in customs and traditions along with layers of formal autonomy, resulted in the region excepting Assam, having vastly superior socio-economic and political empowerment of the tribals than the rest of the country, often among the top rung on some human development indicators (Nayak 2012). For instance, Mizoram, Tripura, Manipur, and Nagaland are far ahead in literacy, in the female literacy rate and with the smallest gap in the literacy rate between the ST population and the population in the country. The Human Development Index of Mizoram was high compared with the national level. These are a result of a history of continued assertion of their territorial rights and successful resistance to physical incursion from the outside, to the present day. The region faces a new form of invasion, of predatory capital, that requires the demise of communitarian governance systems and resource rights as a prerequisite for it to take root and reap profits.

The colonisation of forests

The Permanent Settlement of 1793 began consolidating the intermediate landed interests, the *zamindari* system, in most of India, while the *ryotwari* system[18] of 1820 dealt directly with the tenant peasant and the Mahalwari system[19] of 1833 with one or more villages dealt together for extracting revenue. These effectively commenced the propertification of land, reducing land rights to individual ownership centred on feudal landholdings, ignoring the tenants and the actual cultivators on the one hand, and a whole range and forms of collective and community rights of access and use on the other (Haque and Sirohi 1986). Those lands that were not thus titled as private property became State property, pushing large masses of the marginalised further into the margins and at the mercy of the bureaucracy. In the absence of a law that democratically determines the traditional and customary use of these State lands, the declining marginal concessions, often critical to liveli-hood, is now being denied to them as outlined subsequently, and completely fenced off and made available in the market. These inhabitants are deemed to be 'encroachers' on government land and evicted.

Further, under the eminent domain percept, the State extended its power to expropriate private lands through the *Land Acquisition Act, 1894*.[20] This colonial frame was extended through its incorporation into other legisla-tions to acquire land for specific purposes,[21] continuing its foray even after India became a democratic republic. The forest legislations that consolidated into the *Indian Forest Act, 1927*, continues its reign over the forests even now, with its power derived from this very same colonial land acquisition framework to notify and take over lands as forests, and list out acts prohib-ited in such forests, forest offences, and penalties imposed as punishments. With this, traditional forest dwellers became encroachers and criminals in their own homelands. The traditional and customary rights that forest com-munities exercised became offences, or grossly restricted arbitrarily as con-cessions by administrative diktat of the forest bureaucracy.

The British Colonial Government's custodial and timber-oriented man-agement in the first *Forest Policy of 1894* effectively continued into the post-independence period. The *Forest Policy of 1952* recommended that 33 percent of the country be brought under forest cover while stressing management and protection of forests and wildlife. The *Wildlife (Protec-tion) Act, 1972* (WLPA) extended the scope of the law to protecting wildlife through a protected area regime primarily consisting of national parks as effectively inviolate zones, and wildlife sanctuaries with restricted rights as determined by the forest bureaucracy. 'Forests', a State subject, was brought also as a subject matter of the Central Government by bringing it under the Concurrent List in 1976 by the 42nd Amendment to the Constitution, elevating the importance of forests. This was soon followed by the *Forest (Conservation) Act* in 1980 (FCA) that required mandatory approval of the Central Government before diversion of any forest land for a non-forestry purpose by state governments, with provision for compensatory afforesta-tion, preferably on a non-forest area. Significantly, this Act required that all pre-1980 'encroachers' be settled with the recognition of their land rights, reiterated with a series of guidelines that the Ministry of Environment and

Forest (MoEF) issued in 1990,[22] and eviction of all the rest. Instead, the Act interpreted as the law that outlaws non-forestry activities in the forest became the weapon to put an end to the slow and painstaking process of recognition of rights to land, effectively homestead land of pre-1980 'encroachers', while setting the ground to outlaw and evict the forest dwellers and establish a fortress enclosure approach to forests to prevent the use and access of forests to forest dwellers. Ironically, the Act was to regulate State-initiated forest diversions[23] for development and infrastructure projects by making forest clearance orderly and in strict compliance with the object of conservation. FCA 1980 slowed down the diversion rate from 0.15 million hectares per annum between 1950 and 1980 to as low as 0.038 million hectares per annum by 2004 (Ministry of Environment and Forest 2004: 2). Forestry and Wildlife was shifted from the Ministry of Agriculture to a new Ministry of Environment and Forests in 1985.

Meanwhile, the government notified that forests increased from 59.8 million hectares (1949–50) to 76.74 million hectares (2019), covering 23.34 percent of the total land area (Forest Survey of India, Ministry of Environment, Forests & Climate Change 2019). Forest land under the Protected Area regime also steadily increased from five national parks in 1970 to 104 covering 4,050,103 hectares. Wildlife sanctuaries increased from 62 in 1970 to 543 covering 11,893,180 hectares.[24] Almost a quarter of the forest land is under the Protected Area regime,[25] curtailing severely or completely the rights of forest communities and their access to forests. Carved from within the protected area are the high-priority, tightly guarded Tiger Reserves, an administrative category that has existed since the launch of Project Tiger in 1973, with nine reserves of 911,500 hectares. This number has now risen to 50 Tiger Reserves covering 7,102,710 hectares.[26] The Tiger Reserves were also elevated to a legal category with the amendment to the *Wildlife (Protection) Act* in 2006.

The *Forest Policy, 1988*, made a fundamental shift in its focus by bringing in 'meeting the requirements . . . of the rural and tribal populations' while aiming at the maintenance of environmental and ecological stability, and mobilising people, including women, for achieving the new policy objectives. A separate section entitled 'Tribal people and forests' was introduced, recognising 'the symbiotic relationship between the tribal people and forests', incorporating them into various parts of the policy, particularly in 'Essentials of Forest Managements',[27] and 'Management of State Forests'.[28] But with the launch of neoliberal economic reforms in 1991, these policy objectives were not only abandoned, but also underwent a drastic reversal as never before in history, launching the final assault on the forest and its peoples. The backlash that this generated turned the tide, forcing the State to concretise the democratisation of the forest, freeing a large part of the forest from colonial grip (more on that later).

Forest governance entered a new phase with the *Writ Petition (Civil) No. 202 of 1995* filed by T.N. Godavarman Thirumulpad[29] (popularly known as the 'forest case') in the Supreme Court which sought its intervention to protect a patch of forest in Gudalur of Nilgiri District in Tamil Nadu. The Court, declaring that the forests across the country itself were under threat, expanded the scope of the case, effectively taking control over forest governance (Chowdhury 2014: 177–189). This case led to the evolution of two other laws, the *Schedule Tribes and Other Traditional Forest Dwellers (Recognition of Forest Rights) Act, 2006* (FRA) and the *Compensatory Afforestation Fund Act, 2016* (CAFA). The former, though unintended, was a direct outcome of State aggression on the forest and her peoples that the Court indirectly triggered, and the latter was an intended, direct, Court-induced, and facilitated one. While FRA addresses the 'historical injustice' done to the forest dwellers, CAFA constructed the vehicle to cover up State- and court-sanctioned forest destruction, utilising the monies generated through the Court-initiated and approved formula for monetisation of the forest land that is to be diverted. The former was to serve primarily the collective interests of the forest dwellers, while the latter was to serve the interests of capital.

Framework of democratic governance for the forests

In the aforementioned T.N. Godavarman case, all that the Supreme Court asked of the states on 18 February 2002 was to report on the steps taken to clear the encroachments. The National Democratic Alliance government issued the fateful order on 3 May 2002,[30] stating that 'approximately 1.250 million hectares of forest land is under encroachment' and that 'all encroachments which are not eligible for regularisation' as per the aforementioned 1990 guidelines of the Ministry 'should be summarily evicted' by 30 September 2002. The unprecedented country-wide onslaught by the Forest Department that followed resulted in evictions from 152,400.110 hectares of forest land between May 2002 and March 2004.[31] At least 300,000 forest dwellers would have been evicted during this period, leaving in its wake, death, bloodshed, shattered lives, battered homes, and ravaged habitations. Resistance to this illegal eviction spread, coalesced[32] into a national struggle, and forced the Central Government to concede that there had been a 'historical injustice' because of the government's failure to recognise the traditional rights of the tribal forest dwellers which 'must be finally rectified',[33] the urgent need to recognise rights and the need to enact a new law to surmount the legal impediments posed by existing laws and court orders (Bijoy 2017: 73–93). Opponents in the forest bureaucracy, media, and conservationists who unleashed a campaign that the forests were going to be distributed to the forest dwellers and destroyed fell through because of its lack of credibility. The FRA was enacted in 2006, and Rules (Ministry of Tribal Affairs & UNDP 2014) were notified in 2008. Forest officials and hard-line conservationists immediately challenged FRA in various High Courts and the Supreme Court and presently, all these cases are being heard in the Supreme Court.[34]

About 100 million people live on land classified as forest (Fisher et al. 1997), while an estimated 275 million (World Bank 2006) to 350–400 million (Ministry of Environment, Forests & Climate Change 2009) are forest dependent. A total of 170,379 of the 587,274 villages are located in and around forests and have a mixed population of 147 million. On record are 4,526 forest villages as of 2011, with a population of 2,206,011, of whom 1,332,265 are STs.[35]

This was also the period when legal recognition of tenurial rights over land, forests, and fisheries, both individual and community rights, were gaining traction globally as neoliberal economies unleashed hitherto confined capital to seek primary resources worldwide for investment. Land and natural resource conflicts inevitably led to widespread resistance, particularly so in the indigenous peoples' territories across the world that got reflected into the United Nation and its bodies, particularly its Working Group on Indigenous Populations since its establishment in 1982, the Permanent Forum on Indigenous Issues that was established in 2002, and the United Nations Declaration on the Rights of Indigenous Peoples adopted in 2007. In 2004, FAO (Food and Agriculture Organization) embarked on the development of guidelines on responsible tenure governance which culminated in the adoption of 'Voluntary Guidelines on the Responsible Governance of Tenure of Land, Fisheries and Forests' (FAO 2012) in 2012, the first comprehensive, global instrument on tenure and its administration, prepared through intergovernmental negotiations. The loss of legitimacy that the governments faced when they unleashed repression on the resistance to resource grab in aid of capital, and the consequent economic cost they and investors incurred forced the states to take the primitive accumulation that 'entailed taking land, say, enclosing it, and expelling a resident population to create a landless proletariat, and then releasing the land into the privatised mainstream of capital accumulation' (Harvey 2005: 145–146, 149) to recognising tenurial rights over natural resources so that these become a legally negotiable instrument or commodity in the market on terms that aids accumulation of capital. The World Bank (2006), recognising the huge untapped potential of forests in India, recommended unlocking 'more of the value inherent in Indian forests and boost local livelihoods while also supporting forest conservation policy goals' through strengthening forest rights. International donors have also pitched in to 'rally the business community around the need to accelerate the implementation of FRA' (Halais 2018).

A major shift in the institutional role, responsibilities, and functions of the Ministry of Environment, Forest and Climate Change[36] (MoEFCC) (who had in 2004 acknowledged their failure in the Supreme Court)[37] and the Ministry of Tribal Affairs (MoTA) was made in 2006 with the non-negotiable demand of the forest movement to keep MoEFCC away from being the purveyor of the forest rights law. The *Government of India (Allocation of Business) Rules, 1961*[38] was amended thus: 'The Ministry of Environment, Forest and Climate Change will be responsible for overall policy in relation to forests, except all matters, including legislation, relating to the rights of forest dwelling Schedule Tribes on forest lands.'[39] This exception in business was allocated to MoTA: 'All matters including legislation relating to the rights of forest dwelling Scheduled Tribes on forest lands.'[40] Recognising that the 'forest rights on ancestral lands and their habitat were not adequately recognised, resulting in historical injustice to the forest dwellers who are integral to the very survival and sustainability of the forest ecosystem', it became 'necessary to address the long standing insecurity of tenurial and access rights of forest dwellers including those who were forced to relocate their dwelling due to State development interventions' (Preamble of FRA).

Following the frame of PESA, the habitation-level Gram Sabhas in the forest and its fringes are the statutory authorities in FRA to determine various individual, community, and community resource (territorial) rights in forest land of any kind along with the power to protect and manage them. The law recognised and vested the forest rights on all categories of forest lands irrespective of their current status in law[41] in forest dwelling STs and other traditional forest dwellers who 'primarily reside in' forests for generations, are 'dependent on forest land or forests for bona fide livelihood needs', and have occupied forest land before 13 December 2005, but whose rights could not be recorded. FRA lists 14 sets of 'heritable but not alienable or transferable' rights, including any rights not specified but excluding hunting. Every village is to demarcate its customary and traditional boundary as its community forest resource rights over which the Gram Sabha is to protect, regulate, conserve, and manage. This includes forests, biodiversity, wildlife, cultural and traditional practices, and water resources. Community rights include ownership of minor forest produce,[42] rights to water bodies and fisheries, grazing, seasonal resource access, access to biodiversity, intellectual property rights, traditional knowledge, cultural diversity, and habitat rights of the Particularly Vulnerable Tribal Groups.[43] The individual rights are self-cultivation up to 4 hectares, habitation, restoration of titles, grants and leases if cancelled, disputed lands, alternate land in situ rehabilitation if illegally evicted, and land from where displaced by government acquisition and not used within five years. The FRA lists 13 developmental rights,[44] which are public facilities operated by various government agencies for which up to 1 hectare and felling of 75 trees, with the consent of the Gram Sabha. In effect, the law simply recognises and restores the traditional system of governance where decision making is dynamic that are location and situation specific rather than the rigid prescriptions emanating within the command and control colonial forest bureaucracy.

Excepting individual rights, all others are vested in the Gram Sabha, the village assembly. With the rights holders conferred 'the responsibilities and authority for sustainable use, conservation of biodiversity and maintenance of ecological balance, thereby strengthening the conservation regime of the forests while ensuring livelihood and food security of the forest dwellers', there is a transfer of power over forest land from the State bureaucracy to the Gram Sabha with its open, transparent, and democratic public space to protect forests from any form of destructive practices affecting their cultural and natural heritage, regulate access to community forest resources, and stop any activity that adversely affects forest, wildlife, and biodiversity. These powers extend to the 'customary common forest land within the traditional or customary boundaries of the village or seasonal use of landscape in the case of pastoral communities, including reserved forests, protected forests and protected areas such as Sanctuaries and National Parks to which the community had traditional access'.

Inviolate Critical Wildlife Habitat can be declared after rights are recognised, after fulfilling scientific and objective criteria that the presence of rights holders will adversely impact wild animals and their habitat, after concluding that other options such as co-existence are not available, and after consenting to a resettlement package that ensures 'secure livelihood'. Any violation of the provisions in the law by any official is a punishable offence. The Ministry of Tribal Affairs (MoTA) is the nodal ministry and the Tribal Department of the State is the nodal agency for implementation in the state, with a state-level monitoring committee overseeing the process.

Forced to comply with FRA, recognition of forest rights and consent of the village for all forest diversions were made mandatory for forest diversion since 2009.[45] In addition, the RFCTLARRA, 2013 (*Right to Fair Compensation and Transparency in Rehabilitation and Resettlement Act*) that decolonized and brought in a semblance of democratising land acquisition and on market terms also brought forest rights under FRA under its ambit. Violation of forest rights were brought within the realm of 'atrocities' through an amendment in 2015[46] to the *Scheduled Castes and the Scheduled Tribes (Prevention of Atrocities) Act of 1989*.

Notwithstanding resistance from the bureaucracy, attempts at subversion by the central and state governments and other vested interests (Bijoy 2017: 73–93), as of 30 November 2018, a decade since the law became operational in 2008, a total of 1,894,225 titles were issued for 5,459,102.46 hectares,[47] 13.65 percent of 'around 40 million hectares of community forest resources to village level democratic institutions' (Ministry of Environment, Forests and Climate Change 2009; Rights and Resources Initiative et al. 2015) that the MoEFCC reckoned in 2009.

The co-opted state: subverting democracy

With India adopting a high-growth trajectory in the neoliberal era/post 1991, forests continued to be under increased pressure for a variety of development and infrastructural projects. Forest diversions were carried out with scant regard to FRA. With FRA, now the law that supersedes FCA 1980, combined with political pressure of the forest movement to comply with FRA. Recognition of all rights under FRA and consent of the Gram Sabhas was made mandatory for diversion of forest land for non-forestry purposes in 2009. Just as FRA 2006 was in its final stage of conception, the Parliament amended the *Wildlife (Protection) Act* in September 2006, making Tiger Reserve a statutory category, incorporating various provisions as was being proposed in FRA for Critical Wildlife Habitat. This was in response to the report of the Tiger Task Force constituted by the government on vanishing tigers (Project Tiger, Ministry of Environment, Forests and Climate Change 2005). A total of 31 Tiger Reserves were rapidly notified within days in 2007 to beat the FRA rules notification in 2018, securing 2,925,202 hectares with the ulterior motive of confounding forest rights recognition in Tiger Reserves in gross violation of even the law under which these were notified (Bijoy 2011: 36–41). This has continued to date. Evictions have been and are being carried out without recognising rights. A total of 173 villages were relocated since the inception of Project Tiger on 11 December 2017, relocating 12,327 families (Ghanekar 2017). Of the 2,808 forest villages, 334 villages[48] are located inside the core or Critical Tiger Habitats alone which are to be made inviolate areas under WLPA. Wildlife enclosures provide a captive space for wildlife ecotourism, a fast-growing sector within tourism that the State and the private sector have been promoting.

Of about 6 million hectares (Table 4.1) diverted for non-forest purposes such as mining, development, and infrastructure projects, 1.52 million hectares were diverted under FCA 1980 of which nearly 0.4 million hectares[49] (more than 25 percent) were diverted since 2008 when FRA became operational. The 2009 MoEFCC Order to comply with FRA and Gram Sabha continue to be flouted.[50] In addition, amendments were made to FCA 1980 and orders were issued by MoEFCC and by other Ministries to dilute, violate, and subvert FRA, often illegally, some of which are detailed in Table 4.2.

With forest diversion entering the precincts of the aforementioned Godavarman case, the Supreme Court soon took steps to further regulate the diversion of forests for non-forest purposes under FCA 1980; compensatory afforestation carried out by the Forest Department was made mandatory for forest clearance for projects by incorporating this provision in the FCA

Table 4.1 Forest diversion from 1950 to 2018

Years	Area diverted in hectares (millions)
1950–1980	4.5[1]
1980–2018	1.52[2]
Total	6.02

Notes:
1 MoEFCC, Forests, RF retrieved from www.moef.nic.in/divisions/ic/wssd/doc2/ch9.pdf (22 October 2018).
2 e-Green Watch, FCA Projects, Diverted Land, CA Land Management. Retrieved from http://egreenwatch.nic.in/FCAProjects/Public/Rpt_State_Wise_Count_FCA_projects.aspx (24 December 2018).

Table 4.2 State acts of commission to violate/dilute FRA

Time line	Reference	Remarks
2003	Amendment to replace FCA Rules 1981[51]	Focus shifts to forest clearance[52]
5 February 2013	MoEFCC order exempting linear projects such as roads, canals, pipelines/optical fibres, and transmission lines, etc., from obtaining Gram Sabha consent for forest diversion unless recognised rights of PVTGs are being affected	MoEFCC is not vested with authority over FRA. Neither does FRA provide scope for any exemption
7 March 2014	MoTA clarifies that FRA provides for no exemption	These clarifications continue to be flouted by MoEFCC
2014 and 2016	Amendment to FCA Rules	Settlement of forest rights under FRA and obtaining consent of the concerned Gram Sabhas transferred to the District Collectors who are to issue a certificate to this effect. MoEFCC absolves itself of this responsibility and accountability
28 October 2014	MoEFCC grants District Collectors unilateral powers to sanction diversion of forest land in areas notified as 'forest' less than 75 years before 13 December 2005 and with no record of tribal population as per Census 2001 and 2011	1 MoEFCC does not have the authority to issue such an order exempting FRA 2 Whether rights exist or not can only be determined through the process under FRA 3 The assumption that these are areas free from any claims to forest rights are simply absurd as rights under FRA are on all forest lands irrespective of whether tribal populations are recorded there or not; in fact, in most cases there would not naturally be any human habitation in the area where rights are claimed
12 January 2015	MoEFCC issues guideline exempting five categories of projects from obtaining Gram Sabha consent where statutory consultations were carried out that require a public hearing for environmental clearance	MoEFCC is not vested with authority over FRA. Neither does FRA provide scope for any exemption

(*Continued*)

Table 4.2 (Continued)

Time line	Reference	Remarks
11 August 2015	MoEFCC issues guidelines declaring its intention to lease out 40 percent of forests classified as 'degraded forests', to private companies through joint agreements with the Forest Department, to 'carry out afforestation and extract timber', with access to 10–15 percent of the leased-out area for Minor Forest Produce to tribal communities	1 FRA is applicable to 'degraded forests' 2 Where rights are claimed and recognised, the Gram Sabha is the statutory authority to manage the forest. Leasing out such forest lands without Gram Sabha consent for afforestation and timber extraction is a violation of FRA 3 The MoEFCC and Forest Department do not have the power to decide on any matters regarding Minor Forest Produce as PESA provides for ownership rights in Scheduled Area and FRA, in addition, vested forest rights to forest dwellers
5 January 2017	The Ministry of Mines issues circular to state governments stating that MoTA is not 'insisting on FRA compliance for grant of lease' for mining but instead it is enough that FRA compliance be incorporated into the mining lease deeds for forest clearance by MoEFCC	1 FRA compliance as per the 2009 MoEFCC order on forest diversion under FCA 1980 is mandatory 2 MoTA had made it clear that FRA does not provide scope for any exemption in forest diversion
28 March 2017	The National Tiger Conservation Authority, a wing of MoEFCC, issues a direction barring recognition of rights under FRA in the Critical Tiger Habitats of Tiger Reserves	This violates the provisions under Sec.38 V of WLPA 1972 as amended in 2006 under which the Tiger Reserve is notified and FRA. The Critical Tiger Habitats of Tiger Reserves now cover an area of 4,014,530 hectares
14 March 2018	MoEFCC issues the draft 'National Forest Policy'[53]	1 MoEFCC does not have the sole prerogative over forests as per business rules. MoTA has been vested with the subject of forest rights since 2006. Moreover, more than half of the forests fall within the scope of FRA where MoTA is the nodal ministry. MoEFCC did not even consult MoTA in policy formulation

Time line	Reference	Remarks
		2 The draft outlined forest management that is a commercial plantation–centric investment, seeking forest management through privatisation of forests under the rubric of private and public participation aiming to increase tree cover and productivity to meet industrial and other needs, disregarding the legal reality that more than half of the forest now falls within the jurisdiction of Gram Sabhas59 under FRA 2006
19 June 2018	MoTA writes to MoEFCC on draft National Forest Policy	MoTA, asserting its authority, communicated its displeasure for the aforementioned reasons on 19 June 2018 (Shrivastava 2018)
3 December 2018	MoEFCC clarifies to the Government of Maharashtra that 'compliance under FRA is not required for consideration of in-principal approval' for forest diversion under Forest (Conservation) Amendment Rules, 2016	Settlement of rights and Gram Sabha consent, rather than a pre-condition for consideration for forest diversion, is relegated to being a fait accompli
26 February 2019	MoEFCC issues further clarification on compliance of FRA for forest diversion	Settlement of rights and Gram Sabha consent is now not even required for consideration of in-principle approval (Stage – 1), instead compliance is required *only* for final approval (Stage -2) (Rupawat 2019)
7 March 2019	MoEFCC proposes amending substantially the *Indian Forest Act, 1927.*	Overrides *Forest Rights Act, 2006*, and Gram Sabhas while empowering forest officials to nullify recognised forest rights; legalises commercial plantations and empowers forest officers to use firearms with high immunity (Sethi and Shrivastava 2019)

Rules in 1988 and 2003. This was to compensate for the loss of forest by securing equal non-forest land and if not available, then double the land diverted in degraded notified forests. It was argued that this would act as a disincentive to forest diversion and hence contribute to forest conservation.

Net Present Value, the estimated value for the loss of biodiversity content and environmental services, ranging from INR 0.4 to 1.043 million per hectare (2008) was to be extracted from the user agency primarily for afforestation and regeneration of forests. Its formula for computation began taking shape based on orders of the Supreme Court, taking into account biological and spatial variations in bio-geographical zones and site-specific numerical value based on 'scientific, biometric and social parameters' (Ghosh 2017). Afforestation is to be carried out on double the area diverted if on degraded forest land and an equivalent area if on revenue land which had to be later notified as forest land. The Supreme Court insisted that the money thus accumulated, now more than INR 660 billion, is to be managed through an authority created by law for which the Parliament was to enact a law. The *Compensatory Afforestation Fund Act, 2016*, and *Rules, 2018*, were the outcome. The law went beyond compensatory afforestation, artificial regeneration (plantations), and assisted natural regeneration, and included forest protection, infrastructure development, wildlife protection, and other related activities, and ironically also included relocation of villages from Protected Areas, and planning and rejuvenations of forest cover on non-forest land falling in wildlife corridors without any reference to existing rights of forest dwellers.

This law, by ignoring the very existence of other laws that recognise land and forest rights of tribals with their own statutory bodies, is appropriating the forest and adjacent revenue land by afforesting them. This law empowers the forest bureaucracy to appropriate non-forest lands, the village commons over which people have customary rights, and even individual titled land. The Act and its rules refer to the Village Forest Management Committee, an administrative structure controlled and dominated by forest officials, ignoring the statutory authority of the Gram Sabha as provided under PESA 1996 and FRA 2006. The forest management plan is the 'working plan' approved by forest officials, ignoring the legal fact that in the forest area falling within the purview of FRA, the Gram Sabha, and its Community Forest Rights Resource Management Committee is the statutory authority to develop their management plans which are to be incorporated into the forest working plan. Further, this violation is carried over to the National Working Plan Code 2014.[54] To facilitate forest diversion, MoEFCC ordered state governments on 8 August 2014 and again on 8 November 2017 to identify degraded forest land and non-forest land for creating a land bank under FCA 1980 so that these identified land areas are kept ready for compensatory afforestation. More than 2.68 million hectares were identified in Andhra Pradesh, Chhattisgarh, Madhya Pradesh, Jharkhand, Odisha, Tamilnadu, Rajasthan, and Uttar Pradesh (Tripathi 2017). INR 181,771.9 million[55] have already been released during 2009–10 to 2018. With tree plantations becoming an attractive investment under climate change mitigation through carbon sinks for carbon credit, and India showcasing the National Mission for Green India[56] under The National Action Plan on Climate Change for attracting investment, tree plantations are expected to get a fillip taking over forest lands, and common and individual properties outside the forests. The Mission, launched in February 2014, was to cost INR 460,000 million for increasing forest/tree cover on 5 million hectares of forest/non-forest lands and improve the quality of forest cover on another 5 million hectares (for a total of 10 million hectares) to enhance annual carbon sequestration by 50 to 60 million tonnes in the year 2020.

In effect, forest diversion first deprives people of their rights through coercion, violation of laws, and subterfuge, leading to enforcement of compensatory afforestation over equal or double this land as the case may be, illegally depriving the rights of another set of people. On the other hand, compensatory afforestation, rather than becoming a disincentive, is actually turned around deceptively and through administrative skulduggery as an incentive for forest diversion by neatly circumventing forest rights and forest conservation under cover of FCA 1980 and CAFA 2016. The State and user agency, usually the private sector, collude in this nefarious criminality in the name of growth and national interest.

Afterwards

A wave of nationwide protests broke out in the aftermath of the Supreme Court order of 13 February 2019 to evict the claimants in the rejected claims, which then numbered 1.89 million,[57] 'to ensure that the eviction is made on or before the next date of hearing',[58] which is 24 July 2019. This order pertains to the spate of petitions filed by some wildlife and conservation non-government organisations in the Supreme Court, and by retired forest officials as well as a former *zamindar* in the High Courts immediately on notification of the FRA Rules in 2008[59] which were transferred to the Supreme Court and heard together. Responding to the nationwide outrage and protests both by forest dwellers and wildlife conservationists,[60] the Central Government moved the Court to modify its eviction order.[61] On 28 February 2019, the Supreme Court put on hold the eviction till 24 July 2019,[62] the next date of hearing, while state governments report on the process adopted to reject the claims (Aryan 2019). Reportedly the Court reprimanded the Central Government for being in 'slumber' over these years, not approaching the Court and doing nothing. Though an immediate relief, the threat continues to loom, and forest dwellers vow to continue their struggle for justice by pushing forward the implementation of FRA that promises to undo the historical injustice.

The petitioners in this case questioned the powers of the Parliament to enact the law, the constitutional validity of the law and, its need and argued that this would lead to decimation of the forests and wildlife in the country while encouraging further encroachment of forest. While the Court was not impressed with the argument that the Parliament does not have the powers to enact the law, it is yet to begin examination of the constitutional validity of the law. In past years, the legal counsel of MoTA was silent when present in the hearings and later absented from the hearings, including the one during which the Court passed the eviction order. And this was despite a hue and cry by opposition parties and forest movements through their joint letter[63] alleging an indifferent and callous attitude of MoTA in dealing with this case 'perhaps to appease big corporates or vested interests'. The continued absence of Central Government legal counsels provided the space for petitioners to appeal to the Court to direct the states to evict the claimants in the rejected claims, ironically through a law that the petitioners themselves claimed to be unconstitutional. And the Supreme Court conceded!

Conclusion

The preceding narrative is an accurate reflection of how neoliberal hegemony seeking to transform forest governance – where the final retreat of governmental control through a structure of internal colonialism through the post-independence continuance of colonial forest governance, to a process of decolonised democratic forest governance befitting a democratic republic by a people's democratic struggle – is now being attempted. The roll-out neoliberalism is attempting to supplant the fledgling democratisation of forests by a virtual coupe with State assistance for the takeover of forests and its governance to serve the interests of capital, the business, and investors. The narrative indicates that this is happening not without a fight. The narrative also points to the brewing tensions between forest dwellers and the forces of neoliberal hegemony.

Notes

1 The holders of *jagirs* (large extent of property)
2 Feudal landlords in British India who paid the government a fixed revenue
3 The terms 'ancestral domain' or 'ancestral lands' refers to the lands, territories, and resources of indigenous peoples, particularly in the Asia-Pacific region, which are based on ancestry and relationships beyond material lands and territories, and include spiritual and cultural aspects.
4 These are people who are notified as 'Scheduled Tribe' by the State. They are generally believed to cover those who are referred to as 'Adivasi', literally meaning indigenous, or original, people of India, a commonly recognised and used term to identify this category of social groups, excluding the northeast region where they prefer to be known as 'tribals' and in recent times, 'indigenous peoples'. However not all Adivasi communities are Scheduled Tribes nor are all Scheduled Tribes Adivasis.
5 In the states of Arunachal Pradesh, Mizoram, hill areas of Manipur, and Nagaland, to regulate entry of outsiders and bars acquiring 'any interest in land' by outsiders or residents of other parts of India.

6 Prohibition or restriction of the transfer of land 'by or among members of the Scheduled Tribes' and regulation of the allotment of land to members of the STs in Scheduled Areas through appropriate regulations under the Fifth Schedule of Article 244(1) in any state other than the states of Assam, Meghalaya, Tripura, and Mizoram.

7 Regulate allotment, occupation or use, or the setting apart of land, other than any land which is a reserved forest for purposes likely to promote the interests of the inhabitants of the areas notified as Tribal Areas under the Sixth Schedule of Articles 244(2).

8 Protects these tribal majority states from the application of any act of the Parliament regarding ownership and transfer of land and its resources unless these states take independent decisions on them, safeguarding the religious and social practices of the communities that inhabit these states.

9 Retrieved from https://tribal.nic.in/actRules/PESA.pdf (October 22, 2018).

10 National Front for the Adivasi Self-Rule, initiated by Bharat Jan Andolan and other Adivasi organizations in 1994 led the nationwide struggle. The Late Dr. B.D Sharma, a former bureaucrat, played a critical role in the struggle.

11 The village assembly of all adult members. Under FRA it is a hamlet/habitation or a group of hamlets/habitations. The definition differs, for instance, in the Panchayat Raj Act where it consists of adult members of all the hamlets/habitations falling within the Gram Panchayat which consists of one or more revenue villages with each having one or more habitations.

12 See: The Provisions of *The Panchayats (Extension to The Scheduled Areas) Act, 1996*. Retrieved from https://tribal.nic.in/actRules/PESA.pdf (Accessed on October 21, 2018).

13 According to one of the initial drafts of the National Policy on Tribals, 2006 of the Ministry of Tribal Affairs, 'nearly 85.39 lakh tribals had been displaced until 1990 on account of some mega project or the other, reservation of forests as National Parks etc. Tribals constitute at least 55.16 percent of the total displaced people in the country'. Retrieved from www.prsindia.org/uploads/media/1167469383/bill53_2007010353_Draft_National_Policy_on_Tribals.pdf (accessed on October 21, 2018).

14 The number of districts is 719 as of 2018.

15 The Sixth Schedule Areas are the North Cachar Hills District, the Karbi Anglong District, and the Bodoland Territorial Areas District, the Khasi Hills District, the Jaintia Hills District, and the Garo Hills District in Meghlaya, the Tripura Tribal Areas District in Tripura and the Chakma District, the Mara District, and the Lai District in Mizoram.

16 Rabha Hasing Autonomous Council, Sonowal Kachari Autonomous Council, Mising Autonomous Council, Lalung (Tiwa) Autonomous Council, Deori Autonomous Council, and Thengal Kachari Autonomous Council in Assam, Senapati Autonomous District Council, Sadar Hills Autonomous District Council, Ukhrul Autonomous District Council, Chandel Autonomous District Council, Churachandpur Autonomous District Council, and Tamenglong Autonomous District Council in Manipur, and the Ladakh Autonomous Hill Development Council in Jammu & Kashmir. In Nagaland, Tribal council for each tribe, Area Council, Range Council, and Village Council.

17 Arunachal Pradesh has no Autonomous Councils, but most of the land is community land of various ethnic groups. Assam has three Autonomous District Council areas, viz., the North Cachar Hills, the Karbi Anglong Hills, and the Bodoland Territorial Autonomous Districts under the Sixth Schedule, and Rabha Hasing Autonomous Council. Sonowal Kachari Autonomous Council, Mising Autonomous Council, Lalung (Tiwa) Autonomous Council, Deori Autonomous Council, and Thengal Kachari Autonomous Council which are constituted under

state laws. Each tribe has its own traditional structure and community boundaries. The Manipur Hill Areas have a Hill Area Committee constituted under Article 371C of the Constitution; District Councils and Village authorities are constituted under the *Manipur (Hill Areas) District Council Act, 1971*, and the *Manipur (Village Authorities in Hill Areas) Act, 1956.* Village authorities may be elected or nominated by the Deputy Commissioner, with the traditional chief as the ex-officio head of the authority. Sikkim has no Autonomous Councils; the traditional institutions of ethnic groups are functional. The Tripura Tribal Areas Autonomous District Council under the Sixth Schedule covers an overwhelming 68 percent of the state. The traditional systems of local chieftains continue to exist alongside. Meghalaya, except for the municipality and cantonment of Shillong, is covered by the Sixth Schedule, viz., the Khasi Hills, Jaintia Hills, and Garo Hills Autonomous District Councils. Traditional and customary systems involving a hierarchy of chiefs and headmen prevail with some variations. Mizoram has three Sixth Schedule Areas, viz., the Mara, Lai, and Chakma Autonomous District Councils. The state has elected village councils constituted in most parts of the state, replacing earlier traditions of hereditary chieftainship. Nagaland through the *Nagaland Tribe, Area, Range and Village Council Act* of 1966 provides for the creation of a tribal council for each tribe, an area council for Kohima and Dimapur, a range council where there is a recognized range in the Mokokchung and Kohima Districts, and village councils for one or more villages in Kohima and Mokokchung. The 16 tribes in Nagaland occupy a distinct territory along with their traditional system of self-rule, which is diverse. Every village constitutes an authority. Village councils are constituted by the villages according to customary practices for five years under the provisions of the *Nagaland Village and Area Councils Act, 1978* (compiled from Bijoy, 2015).

18 A land tenure system in British India used to collect revenues from the cultivators of agricultural land
19 A revenue system of land tenure in British India for a compact area containing one or more villages which were called 'estates'.
20 This act was repealed and replaced by the much more liberal *Right to Fair Compensation and Transparency in Land Acquisition, Rehabilitation and Resettlement Act, 2013* (RFCTLARR) after decades of resistance that often resulted in violent bloodshed. For the law, see https://indiacode.nic.in/bitstream/123456789/2121/1/201330.pdf (Accessed on 21 October 2018)
21 For instance, mining, coal bearing areas, ancient monuments and archaeological sites and remains, national highways, atomic energy, etc.
22 Dated 18 September 1990, these guidelines dealt with (1) review encroachments on forest land; (2) review of disputed claims over forest land, arising out of forest settlement; (3) disputes regarding pattas/ leases/grants involving forest land; and (4) conversion of forest villages into revenue villages and settlement of other old habitations, Retrieved from http://wrd.bih.nic.in/guidelines/awadhesh02a.pdf (Accessed on 21 October 2018)
23 Pre-1980, diversion of forest was primarily for cultivation. More than half of about 4.3 million hectares of forests diverted between 1951 and 1980 was for agriculture (Ministry of Environment and Forests, Government of India 2004: 58).
24 For current data, see 'Protected Areas of India from 2000 to 2018 (as on July, 2018)', Retrieved from www.wiienvis.nic.in/Database/Protected_Area_854.aspx (Accessed on 22 October 2018)
25 Together with 77 conservation reserves (259,403 hectares) and 46 community reserves (7,261 hectares), 23.1 percent of the forest.
26 See: *Tiger Reserves* for the latest figure, Retrieved from http://wiienvis.nic.in/Database/trd_8222.aspx (Accessed on 22 October 2018).

27 Protection, improvement, and enhanced production of minor forest produce to generate employment and income for tribal and other communities (Sec.3.5)

28 The holders of customary rights and concessions, specifically the tribals, in forest areas are to protect and develop the forests while using them for their bona fide needs as 'rights and concessions' (Sec.4.3.4.2).

29 He belonged to the Nilambur Kovilakam, the *Janmi* (a feudal land-holding family) who once owned huge tracts of land in these parts of the Western Ghats.

30 Ministry of Environment, Forest and Climate Change, Government of India, Letter No.7–16/2002-FC dated 3 May 2002, Sub: Evictions of illegal encroachments on forest lands in various States/UTs time bound action Plan. Retrieved from http://mpforest.gov.in/img/files/Prot_New79.pdf (Accessed on 22 October 2018).

31 Reply by MoEFCC on 16.08.2004 to the Lok Sabha starred question No.284 regarding 'Regularisation of encroachments on forest land'. Retrieved from http://164.100.47.192/Loksabha/Questions/QResult15.aspx?qref=2276&lsno=14 (Accessed on 22 October 2018).

32 For further details, see https://forestrightsact.com/about/

33 In IA No. 1126 in IA No. 703 in Writ Petition (C) No. 202 of 1995 dated 21.07.2004.

34 See: *Court Cases* at https://forestrightsact.com/court-cases/

35 Lok Sabha unstarred question no.2487 of 31.07.2017, Retrieved from http://164.100.47.190/loksabhaquestions/annex/12/AU2487.pdf (Accessed on 22 October 2018)

36 The Ministry of Environment & Forests was renamed in 2014.

37 MoEFCC on 21 July 2004 filed an affidavit IA No. 1126 in IA No. 703 in Writ Petition (C) No. 202 of 1995 in the Supreme Court in the 'forest case', conceding that there has been a 'historical injustice' because of the government's failure to recognise the traditional rights of the tribal forest dwellers which 'must be finally rectified'.

38 Government of India (Allocation of Business) Rules, 1961 (As amended up to 28 December 2017), Cabinet Secretariat, p. 52, Retrieved from https://cabsec.gov.in/writereaddata/allocationbusinessrule/completeaobrules/english/1_Upload_1368.pdf (Accessed on 24 October 2018).

39 Inserted vide Amendment series no.285 dated 17.03.2006

40 Inserted vide Amendment series no.285 dated 17.03.2006

41 Includes unclassed forests, undemarcated forests, existing or deemed forests, protected forests, sanctuaries, national parks, and tiger reserves, and 'forest' as understood in the dictionary sense, that is, any area recorded as forest in the government record irrespective of any other official classification.

42 Minor forest produce is defined in FRA [Sec.2(i)] as that which 'includes all non-timber forest produce of plant origin including bamboo, brush wood, stumps, cane, tussar, cocoons, honey, wax, lac, tendu or kendu leaves, medicinal plants and herbs, roots, tubers and the like'.

43 A total of 75 STs are notified as Particularly Vulnerable Tribal Groups

44 These facilities are (a) schools; (b) dispensary or hospital; (c) anganwadis; (d) fair price shops; (e) electric and telecommunication lines; (f) tanks and other minor water bodies; (g) drinking water supply and water pipelines; (h) water or rain water harvesting structures; (i) minor irrigation canals; (j) non-conventional source of energy; (k) skill upgradation or vocational training centres; (l) roads; and (m) community centres.

45 Ministry of Environment, Forest and Climate Change, Government of India, Letter F.No.11–9/1998-FC(pt) of 03.08.2009, Sub: Diversion of forest land for non-forest purposes under the *Forest (Conservation) Act*, 1980, ensuring compliance of the *Scheduled Tribes and Other Traditional Forest Dwellers*

(Recognition of Forest Rights) Act, 2006, Retrieved from www.moef.nic.in/divi sions/forcon/3rdAugust2009.pdf (Accessed on October 23, 2018).

46 The *Scheduled Castes and the Scheduled Tribes (Prevention of Atrocities) Amendment Act*, 2015, Retrieved from https://tribal.nic.in/DivisionsFiles/mj/4-preventionofAtrocities.pdf (October 23, 2018).

47 Only 19 states have actually begun implementing FRA. While Mizoram has extended the law to the state, the Nagaland assembly has yet to decide on its extension to the state. In Jammu & Kashmir, a private member's bill is under consideration by its legislative assembly. See: Status report on implementation of the *Scheduled Tribes and Other Traditional Forest Dwellers (Recognition of Forest Rights) Act*, 2006, for the period ending 30.11.2018, Retrieved from https://tribal.nic.in/FRA/data/MPRNov2018.pdf (Accessed on 3 March 2019).

48 Lok Sabha Unstarred Question No. 816 answered on 14.12.2018.

49 Ibid.

50 The few cases that have come to the courts overturned decisions to divert forest land for violating FRA and the 2009 order such as Writ Petition (Civil) No. 180 of 2011 *Orissa Mining Corporation vs. Ministry of Environment & Forest and others*, Judgement of 18 April 2013, available at http://sci.gov.in/jonew/judis/40303.pdf. Since then there have been other such judgments as the Kashang hydroelectric project of Himachal Pradesh and the Mapithei dam of Manipur.

51 Retrieved from www.envfor.nic.in/legis/forest/gsr23(e).pdf (Accessed on 23 October 2018).

52 Also see the list of initiatives 'taken for granting of early forest clearance' provided as answer to Rajya Sabha Question No.1251 of 04.12.2014. Retrieved from http://164.100.47.4/newrsquestion/ShowQn.aspx (Accessed on 28 October 2018).

53 Ministry of Environment, Forest and Climate Change, Retrieved from www.moef. nic.in/sites/default/files/Draft%20National%20Forest%20Policy%2C%20 2018.pdf (Accessed on 23 October 2018).

54 National Working Plan Code, 2014, Retrieved from http://envfor.nic.in/sites/ default/files/National%20Working%20Plan%20Code%202014.pdf (Accessed on 23 October 2018).

55 Lok Sabha Unstarred Question No.865 answered on 14.12.2018.

56 National Mission for Green India, Retrieved from www.moef.gov.in/sites/default/ files/GIM_Mission%20Document-1.pdf (Accessed on 16 November 2018).

57 The number of rejected claims then available was of October 2018, Retrieved from https://tribal.nic.in/FRA/data/MPROct2018.pdf (Accessed on 4 March 2019).

58 Retrieved from www.sci.gov.in/supremecourt/2008/8640/8640_2008_Order_ 13-Feb-2019.pdf (Accessed on 4 March 2019).

59 In addition to Wildlife First, the Wildlife Trust of India, Nature Conservation Society, Tiger Research and Conservation Trust, Bombay Natural History Society, retired forest officials from Andhra Pradesh, Karnataka, Maharashtra, Orissa, and Tamilnadu, and T.N.S. Murugadoss Theerthapathi, ex-*zamindar* of Singampatti in Tamilnadu; see *Centre Again Totally Silent in Anti-FRA Case, Supreme Court Asks for Reports on Forest Rights Act*. Retrieved from https://forestright sact.com/2019/02/13/centre-again-totally-silent-in-anti-fra-case-supreme-court-asks-for-reports-on-forest-rights-act/ (Accessed on 4 March 2019).

60 See their protest note, *Conservationists Speak Out Against Evictions, Say This Is Not Pro-Conservation*. Retrieved from https://forestrightsact.com/2019/02/27/ conservationists-speak-out-against-evictions-say-this-is-not-pro-conservation/ (Accessed on 4 March 2019).

61 This application can be accessed in the article *SC Agrees To Hear Tomorrow Centre's Application For Stay Of Eviction Of Forest Dwellers*. Retrieved from www.livelaw.in/top-stories/sc-agrees-to-hear-tomorrow-centres-application-for-stay-of-eviction-of-forest-dwellers-143203#.XHYmGIb9j3I.facebook (Accessed on 4 March 2019).

62 The Supreme Court order was not available in the public domain at the time of writing though widely reported in the media.
63 The letter is available at *Opposition Leaders, People's Organisations Ask if Govt Has Decided to Sacrifice Forest Rights Act*. Retrieved from https://for-estrightsact.com/2019/02/04/opposition-leaders-peoples-organisations-ask-if-govt-has-decided-to-sacrifice-forest-rights-act/ (Accessed on 4 March 2019).

References

Akerkar, Supriya. 1996, 30 March. 'Attaining autonomy'. Retrieved from www.indiaenvironmentportal.org.in/content/1608/attaining-autonomy accessed on 16 November 2018.

Aryan, Aashish. 2019, 28 February. 'Supreme court stays February 13 order to evict nearly 1.89 million tribals'. Retrieved from www.business-standard.com/article/current-affairs/supreme-court-stays-its-earlier-order-to-evict-forest-dwelling-tribes-119022800811_1.html accessed on 3 March 2019.

Bakshi, G.D. 2009. *Left wing extremism in India: context, implications and response options*. Manekshaw paper no. 9. Retrieved from www.claws.in/administrator/uploaded_files/1249630947Manekshaw%20Paper%20%209%20%202009.pdf accessed on 14 November 2018.

Bijoy, C.R. 2008. 'Forest rights struggle: the Adivasis now await a settlement', *American Behavioural Scientist*, 51(12): 1755–1773.

Bijoy, C.R. 2011. 'The great Indian tiger show', *Economic and Political Weekly*, 46(4): 36–41.

Bijoy, C.R. 2017. 'Forest rights struggle: the making of the law and the decade after', *Law, Environment and Development Journal*, 13(2): 73–93. Retrieved from www.lead-journal.org/content/17073.pdf accessed on 22 October 2018.

Bijoy, C.R. et al. 2010. *India and the rights of indigenous peoples*. Thailand: Asia Indigenous Peoples Pact (AIPP) Foundation.

Bijoy, C.R. 2015. *Forest rights in the Himalayan mountain states: status and issues*, (Unpublished). Retrieved from https://www.academia.edu/17019990/Forest_Rights_in_The_Himalayan_Mountain_States_Status_and_Issues accessed on 25 March 2020.

Chowdhury, Nupur. 2014. 'From judicial activism to adventurism – the Godavarman case in the Supreme Court of India', *Asia Pacific Journal of Environmental Law, Australian Centre for Climate and Environmental Law*, 17(1): 177–190.

FAO. 2012. 'Voluntary guidelines on the responsible governance of tenure of land, fisheries and forests in the context of national food security', *FAO*, Rome. Retrieved from www.fao.org/docrep/016/i2801e/i2801e.pdf accessed on 22 October 2018.

Fisher, R.J., Somjai Srimongkontip and Cor Veer. 1997. *People and forests in Asia and the Pacific: status and prospects, Asia-Pacific forestry sector outlook study*. Working paper no. APFSOS/WP/27, Forestry Policy and Planning Division, Rome: FAO. Retrieved from www.fao.org/3/a-w7732e.pdf accessed on 22 October 2018.

Forest Survey of India, Ministry of Environment, Forests & Climate Change, Government of India. 2019. *India state of forest report 2019*. New Delhi. Retrieved from http://fsi.nic.in/isfr19/vol1/chapter1.pdf accessed on 25 March 2020.

Ghanekar, Nikhil M. 2017, 27 December. 'NCST to examine freezing of tribal rights in tiger reserves, compensation, with MoEFCC', *DNA*. Retrieved from www.dnaindia.com/india/report-ncst-to-examine-freezing-of-tribal-rights-in-tiger-reserves-compensation-with-moef-2570828 accessed on 22 October 2018.

Ghosal, Somnath. 2011. 'Pre-colonial, and colonial, forest culture in the presidency of Bengal', human geographies', *Journal of Studies and Research in Human Geography*, 5(1): 107–116. Retrieved from http://humangeographies.org.ro/arti cles/51/5_1_11_8_ghosal.pdf accessed on 21 October 2018.

Ghosh, Soumitra. 2017. 'Compensatory afforestation: "Compensating" loss of forests or disguising forest off sets?' *Economic and Political Weekly*, 52(38): 67–75.

Government of India. 1996. *The Provisions of The Panchayats (Extension to The Scheduled Areas) Act 1996 (PESA 1996)*. Retrieved from https://tribal.nic.in/actRules/PESA.pdf accessed on 25 March 2020.

Government of India. 2002. *Tenth five year plan (2002–2007), Vol. II, sectoral policies and programmes*. New Delhi: Planning Commission. Retrieved from http://164.100.161.239/plans/planrel/fiveyr/10th/volume2/10th_vol2.pdf accessed on 25 March 2020.

Government of India. 2008. *Development challenges in extremist affected areas, report of an expert group to planning commission*. New Delhi. Retrieved from http://planningcommission.nic.in/reports/publications/rep_dce.pdf accessed on 23 October 2018.

Halais, Flavie. 2018, 24 July. 'In India, making the business case for community forest rights', *DEVEX*. Retrieved from www.devex.com/news/in-india-making-the-business-case-for-community-forest-rights-90595 accessed on 22 October 2018.

Haque, Tajamul and Amar Singh Sirohi. 1986. *Agrarian reforms and institutional changes in India*. New Delhi: Concept Publishing Company.

Harvey, David. 2005. *A brief history of neoliberalism*. New York: Oxford University Press.

Mathur, H.M. 2008. 'Introduction and overview', in H.M. Mathur (ed.), *India social development report 2008: development and displacement* (pp. 3–13). New Delhi: Council for Social Development and Oxford University Press.

Menon, Ajit and C.R. Bijoy. 2014, January. 'The limits to law, democracy and governance', *Yojana*, pp. 9–12.

Ministry of Environment & Forest. 2004. *Handbook of Forest (Conservation) Act, 1980 (with amendments made in 1988), forest (conservation) rules, 2003 (with amendments made in 2004), guidelines & clarifications (up to June, 2004)*, New Delhi, p. 2. Retrieved from http://wrd.bih.nic.in/guidelines/awadhesh02c.pdf accessed on 23 October 2018.

Ministry of Environment, Forests and Climate Change. Government of India. 2009. 'Asia-Pacific forestry sector outlook study II', in *India forestry outlook study* (pp. 75–76). Bangkok: FAO. Retrieved from www.fao.org/docrep/014/am251e/am251e00.pdf accessed on 23 October 2018.

Ministry of Tribal Affairs, Government of India & UNDP, India. 2014. *Forest Rights Act, 2006: act, rules and guidelines*. Retrieved from https://tribal.nic.in/FRA/data/FRARulesBook.pdf accessed on 23 October 2018.

Nayak, Purusottam. 2012, August. *Human development in north-eastern region of India: issues and challenges*. MPRA paper no. 41582, Munich Personal RePEc Archive. Retrieved from https://mpra.ub.uni-muenchen.de/41582/1/MPRA_paper_41582.pdf accessed on 23 October 2018.

Project Tiger, Ministry of Environment, Forests and Climate Change, Government of India, 2005. *The report of the tiger task force. Joining the dots*. Retrieved from https://projecttiger.nic.in/WriteReadData/PublicationFile/Joning%20The%20Dots.pdf accessed on 25 March 2020.

Rights and Resources Initiative, Vasundhara and Natural Resources Management Consultants. 2015. *Potential for recognition of community forest resource rights under India's Forest Rights Act: a preliminary assessment.* Washington, DC, USA. Retrieved from http://rightsandresources.org/wp-content/uploads/Community Forest_RR_A4Final_web1.pdf accessed on 23 October 2018.

Rupawat, Prudhviraj. 2019, 14 March. 'FRA: how Modi chose corporate interests over tribal rights', *NewsClick.* Retrieved from www.newsclick.in/fra-how-modi-chose-corporate-interests-over-tribal-rights accessed on 21 March 2019.

Sethi, Nitin and Kumar Sambhav Shrivastava. 2019, 21 March. 'Centre drafts stricter alternative to colonial-era Indian forest act, 1927', *Business Standard.* Retrieved from www.business-standard.com/article/economy-policy/centre-drafts-stricter-alternative-to-colonial-era-indian-forest-act-1927-119032001071_1.html accessed on 21 March 2019.

Shrivastava, Kumar Sambhav. 2018, 17 July. 'Tribal affairs ministry opposes centre's draft national forest policy for its "privatisation thrust"', *Scroll.in.* Retrieved from https://scroll.in/article/886708/thrust-on-privatisation-tribal-affairs-ministry-opposes-centres-draft-national-forest-policy accessed on 23 October 2018.

Tripathi, Bhasker. 2017, 19 September. 'As states create land banks for private investors, conflicts Erupt across India', *The Wire.* Retrieved from https://thewire.in/banking/states-create-land-banks-private-investors-conflicts-erupt-across-india accessed on 23 October 2018.

Veeresha, Nayakara. 2017, 19 September. 'Governance of the fifth schedule areas: role of governor', *The Indian Journal of Public Administration*, 63(3): 444–455.

World Bank. 2006, 6 February. *India. unlocking opportunities for forest – dependent people in India.* Report No. 34481 – IN, Agriculture and Rural Development Sector Unit South Asia Region.

5 Maharashtra Agricultural Land Leasing Bill, 2017

Exploring opportunities for landless and women's collectives

Seema Kulkarni and Pallavi Harshe

One of the biggest threats to landownership in the present day, especially among small and marginal farmers, has been the large-scale conversion of agricultural land for non-agricultural purposes or distress selling because agriculture has become unviable. The 'land use statistics' between 1991–92 and 2012–13 (Ministry of Agriculture 1991–92 and 2012–13, cited in Rao and Behera 2017: 21) reveals that nearly 3.16 million hectares of agricultural land was lost to other sectors. To free up land and make way for industrial development and large infrastructure projects, several states in India are either amending older laws or bringing in new ones. In consonance, changes in land record management, land ceiling laws, land acquisition laws, land leasing laws, and property laws are observed.

Among the various legal reforms proposed is the land lease law, which aims at liberalising land leasing by setting land free from tenancy laws that allow the tillers to stake their claim to land. The discourse on land leasing by its advocates calls for a scrapping of the old tenancy laws, arguing that tenancy laws have become redundant. They further the argument, saying that liberalising land leases would provide the necessary incentive to formalise leases and ensure security to both the owner and tenant. NITI Aayog Report 2016 advocates for a land lease law; it mentions the commendable work done by women's collectives and, as examples of group leasing, under the Kudumbashree programme in Kerala, and under the Society of Elimination of Rural Poverty Programme (SERPP) of the undivided Andhra Pradesh in Telangana. Based on our work experience, we curiously ask – among landless women tenants belonging to socially marginalised groups, who enters informal land leases? Does this ensure women's tenure rights and works as a solution for access to agricultural land for livelihood? We examine this question in the context of a draft land lease bill introduced by the Maharashtra Legislative Assembly in April 2017, as a measure to bring in equity and efficiency in agriculture and creating a pathway for rural transformation.

Land reform and India's 'agricultural growth' story

In post-independent India, broadly speaking, three major types of land reform legislation have been enacted in most of the states: (1) abolition of intermediary tenures; (2) regulation of the size of holdings through land ceiling or land consolidation reforms and the settlement and regulation of tenancy to transfer land to the tiller; and (3) increase the security of tenure for tenants and regulation of rent seeking by large landlords (NITI Aayog Report 2016: 4). Social justice and poverty alleviation, addressing inequalities in landholding by transferring land to the tiller and improving efficiency in agricultural productivity were some of the objectives for introducing these reforms. Barring a few states, such as West Bengal and Kerala, overall, the land reform agenda has not attained what it set out to achieve. It was generally abandoned by most political parties after a decade following independence.

In the current neoliberal paradigm, the agenda for land reform and distribution has witnessed a new set of challenges. The process of land acquisition, trading of water, and access to other natural resources has become easy because of the introduction of various government policies. The growing number of special economic zones (SEZs) and mushrooming of industrial zones, development projects such as the golden corridor, etc., have meant that land is being acquired through the State arm, thereby dispossessing the poor of their meagre resources. As Harvey (2004) puts it, accumulation by dispossession consists of the commodification of goods that were not seen as part of the market before, because of the needs of capital to find new avenues for investment, to keep reproducing and therefore growing (and accumulating). In Harvey's terms, current reallocations of resources can be seen as a new round of enclosure of the commons, referring to processes of dispossession of resources that release labour, land, and water at a very low cost. The coercive powers of the State play a crucial role in backing and facilitating these processes, as it is responsible for altering regulations or laws and institutions, favouring, privileging, and even promoting such forms of capitalist accumulation as forms of economic growth, progress, and development. State politics and ideology are central to these forms of dispossession. The State, for instance, actively appropriates land, freeing it for leasing or for contract or corporate farming.

Liberalising land leases in India

It has been argued from different quarters that reform in tenancy is warranted to improve efficiency in agricultural productivity. Advocates of this school say that tenancy reforms had a role to play in the immediate post-independence period when landlordism characterised the agrarian society. Now, the situation has changed and although land leasing continues, the fear of losing land to the tenant has forced an increase in the number of landless, small, and marginal farmers entering into informal contracts with landowners.

Land leasing or sharecropping is not new to India, and there is enough evidence to show its existence in ancient India as well (Byres 1983). Literature is replete with theoretical and empirical work which explains the rationale behind sharecropping contracts, costs of sharing, terms of contract, etc. See for example the work of Eswaran and Kotwal (1985), Newbery (1977), Stiglitz (1974), and Singh (1989), among others that speak of the risk-sharing properties of sharecropping or existence of what is referred to as moral hazards and adverse selection. They further go on to explain the various factors that determine such contracts. Chaudhari and Maitra (2000) through their empirical study have shown how the terms of cost sharing depend on availability of employment opportunities outside the tenancy, the proportion of inputs costs shared by the owner, and the possibility of assured market linkages.

Bansal et al. (2018) in their detailed analysis of NSSO (National Sample Survey Organisation) data show that a substantial increase in the incidence of agricultural tenancy has occurred between 2002–03 to 2012–13. From 6.7 percent in 2002–03 to 11 percent, the increase in the area leased-in is the highest reported in the past four decades. The proportion of tenants also has increased from 11.4 percent (2002–03) to 15 percent (2012–13). The study highlights that fixed rent is the preferred form of sharing, which indicates that the higher income groups are entering into the leasing market, thereby pushing out smaller landless tenants. There is exclusion of dalits and Muslims from both landownership as well as access to land for tenancy; tenancy does not mitigate caste disparities.

It is evident from NSSO data and other micro-studies that land leasing is on the rise and this is especially so in the states of Andhra Pradesh and Telangana. Both states have introduced legal provisions in the past decade to protect the rights of tenants and owners, but without any significant success in doing so. Data from a survey done by the Rythu Swaraj Vedika, a Telangana-based farmer's organisation along with students of TISS (Tata Institute of Social Sciences) in 2018 shows that 75 percent of farm suicides were of tenant farmers (Kurmanath KV 2018).

It is against this backdrop of increasing informal tenancies that the Expert Committee on Land Leasing under the chairmanship of Dr Tajamul Haque was set up in 2015. It proposed the *Model Land Lease Act, 2016*, by pointing to stringent tenancy laws and the resultant loss of land available for cultivation. The committee argued that land redistribution no longer is relevant as the old feudal structures no longer exist; however, concealed land leases need to be formalised to protect both the tenant and the owner. On 11 April 2016, the Expert Committee presented its report to NITI Aayog, including the *Model Land Leasing Act*. The Model Act limits itself to land leasing in the context of agriculture and allied activities as well as only for farmers and farmers' collectives. The report makes a case for why legalising of land leasing is necessary both from the tenant's point of view and the landowners. It says that there is a strong case for legalisation and liberalisation of land leasing as it would help promote agricultural efficiency, occupational diversification, and rapid rural transformation (NITI Aayog Report 2016: 11). Pointing out the negative impact of the tenancy reforms on both tenant and owner, the report states:

> Legal restrictions on land leasing have affected agricultural efficiency in several ways. First, legal ban or restrictions on land leasing have led to concealed tenancy in almost all parts of the country. Informal tenants are most insecure, as they either have short duration oral leases or get rotated from plot to plot each year so that they cannot prove continuous possession of any particular piece of land for any specified period which could give them occupancy right, according to law of a state. This provides a disincentive to tenant farmers to make any investment in land improvement for productivity enhancement. Legalisation of land leasing would ensure security of landownership right for the landowners, which in turn would provide security of tenure to the tenants.

Hence, efficiency and productivity arguments are extended to justify the need to formalise land lease agreements in the *Model Land Lease Act*. As Mani (2016: 4) points out:

> The salient features of the Act included: (i) legalise land leasing to promote agricultural efficiency, equity and poverty reduction; (ii) legalise land leasing to ensure complete security of land ownership right for land owners and security of tenure for tenants; (iii) remove the clause of adverse possession of land in the land laws of various states; (iv) allow automatic resumption of land after the agreed lease period; (v) allow the terms and conditions of lease to be determined mutually by the land owner and the tenant; (vi) facilitate all tenants to access crop insurance and bank credit; and (vii) incentivise tenants to make investment in land improvement.

It also lays the dispute redressal mechanism in case of disputes between tenant and owner.

Maharashtra interestingly shows a decline in both the proportion of tenants among cultivator households and the proportion of the leased-in area of the operated land. For Maharashtra in 2002–03 the proportion of tenants was 7 percent and the leased-in area was 4.7. In 2012–13, it has come down to 4.9 and 3.3 percent, respectively. It is thus not clear why the government is in a tearing hurry to revoke the tenancy laws and replace them with the Land Lease Bill modelled on the Model Land Lease law proposed by NITI Aayog.

Exploring potential for women farmers

More than 50 percent of the population depends on agriculture; its contribution to the economy is less than 18 percent, contributing to the agrarian crisis. As per the Agriculture Census data of 2015–16, the number of small and marginal holders operating smaller areas of land is increasing. It shows that about 86 percent of the operational holders are small and marginal (0.0–2.0 ha), operating only 47 percent of the land, while semi-medium and medium farmers, who constitute about 13 percent of all the operational holders (2.00–10.0 ha), operate 44 percent of the land, and larger holders, who constitute about 0.57 percent of the operational holders, operate about 9 percent of the land. High dependence on agriculture, inequalities in access to land, decline of agriculture's contribution to the economy, and declining investments in agriculture are among the key reasons for the current agrarian crisis.

Agrarian transition has largely been a gendered one, with large-scale male outmigration from rural areas as a result of agrarian distress. As men move into non-farm jobs, women are forced to look after the fields but under extremely adverse conditions and doing unpaid labour. Though women are seen on the farms, they are not paid for the work they do. This is evident from the NSSO data on employment done over a period of years that show a decline in rural women's employment. In 1999–2000, about 41 percent of rural working-age women were employed in agriculture. In 2011–12, this declined to 28 percent. There was no parallel increase in employment in any other sector as well for rural women, clearly indicating that they were not being absorbed elsewhere (Rawal and Saha 2015). The recent Periodic Labour Force Survey (PLFS), 2017–18 data shows that only 18 percent of women participate in the labour force (MOSPI 2019).

In the face of increasing agrarian distress, with marginalisation of small, marginal, and landless farmers; the coexistence of feminisation of agriculture; and a decline in rural women's employment; clearly new models are needed in agriculture – both in form and content.

In rural India, access to cultivable land with access to water is considered equally important from the point of view of economic well-being. Considering that women's ownership of land is very poor despite amendments in some of the personal laws, addressing the rural women's question becomes a rather vexing issue.

To understand women's ownership through operational holdings, the Agriculture Census is the main source of information. The most recent Agricultural Census data for 2015–16 shows that 14 percent of all the operational landholders are women, operating about 11 percent of the area. Over a decade there was a marginal increase – from the 2005-06 census, 13 percent operational holding to 14 percent in 2015–16. Women operating 10 percent of operated areas does not reflect the overwhelming presence of women in agriculture; this contrasts with the NSSO data that show a decline in rural women's employment in the past decade.

Poor landownership among women on one hand, and an increased presence on the farms on the other, indicates that solutions need to be found to strengthen ecological agriculture and the recognition of women as farmers. In this situation, a key question is: If this were to be pursued, what are the institutional models or forms that could address gender gaps in landownership and access to entitlements associated with ownership? Can group farming or collective farming with support from the State be an answer? Can then there be legal provisions that ensure tenure security for women leasing-in land for group farming?[1] Can the proposed land lease bill for Maharashtra open such possibilities? We explore this by understanding the provisions in the bill in the context of the field work done in Maharashtra.

Increasing empirical evidence from Kerala and Telangana highlighted by Bina Agarwal (2018) suggests that group farming or collective farming is a possible solution to address some of the questions raised. There are also less-documented evidences from various other states where the women collectives have been formed for sharing various resources, including knowledge and information. She argues in her paper (2018) that group farming does provide an effective alternative provided the State makes available the necessary supports. If the Kudumbashree and SERPP models were to be scaled up, a legal provision to ensure tenure security would need to be in place.

Tenancy reform in Maharashtra State

Maharashtra enacted the *Bombay Tenancy & Agricultural Lands Act* in 1948. It has been revised several times (in 1951, 1964, 1965, 2014, 2016) and is now referred to as the *Maharashtra Tenancy and Agricultural Lands Act, 1948* (MTALA), which covers the entire state. Section 32 of the Act ensured that tenants who were cultivating land on 1 April 1957, 'tillers day', will be made the owners of the land after paying a nominal amount which could also be paid in instalments.

Different acts were applicable to different parts of Maharashtra before the enactment of the MTALA. Western Maharashtra had a *Bombay Small Holders Relief Act, 1938*, which prevented eviction of tenants who had cultivated the land continuously for more than six years. Further amendments to this Act allowed for security of tenure and regulation of rent, but its implementation was poor. In the Berar Division, Vidarbha region of Maharashtra, the *Berar Regulation of Agricultural Leases Act, 1951*, allowed for some protection to tenants by determining reasonable rents and a term for lease, and the *Central Provinces Tenancy Act, 1883*, which recognised different types of tenants such as absolute occupancy tenants, ordinary tenants, sub-tenants, village service tenants, etc. Different types of tenants were protected, except the ordinary tenants who were unable to pay rent. These were later protected through the *Bombay Vidarbha Region Agricultural Tenants (Protection from Eviction and Amendment of Tenancy Laws) Ordinance* in 1957. Later, more comprehensive legislation, *The Bombay*

Tenancy and Agricultural Lands (Vidarbha Region) Act, 1958, was passed. The tenancy in Marathwada region was regulated by *Asami-Shikmi Act, 1354 F.* Asami Sikhmis was a class of protected tenants as created by the Act. After independence, the erstwhile Hyderabad State passed a comprehensive tenancy act named the *Hyderabad Tenancy and Agricultural Lands Act, 1951* (Mokashi 1978: 186–188).

At present, tenancy is not completely banned in Maharashtra, but the tenant acquires the right to purchase the leased land from the owner within a specified period of creation of tenancy (Haque n.d.). Section 43 of the MTALA also lays restriction on the transfer of land through sale, gift, exchange, mortgage, lease, or assignment without the prior permission of the Collector. These restrictions were imposed to ensure that the tenants do not sell the land for profits, as the land was intended for livelihood purposes; also, to ensure that others do not take undue advantage of them and buy the land at lower rates. This provision was later amended in 2014 under which the need for permission of the Collector to sell the land was removed in cases where the land had been purchased ten years before.

Implementation of tenancy reforms is indicative of concerns for tenants. Until 2006, 4 percent of land rights were conferred on the tenants; 33 percent of the tenants were evicted from the land they were tilling to prevent them from acquiring occupancy rights, resulting in a general worsening of their tenure security (Appu 1997, cited in Mearns 1999). NSSO data in different rounds have indicated that land leasing has been on the decline, and this is largely attributed to stringent tenancy laws. However, various studies point to the fact that land leases/reverse tenancy are in fact increasing (Jodha 1981; Mearns 1999); none of them are formally recorded as a result of the stringent laws. Concealed tenancy arrangements often lead to insecure tenures for tenants, pushing them to the margins (Mearns 1999: 6).

Maharashtra Land Leasing Bill, 2017

Following the *Model Land Lease Act*, Maharashtra State proposed a bill entitled *A Law Relating to Agricultural Land Leasing in the State of Maharashtra* on 7 April 2017 in the State Legislative Assembly. The bill echoes the statement of object of the *Model Land Lease Act, 2016*, stating that the prohibitions and restrictions under existing state tenancy laws governing agricultural land leasing have forced landowners and tenant cultivators to have informal agreements, thereby depriving the tenant cultivators of the benefits which are normally due to them. The Model Act provides rationale that the existing laws create insecurity among landowners to lease-out agricultural land, thereby reducing access to land by landless poor, small, and marginal farmers and others by way of leasing. Moreover, agricultural land leasing would improve agricultural efficiency and equity by promoting access to land for the landless, small, and marginal farmers. By providing recognition to the tenants, they will be able to access institutional credit, insurance, disaster relief, and other support services provided by the government, while also protecting fully the land rights of the owners.

The Maharashtra bill mainly subscribes to the Model Act but makes it mandatory for a written lease agreement (section 3, sub-section 4), a departure from the Model Act. As per the bill, the written agreement should be registered under the provisions of the *Registration Act, 1908*. In subsection 8 of section 3, it is also mentioned very explicitly that the lease agreement will not be registered under the Record of Rights but a separate register would be maintained by authorised officials, and the lease agreement would be registered in that register maintained in a prescribed format by related officials. Section 3, sub-section 9, clarifies that registration of tenancy under the *Registration Act* will not lead to any right over land for the tenant. The tenant will not get any of the following rights: (a) protected tenancy, (b) occupancy right, (c) any other right against eviction, and (d) right against lease termination except for those mentioned in the lease agreement. Similarly, the entry in register or under the *Registration Act* cannot be used in any court of law to establish permanent right over land. It is thus evident that the land rights of landowners are secured. Section 3 also states that the lease period and the lease amount in cash or kind or share is to be decided mutually by the tenant and the owner. Sub-section 10 of section 3 underlines the automatic reversion of the land to the landowner once the lease agreement ends.

Section 4 of the bill largely speaks of the rights and responsibilities of the landowner which includes the right to get back the land in the event the tenant carries out any of the default actions such as failure on the part of the tenant to make the payment, or in case the tenant causes damage to the soil health or if the land is used for purposes not mentioned in the lease agreement. Similarly, landowners are entitled to the lease amount on time and the right to automatically get the land back after the expiry of the lease agreement, to transfer the land without disturbing the cultivation rights of the tenant till the end of the lease period. The bill specifies that the owner should not interfere in the use of the land until the expiry of the lease period. The owner is responsible for paying the taxes, cess levied on the land.

Section 5 is about the rights and responsibilities of the tenant. According to section 5, the tenant is entitled to have undisturbed possession and use of the agricultural land until the expiry of the lease agreement. The tenant will only have those rights as mentioned in the lease agreement and cannot have the right over land because of the lease agreement. The tenant does not have the right to sub-lease the land, make changes to the soil or land unless mentioned in the agreement, build any structures or fixtures on the land without the permission of the landowner, and disturb the boundaries of the land during the lease period. The right to get credit or benefits of crop insurance, etc., is dependent on mutual agreement either between the financial institution and tenant or the tenant and owner. When there is need of credit facilities from banks, cooperatives, or any other financial institutions, sub-section 'e' of section 5 stipulates that the credit can be taken without mortgaging the land. In such cases, the institution and tenant mutually agree that he/she can use the expected value of production/returns from leased-in land during the lease period as collateral for advancing the loan. Regarding the need to get the benefits of crop insurance, disaster relief, or any other benefits or facilities provided to farmers by the State or Central Government, sub-section 'f' of section 5 states that it is to be based on mutually agreed terms between the tenant and owner.

Section 7 of the bill states that the lease can be terminated under the following conditions: (a) expiry of the lease period, (b) failure to pay lease consideration after three months from the due date, (c) use of the land for purposes other than agriculture and allied activities or as mentioned in the lease agreement, (d) tenant sub-leases the land, (e) tenant damages the land, (f) both parties mutually agree to terminate the lease, (g) tenant dies, and (h) tenant voluntarily surrenders the leased-in land.

An important mechanism as laid down by the bill is the dispute redressal mechanism. Section 8 of the bill mentions that there will be competent authority nominated by the State to enforce the lease terms and will be responsible for implementation of the terms of lease and to return back the leased-out land to the owner after completion of the lease agreement. Three layers of a dispute resolution mechanism are mentioned in the bill, including competent authority that will be specified by the State. The second appeal point would be the District Magistrate, and the final redressal mechanism would be the Maharashtra Revenue Tribunal. All of them have been given the rights to pass interim orders which cannot be challenged. For other orders, appeal can be made to higher appeal structures. Section 12 also explicitly states that, except for a decision affecting the legal title of land of an owner, no other decisions made under this Act by competent authorities can be challenged in a Civil Court. Similarly, no Civil Courts have the jurisdiction to resolve disputes under this Act. Section 13 states that no suit, prosecution, or other legal proceedings can be used against an officer of the government for doing anything which is done or intended to be done in good faith, thereby offering protection.

Field study on land leasing

In July 2018, field work was done in the Osmanabad District of the Marathwada region of Maharashtra to study the prevalent forms and terms of lease agreements, labour, and other input- and produce-sharing arrangements to articulate the tenants' perspective and also to understand the social composition of those who lease-in land and whether women engage in any group leasing activities. Based on the findings, the study attempts to explore whether there are opportunities for ensuring tenurial rights of landless families and women's collectives in Maharashtra State.

Methodology and sample

The study was conducted in three villages, namely, Apsinga, Kamtha, and Katri in Tuljapur Taluka,[2] of the Osmanabad District. Purposive sampling was used for selection of villages and the respondents, such as presence of known activists in the village[3] and availability of lessee. Of a total of 72 land leases that were identified, 32 were interviewed. Three of the seven households interviewed in Kamtha who cultivated leased land stopped subsequently because of oppressive terms set forth by the landowner. During eight interviews, the wives of the farmers were also present and contributed to providing information.

We use the term 'owner' for the term 'lessor' referred to in the bill and 'tenant' for the term 'lessee', that is, the one who has leased-in the land as referred to in the bill.

Of the 32 tenants interviewed, 21 are from Apsinga, five from Kamatha, and six from Katri. The gender profile shows that 27 are men, while only five are women. Of the five, two single women were cultivating the land themselves; three women are married and interacted as respondents as their husbands were not available at the time of the interview. Two married women were not aware of the financial arrangements of the leasing-in. Of 32 tenant farmers, 26 farmers are Hindu, six are Muslims. All the Muslims are from Apsinga village. The details regarding social strata and caste of the Hindu tenants is as follows: 12 belonged to the general category (Maratha); three belonged to the OBC category (Mali, Fulmali, and Lingayatmali); and 11 belong to the SC community (Matangs and neo-Buddhists). Among SCs, a greater number of neo-Buddhist families are leasing-in land and cultivating (Table 5.1).

Table 5.1 Profiles of tenant farmers interviewed in the study villages

Village	No. of interviewed tenants	Gender distribution of interviewed tenants		Social strata			
		Males	*Females*	*General*	*OBC*[4]	*SC*[5]	*Muslim*
Apsinga	21	17	4	6	3	6	6
Kamatha	5	4	1	0	0	5	0
Katri	6	6	0	6	0	0	0
Total	32	27	5	12	3	11	6

Source: All tables in this chapter are prepared by the authors based on primary data collection, unless specified otherwise

The social strata of landowners – 26 are from the open category (Brahmin, Maratha,[6] and Vani)[7]; eight belong to the Other Backward Classes (OBC) category (Mali,[8] Mahadev Mali, and Teli[9]); three belong to either SC (dalit) or Nomadic Tribes (NT) (D)/(C) category (Chambhar,[10] Dhangar[11] and Vanjari[12]), and one has leased-in land from Shri Shivaji Shikshan Prasarak Mandal registered under the *Societies Registration Act, 1860*. All open-category farmers are Marathas, and all the OBC farmers have self-owned land. Of the total households from the SC (Scheduled Castes, mentioned as 'dalit' henceforth) community interviewed, only one has self-owned land. The other four SCs (all neo-Buddhists) are also cultivating encroached grazing lands[13] and *hadki hadvala*[14] (Dhasal 1987). One of the Muslim households was cultivating *devsthan inam* land[15] in exchange for service they provide in an annual religious procession (Table 5.2).

Profile of the study villages

Marathwada is a drought-prone area of Maharashtra and comprises eight districts. It is home to 423,203 (14 percent of the total population) SC households, of which 337,740 (79 percent) are deprived[16] with regard to various criteria as per the socio-economic caste census (SECC) 2011. Of the SC households in Marathwada, the SECC 2011 data show that 61,228 (15 percent) of dalit households are dependent on cultivation, while 244,812 (57 percent) of households are landless and are dependent on manual casual labour. For Osmanabad District, there are 47,749 (16 percent) dalit households among whom 37,754 (79 percent) are deprived, and 27,931 (58 percent) dalit households are landless and are dependent on manual casual labour as their main income source. As per Census 2011, the dalit population of the three villages under study is greater compared with the percentage of the SC population in Osmanabad District (16 percent) or Tuljapur Taluka (16.8 percent). Apsinga village has the highest SC population at 1,338 (29 percent) followed by Katri with 321 (27.4 percent) and Kamatha with 440 (23.6 percent) villages (Table 5.3).

Table 5.2 Caste-wise details of other kinds of land cultivated by tenants

Religion/caste category	Total number of lessees	Number of tenants cultivating other than leased-in land[17]
General	12	12
OBC	3	3
SC	11	5
Muslim	6	2
Total	32	22

Table 5.3 Area and population details in the study villages

Region	Total geographical area (in hectares)	Total population	Total households	Total SC population[18]
Osmanabad District total	772,550.45	1,376,519	296,494	221,325 (16.1)
Tuljapur District total	156,884.79	226,527	47,223	38,051 (16.8)
Katri village	769	1,170	236	321 (27.4)
Apsinga village	2534	4541	920	1338 (29.4)
Kamatha village	1155	1867	386	440 (23.6)

Source: Census 2011

Table 5.4 Land ownership in the study villages

Village	Katri	Apsinga	Kamtha
Total households	241	928	408
Households owning land	144	341	152
Percent of households owning land	59.8	36.7	37.3
Households owning 2.5 acres or more irrigated land with at least one piece of irrigation equipment (in percent)	4.2	1.4	2.2
Households owning 5 acres or more land irrigated for two or more crop seasons (in percent)	3.7	3.2	2.2
Households owning 7.5 acres or more land with at least one irrigation piece of equipment (in percent)	3.3	0.8	2.2
Landless households deriving major part of their income from manual casual labour (in percent)	29.9	37.9	44.9

Source: SECC data 2011

Landownership and labour

As per the SECC 2011, the households owning land in Katri village number 144 (60 percent), 341 (37 percent) in Apsinga, and 152 (37 percent) in Kamtha, indicating a high percentage of landlessness (Table 5.4).

The SECC data, 2010–11, show that in Katri village, 118 households (49 percent) are engaged in cultivation, while 99 households (41.1 percent) derive their income from manual casual labour. In Apsinga village, 338 households (36.4 percent) earn their income from cultivation and 437 households (47.1 percent) from manual casual labour. In Kamatha village, 131 households (32.1 percent) are engaged in cultivation, while 270 (66.2 percent) are engaged in manual casual labour. Households dependent on manual casual labour for their livelihood are more numerous in Kamatha and Apsinga, while in Katri more households are dependent on cultivation rather than manual casual labour (Table 5.5).

Table 5.5 Household sources of income in the study villages

Village	Total number of households	Main source of household income – cultivation (%)	Main source of household income – manual casual labour (%)
Katri	241	49.0	41.1
Apsinga	928	36.4	47.1
Kamatha	408	32.1	66.2

Source: SECC data, 2010–11

Land use, irrigation, and cropping patterns

Land use data from Census 2011 show that out of the total geographical area in Osmanabad,700,987.4 hectares (90.7 percent) are the net area sown which are almost equal to Tuljapur taluka (141,828 hectares [90.4 percent]). For the villages, the percentage of net sown area is less compared with the district and taluka percentages. For Katri village, the net area sown is 642 hectares, or 83.5 percent); for Apsinga village, 934 hectares (36.9 percent); while for Kamatha village, it is 873 hectares (75.6 percent). The lowest net sown area is in Apsinga village, which has 454 hectares (17.9 percent) of forest area, while 828 hectares (32.7 percent) is barren and uncultivable land area. As per the District Socio-Economic Survey 2017, Osmanabad District, irrigated area is 11.62 percent, and for Tuljapur taluka, irrigated area is 15.81 percent.

The District Socio-Economic Survey from 2006 to 2017 shows an increase in area for crops such as soya bean, onions, fruits, total crushed grains, fibrous crops, cotton, vegetables, pulses, tur, Bengal gram, corn, and sugarcane, while there is a decrease in area under cultivation for rice, Jowar, Bajra, chillies, spices, groundnut, sunflower, etc.

In 2006, there was no area under soya bean cultivation, but in 2017 the area growing soya bean was reported to be 208,966 hectares for Osmanabad District. The area under onion cultivation increased from 2,805 hectares in 2006 to 7,085 hectares in 2017 for the district. The area under Jowar cultivation for both Osmanabad district and Tuljapur taluka was 53,365 hectares in 2006; this was reduced to 46,907 in 2017. This shows a shift from traditional food crops to more cash crops which can provide some cash in hand.

Key findings of the study

Leasing patterns

The 32 tenants who were interviewed under the study had leased-in land from 45 landowners.

Table 5.6 Duration of leases in the study villages

Village	1–5 years	6–10 years	11–20 years	Not available
Katri	2	3	0	1
Apsinga	11	8	5	6
Kamatha	3	2	0	4
Total	16	13	5	11

Analysis regarding the leasing pattern reveals that the majority of tenants lease in land from a single owner (22); eight tenant farmers stated that they have leased in land from two to three owners. The total area of land leased in by a tenant ranges from 1 acre to 10 acres. Out of 32 tenant farmers, seven have leased in land between 1 to 2.5 acres, eight between 2.5 to 5 acres, ten between 5 to 10 acres, and seven above 10 acres.

As shown in Table 5.6, a total of 18 tenants cultivated land between six and 20 years from one owner. Three dalit tenants complained that they were not allowed to cultivate the land for longer periods, as the landowners feared that the tenants might claim rights on the leased-out land. The landowners preferred to change the tenants every alternate year. This break in contracts prevented the tenants from making any long-term investments for improving the production as the landowners kept changing almost every year or two. All of them were oral contracts. One local activist explained that this trend is common among the dalit tenants, as they are not recognised as 'traditional cultivators', that is, being a landed caste and agriculture being the primary occupation. They take the land on lease; if they find that cultivation would help them make a profit in a particular year, they go for leasing in the field; otherwise, they will leave it as soon as it becomes unaffordable. He also shared his observation that dalits do not have enough equipment to continue working in agriculture; hence, they cannot sustain operations for a longer period and have to leave farms in between. Regarding leasing patterns, the tenant farmers of Kamatha village expressed their view that leasing terms and conditions are many times unfavourable, leading contracts with shorter durations.

Terms and conditions prevalent under informal arrangements

Types of contracts

Of land leased from 45 owners, the contracts were verbal in 42 cases and written in three cases (Table 5.7). Verbal contracts are done both in the case of sharecropping or leasing-in based on a fixed rent. But all the sharecroppers have necessarily entered into verbal contracts. In two cases, the

Table 5.7 Type of contract and terms of leasing-in

Type of contract	Lease arrangements		
	Rent	Sharecropping	Exchange of loan/monetary help
Verbal	2	39	1
Written	1	0	2
Total	3	39	3

landowner leased out land in exchange for monetary help extended by the tenant; in these cases, the tenant farmers were entitled to share in the whole harvest. In the three cases in which a written agreement was produced, the terms were recorded on a simple piece of paper; not having the contract on stamped paper reduces its legal value to nil. These written agreements are mainly prepared either when the owner leases out the land in exchange for help extended by the tenant and subsequently allows the tenant to cultivate the land for a mutually agreed-on period or when the land is leased out for a fixed annual/more than a year rent.

Cost- and produce-sharing arrangements between tenant and owner

Discussions regarding cost- and produce-sharing arrangements with tenants revealed that there are many unwritten yet normative rules that are prevalent among tenants and owners; it is expected that both will abide by these norms. In all verbal contracts, sharecropping arrangements were such that the input costs were shared by the owners and tenants; these shared costs were always unequal, with the tenant bearing the larger burden. For example, in the case of Karim Kajhi, a tenant from Apsinga, the owner shares the costs of land preparation if the ploughing is done by tractor, sowing as well as other inputs such as seeds, fertilizers, insecticides, and all costs related to the harvest and post-harvest of onions. All labour-intensive costs such as weeding, trenching, preparing raised beds, and similar tasks are paid for by the tenant. These together constitute about 75 percent of all the tasks involved in onion cultivation. The owners in Kamatha rarely shared the input costs yet made sure that the quality of inputs used – seeds, manure/fertiliser, etc., were good. Uttam Gore, one of the tenant farmers said that:

> Sharing of inputs is a very recent trend prior to which all the expenses had to be incurred by the tenant. Until two years ago tenants were not bargaining, but when the input costs were higher than the returns, we started arguing with the owners and negotiated with them to share

some of the input costs. This forced the owners to at least share part of the input costs.

Crop-related arrangements are different for each crop. For example, input costs for onion and soya bean were shared 50/50 for some tasks/inputs between owner and tenant. Fifteen tenant farmers shared this information. The costs of ploughing by tractor, seed, fertilisers, and pesticides were split equally pre-harvest, and so were the harvesting and post-harvesting costs such as grading, sorting, transportation, etc. Labour costs for sowing, weeding, etc., which is largely family labour, was borne by the tenant farmer.

For food crops, such as Jowar, the cost was largely borne by the tenant farmer. In four of the 12 cases where Jowar was grown, the costs of fertiliser were shared evenly and in two cases seed costs and harvesting costs were shared by the owner. Choice of crops usually remains at the owners' discretion; the tenants do not always accept the choice whole-heartedly. Popat Rokade, an SC from Kamatha village, said that:

> If we are allowed to take Jowar after the onion, we could easily produce 10–15 sacks of Jowar. We also get fodder by cultivating Jowar. It is profitable for us but owner does not allow us to cultivate it.

The terms of contracts in each of the three villages varied. Kamtha village had the most unfavourable sharing agreements as far as the tenant was concerned. The relationship between owner and tenant was tense and according to Vasant Rokade, former sarpanch (Gram Pradhan – elected representative as a village head under Panchayati Raj, local governance system) of the village, Kamtha had few people employed in cities and away from their villages compared with Katri and Apsinga villages. The requirement for leasing out land for the absentee landlords was thus greater in Apsinga and Katri. In Kamtha village, the farmers prefer to cultivate their own land and are thus in a better bargaining position when leasing out their lands; the reverse is true in Apsinga and Katri villages. Large landowning size and non-availability of labour for farming determines the terms and conditions of the contract. Terms of leasing are better when landowners have some compelling reasons to lease out their land.

With regard to leasing-in on rent, one case had a written agreement while the other had a verbal contract. One tenant gave an example of how the rent on the land he had leased in was raised ad hoc when he reaped a good profit from onions in one year. The owner increased the rent and the tenant could then no longer afford it but still continued to lease in the same land in the hope of realizing a profit in subsequent years. Although this study does not build adequate evidence on the relationship between caste and the terms of lease, dalit tenants from Kamatha village did complain of unfavourable terms and conditions. This has also been highlighted by a study done by

Sukhdev Thorat in 2003 in three villages in the states of Odisha, Gujarat, and Maharashtra, where he shows that the 22 dalits who had taken agricultural land on lease to cultivate faced differential treatment either in the form of refusal to rent land by the upper castes or through renting of land on unfavourable terms and conditions (Thorat et al. 2011). Caste thus does impact the nature of leases and the terms and conditions of the lease arrangements. In the current scheme of the bill, this understanding of caste dynamics and resultant effects on mutual agreements is completely missing.

Verbal contract: insecurity of tenure

Verbal contracts were preferred by owners over written ones as they feared that they would lose their rights under the stringent tenancy law of the State.

Tenants initially were not forthcoming about the problems they have with oral contracts. Initially, they responded that most agreements are based on mutual trust and long-standing relationships with the owners; on further probing, they did discuss the problems they faced because of verbal contracts. When asked why they don't insist on a written contract, Madhukar, a tenant farmer responded, 'None of the owners give land to cultivate on written contract. If we insist for written contract, they will not give their land for cultivation'. Others said that whenever they have asked for a written contract, the owner has rebuked them by saying, 'If you want to cultivate, then do it without a written contract or else leave it'. Tenants who are keen on leasing in therefore have refrained from asking for a written contract. This indicates that tenants do not have the bargaining power to decide on either the terms of the contract or the nature or decision making around crops. In this context, the Land Lease Bill in Maharashtra State would make compulsory the registration of the written agreement, in the hope of helping the tenants.

There were many examples of tenants leasing in from one particular owner and that too for many years. The exceptions were the tenants from the neo-Buddhist community – many of them complained that they were not allowed to cultivate for longer durations, that is, more than 12 to 24 months. Other tenants said that they lease in only if the owner is trustworthy. When they were asked the implications of the absence of a written contract, they said that they themselves did not have any negative experience but had seen injustices happen to others. Tenants expressed fear of an ad hoc termination of a lease, abandoning the agreement when the crop is standing in the field, or the owner usurping the entire produce, cheating in an economic transaction. They also expressed their helplessness in such situations, saying that they were left only with the option of not leasing-in land from the owner in the subsequent year.

Uttam Gore from Apsinga village shared his experience:

> If the owner keeps all the produce and doesn't give anything to the tenant, the tenant is not left with any option. I was cheated by my previous

landowner. I spent from my own pocket and grew sugarcane on leased in land. I did all the hard work and when the crop was ready for harvest, the owner sold the produce without consulting me. I suffered a loss of 2–3 lakhs. I refused to lease in his land for the next cultivation year. What else could I do? I didn't have any documents to prove.

With no evidence in hand and no money to fight in court, Uttam had to bear the losses. Uttam Kadam from Katri village was also cheated by the owner, who refused to share the Jowar crop with him. When Uttam asked him for his share, the owner asked him to show the proof that he had cultivated the land. He subsequently stopped cultivating that owner's land.

In the case of crop failure resulting from various causes, it is the owner who receives the compensation; this is not shared with the tenant. Saiyyad said, 'If we incur loss due to natural calamity, we can't do anything. It's our bad luck. Neither the government nor the owner listens to us. No one takes responsibility.' Saiyyad tried to put up a fight and argued with the owner. He even went to the bank manager to tell him that the compensation amount had to be shared with him as a tenant. However, lack of documentation forced Saiyyad to stay quiet and eventually withdraw.

One of the respondents had a positive experience with the owner who did share the compensation with him; however, in the past two years the owner has stopped doing that.

The written contract on simple paper also has its limitations. Madhukar Vidhate from Apsinga village said that 15 years ago he had leased in land on rent for five years through a written contract. But the very next year the owner's brother applied pressure and took back the land after holding a *panchayat* meeting and ending the contract. The tenant was from the dalit community. Subsequently, he preferred taking on land for short-duration leases. He added that owners also prefer short leases over long ones.

Cropping and irrigation patterns in leased-in land

Most of the tenants prefer to take irrigated lands on lease. Of the 45 landowners from whom land was leased in, 22 had partially irrigated land which had some source of irrigation for part of the year; 16 owners had irrigation year-round, and only three of them had non-irrigated lands. So, the majority of tenants had leased-in land with irrigation sources, with a few who had leased in non-irrigated land as well. Irrigated land helps them to sustain livestock which is one of the reasons for leasing in land for cultivation. Subhash from Apsinga said, 'I have leased in land which has a bore-well, although it goes dry in summers. I can provide water to my livestock and they also get fodder'.

Reasons for cultivating leased-in land

Leasing has not been very profitable for tenants, especially for those cultivating onions. The cost of cultivation of onion as outlined by the tenants is in the range of INR15,000–135,425 per season. Of the nine farmers cultivating onions, six had incurred losses. Yet, onions are cultivated partly because the owners insist and partly also because tenants hope that at least one year will provide them with good profits to make up for earlier losses. One of the tenants mentioned that two to three years ago, the rate of onion went up to INR 60 per kilogram and that allowed him to turn a decent profit and invest it in agriculture, such as purchase of land or, more commonly, towards renovation of their house, daughters' marriage, etc.

Other reasons outlined by the male tenants leasing in land included livelihood for family, meaningful work for themselves and their families, availability of water and fodder for livestock for the whole year, etc. For some it was more respectable to lease in land rather than work as wage labourers elsewhere. Conversely, many of the women were against leasing in land. Their argument was that by working as labourers, they were able to earn wages, while if they worked the leased-in land, it was usually unpaid labour for them, as the entire control of the land was with the men of their households and the landowner. Women also believed that the uncertainty of agriculture did not guarantee profits, and hence they often tried to convince their husbands not to lease in land. For men, the lack of meaningful and gainful employment outside was a compelling reason to lease in land.

Upper-caste farming families who are traditionally cultivators are fully prepared and have all the assets for cultivation. They lease in land with the hope that it will increase their income. The number of family members who can work in the field also is a reason why tenants lease in land as it reduces the burden of renting labourers and reduces the cost and provides work to all family members.

Reasons for leasing out land

Landowners were not forthcoming about sharing information and therefore the perspective regarding leasing out is largely that of the tenants, not of the owners. Some of the chief reasons that owners leased out their land were: the non-availability of labour in the villages, absentee owners who did not want to keep their land fallow, and owners who were single women.

According to Kumar Kadam, an upper-caste tenant farmer, 'Presently the young generation is attracted towards cities; hence there is lack of labour in the village. The educated youth do not prefer to work on their respective fields. Hence, there is more demand and less supply of labourers.' According to Kadam, the situation is such that 20 farmers require labour at the same time. Every farmer requires approximately 10 women agricultural labourers but get only five. Hence, their rates increase, and sometimes they have to pay wages up to INR 200–300 per day. In the onion season, this rate can be as high as INR 500 per day. Similarly, to keep the labourers happy and call them on their fields, owners need to accept other demands of the labourers, which increases the petty expenditures of the farmer as well. On the whole, this landowner, who is also a tenant, thought that the labourers – referring especially to the dalits – had become ungrateful and arrogant. However, Vasant Rokde, a former sarpanch and a tenant himself belonging to the dalit community, thought otherwise. He said that times have changed, and the dalits are not going to take everything lying down. The young among the community are engaged in construction work and have moved to towns or cities. Some are educated and in jobs outside the village. This has meant that landless labour is not available to the farmers anymore. Their women are forced to come out and work in the fields, something that had never happened earlier. They themselves have now had to labour in the fields, and this is what makes them speak of the dalits in such a manner.

Demands of tenants

One of the demands emphasised by tenants was the need for a minimum support price for the produce. Markets are volatile and, despite a good harvest, often the returns are not good because of poor price support. On several occasions tenants have had to throw away the produce. The second demand was related to the compensation given by the government in case of crop failure. The owner has access to the entire amount of compensation despite the fact that the costs have been incurred by the tenant. Tenants also believed that contracts should be written out, not verbal, so that they have proof of the arrangement. They were, however, sceptical as to whether such a change would ever come about. Another set of demands included land for the landless (emphasised by dalit women), support for dairy farming, access to loans, government schemes for tenant farmers, government support for sowing, and several other inputs to make farming a viable activity.

Discussion: Is protecting tenants or landowners in the neoliberal era possible?

The entry point for the present study was to explore whether or not the Land Lease Bill would protect the rights of tenants and if so, would it actually open up spaces for women's collectives or small, marginal farmers and landless peasants to individually or collectively take land on lease for meeting livelihood needs by providing the security of tenure. However, the bill seems to do the reverse as it pushes back the land reform agenda and brings in economic contracts on mutually agreed terms, thereby leaving the tenant helpless. The increasing number of farm suicides and the rise in rural unemployment are, as we have seen earlier, the manifestations of such a crisis.

The verbal nature of contracts, the unfavourable terms of cost- and produce-sharing, the lack of choice in cultivation of crops, and the lack of access to institutional credit and insurance for crop failure are clearly emerging as concerns for tenant farmers. These unfavourable terms have often meant huge losses for them; therefore, there is little or no incentive for them to reinvest in tenant farming.

Women from these households have preferred paid wage labour over unpaid wage work that they must do on the leased-in farms. Can the Land Lease Bill of 2017 address these concerns? Evidence from this study and other secondary sources suggest that the Government of Maharashtra should promptly address the question of land reform by settling several claims on ceiling surplus, tenancies, *gairan* (pasture) lands, and forest rights, for example; it should commission a study on the extent of land leasing in the state and call for a wider consultation on the issue before introducing legislation. Yet, we think that we need to find answers to provide support to increasing instances of collective farming, especially among women's groups who are left to fend for themselves on their own fields or labour in the fields of others. Can there be a model that provides them secure tenancy agreements?

Mutually agreed but unequal!

Section 3(4) of the bill mandates that lease agreements must be written and registered under the relevant law. While this is a welcome step, it is important to understand that the Act leaves the rest of the terms of understanding entirely to a mutual agreement. So, while the bill states in its objects that efficiency and equity are its goals, it assumes that, in a society based on social and economic discriminations, the terms of agreement would be in the interests of both concerned parties. Study findings clearly show how gender, class, and caste intersect to determine the terms and nature of the contracts. Tenants are unable to set the terms with reference to cost- and produce-sharing or even in matters of choice of crops and the inputs to be used.

If leasing were to be formalised, the mutuality clause would have to be removed and a clear instruction to fix a range – the upper and lower limits for a sharing arrangement, whether in cash or kind – would have to be stated. Floor and ceiling lease rates would have to be decided for different states and for differently endowed regions as well. For example, rain-fed areas may need a different set of rates compared with irrigated areas. Such floor and ceiling rates are more likely to protect the tenants, especially as seen in the case from the present study in which the owner increased the land rent ad hoc in response to the profits drawn by the tenant.

Access to credit and crop insurance

The right to get credit under sub-section 'e' of section 5 of the bill is based on very uncertain criteria. Here, the onus to decide whether to accept the expected value of production of leased-in land as collateral lies on the institution. The criteria seem to be very uncertain, and hence there would only be rare occurrences in which the tenant would benefit from provisions in this section.

The provision for crop insurance, disaster relief, or any other benefits or facilities provided to the farmers by the State or Central Government is mentioned in sub-section 'f' of section 5. However, this is based on the mutually agreed lease agreement which does not favour the tenant. Here the State needs to play a strong proactive role to protect the interests of the tenant rather than an ambiguous one which favours the owner. Unfortunately, the bill does not take into consideration the unequal power relations between the owner and the tenant based on caste and class and its negative implications on bargaining capacities of tenants in such negotiations.

The Maharashtra Bill and the Model Act did not build in clauses that would have protected the interests of tenants, for instance, while the NITI Aayog's report of the Expert Committee on land leasing talks about facilitating all tenants to access insurance and bank credit against pledging of expected output, the Act leaves it to the tenants' own efforts to access these support systems. Institutional credit and protection against crop failure were two of the main demands that tenants have articulated. The bill does not have a robust mechanism to include this in a definitive way. The volatility of prices and the increasing cost of production make the tenant farmer far more vulnerable than the one with a land title.

Many farm movements have been asking for more express guidelines from the RBI (Reserve Bank of India) to bankers regarding greater support to tenant farmers and for the government to set up a credit guarantee fund to bolster banker confidence. Further, the Bhoomiheen Kisan Credit (credit scheme for landless farmers) can be scaled up to cover tenant farmers in a joint liability groups (JLG) approach but with more investments built into building up the JLG of such tenant farmers into workable institutions.

In its current form, the entire onus of a successful lease arrangement rests on the shoulders of the owner and the tenant, with the State only possibly facilitating the process. The Rural Development, Agriculture, and the Revenue departments do not seem to have a role in registering the leases and/or regulating and monitoring them. The bill should have mandated these state government departments to proactively record and register all lease agreements and share the database on a seasonal or yearly basis with bankers for credit, run special camps to enrol tenant farmers for crop insurance, ensure that at the time of disaster relief payments, such data are accessed by the competent authorities preparing the cheques, etc.

Undivided Andhra Pradesh introduced the *Land Lease Cultivation Act, 2011*, and issued loan eligibility cards to all registered lessees. However, the implementation of the Act has not been very successful so far (Revathi 2016).

Potential for women farmers' collectives

One of the potentials of the bill in the context of collective land leasing, especially for women farmers, is similar to the Kudumbashree in Kerala and SERPP model in Andhra Pradesh, as mentioned in the NITI Aayog report. However, in the current context of Maharashtra, the bill in its present form provides no hope for women farmers' collectives for land leasing. The much-cited example of Kudumbashree should be understood in the light of the strong support of the state in ensuring equity and efficiency in use of resources in an ecologically sound way. Convergence of rural employment schemes, agricultural credit and other inputs, and strengthening of local self-government has created a pathway for success in Kudumbashree, thereby underscoring the role of the welfare state rather than its withdrawal, representing a typical feature of neoliberalism.

Land to the tiller: missing agenda

The slogan, 'land to the tiller', became important soon after independence, especially with regard to recognising the occupancy rights of tillers. The starting point of the Land Lease Bill, however, is to negate the rights of tenants on the ground – the current tenancy laws constrain the landowner and the tenant from entering into formal contracts. In a bid to protect the rights of the owners, and make land available for the landless for cultivation, the bill states that all existing acts related to tenancy would be overruled by the 2017 bill. However, the pending claims of tenants under the tenancy laws would be protected. This clause misses out on the fact that claims are being continually filed by tenants for ownership rights. If the 2017 bill does become a law, such new claims would then not be entertained, which effectively means that land redistribution would not take place – this also indicates the changing role of the State in the neoliberal era.

Concluding comments

The Maharashtra Bill represents the neoliberal state in many ways – first, it falls short in protecting the tenants' rights. Second, although it stresses the registration of leases, it allows for lease agreements to be mutually decided between the landowner and the tenant. By doing so, it undermines the role of unequal power relations among castes, class, and genders in determining the terms and nature of contracts. Third, the bill leaves several questions unanswered with reference to the 'land to the tiller' agenda, which is still actively being pursued by tenants in different parts of the state. Fourth, it does not engage with the question of landless/women farmers' collectives that are looking at security of tenure even for the short duration leases that they enter to. By undermining the role of the State in promoting the welfare of landless and women farmers, the Land Lease Bill seems to be promoting an agenda for liberalising leases and freeing up land for capitalist forms of agriculture.

All the findings of the field study suggest that State regulation in tenancy needs to be in favour of poor tenants. A withdrawal of tenancy laws as recommended by the Expert Committee on Land Leasing, 2016, would work against the interests of the poor.

Notes

1 These are the questions that the national-level network Mahila Kisan Adhikar Manch (MAKAAM), agriculture researchers working with women farmers, advocates of rights of women farmers working on the question of land, water, women, and marginalised groups, ask, in order to bring about change.

2 An administrative term, used to indicate a geographical territory – *taluka* (block), *tehsil* (sometimes equivalent to a district)

3 One of the authors of the article has also worked in all the three study villages for more than ten years.

4 Other Backward Classes

5 Scheduled Castes

6 Marathas are famed in history as warriors and consider themselves as a sub-caste of kshatriya, one of the *varnas* of Hinduism. Their homeland is the present state of Maharashtra. Within the Marathi-speaking region, the social designation 'Marathas' refers to the single dominant Maratha caste or to the group of Maratha and Kunbi castes. Retrieved from www.britannica. com/topic/Maratha (Accessed on 12 September 2019).

7 Vani is an occupational community of merchants, bankers, money lenders, dealers in grains or in spices, and in modern times numerous commercial enterprises. It is a sub-caste of Vaishyas, one of the *varnas* of Hinduism. Retrieved from www.revolvy.com/page/Bania-%28caste%29 (Accessed on 12 September 2019).

8 Mali is an occupational caste found among the Hindus who traditionally worked as gardeners and flourists. In the Hindu *varna* system, they are a sub-caste of *shudras* (the *varna* at the bottom).

9 Traditionally, the Teli are an occupational caste of oil-pressers. Retrieved from https://peoplegroupsindia.com/profiles/teli/ (Accessed on 12 September 2019). In the Hindu *varna* system they are a sub-caste of *shudras*.

10 'Chambhar' is the word for Chamar in Maharashtra. Their hereditary occupation is tanning leather. Members of the caste are included in the officially designated Scheduled Castes (also called 'dalits'); because their hereditary work obliged them to handle dead animals, the Chamars were among those formerly called 'untouchables'. Retrieved from www.britannica.com/topic/Chamar (Accessed on 12 September 2019).

11 Dhangar is the shepherd caste of Maharashtra. In Maharashtra, they are classified as Nomadic Tribes.

12 Vanjaris were grain carriers and traders of commodities.

13 Grazing land or community land is a part of the common property resource of a village. The major purpose of grazing lands is to ensure common land for grazing of the cattle of the village.

14 Namdeo Dhasal has defined it in his novel 'Hadaki Hadwala' as the collective *inam* land given to Mahars.

15 *Devasthan land* means a village, portion of a village, or land held under a *devasthan inam*.

16 The SECC 2011 measures deprivation using criteria such as the number of deprived households with deprivation criteria: Only one room with kucha walls and kucha roof, no adult member between the ages of 16 to 59, female-headed households with no adult male member between the ages of 16 to 59, disabled member and no able-bodied adult member, SC/ST households, no literate adult

above the age of 25 years, and landless households deriving a major part of their income from manual casual labour.
17 Self owned, *hadki hadvala*, encroached grazing land, *devsthan* land
18 The percentage of the SC population to total population of a village is shown in brackets.

References

A Bill to enact the law relating to agricultural land leasing in the state of Maharashtra 2017 (India). Retrieved from https://egazzete.mahaonline.gov.in/Forms/Gazet teSearch.aspx accessed on 12 December 2018.

Agarwal, B. 2018. *Can group farms outperform individual family farms? Empirical insights from India.* Retrieved from https://doi.org/10.1016/j.worlddev. 2018.03.010 accessed on 12 September 2019.

Bansal, V., U. Yoshifumi and V. Rawal. 2018. *Agricultural tenancy in contemporary India: an analytical report and a compendium of statistical tables based on NSSO surveys of land and livestock holdings.* New Delhi: Society for Social and Economic Research.

Byres, T. 1983. 'Historical perspectives on sharecropping', in T. Byres (ed.), *Sharecropping and sharecroppers.* London: Frank Cass and Co. Ltd.

Chaudhari, A. and P. Maitra. 2000. 'Sharecropping contracts in rural India: a note', *Journal of Contemporary Asia*, 30(1): 99–107. doi:10.1080/00472330080000071 accessed on 12 April 2019.

Dhasal, N. 1987. *HadakiHadwala.* Pune: Asmita Publication.

Eswaran, M. and A. Kotwal. 1985. 'A theory of contractual structure in agriculture', *American Economic Review*, 75(3): 352–367.

Haque, T. n.d. *Impact of land leasing restrictions on agricultural efficiency and equity in India.* Retrieved from www.landandpoverty.com/agenda/pdfs/paper/haque_full_paper.pdf accessed on 12 December 2018.

Harvey, D. 2004. *The 'New' imperialism: accumulation by dispossession.* Retrieved from https://socialistregister.com/index.php/srv/article/view/5811 accessed on 14 December 2018.

Jodha, N. 1981. 'Agricultural tenancy: fresh evidence from dryland areas in India', *Economic and Political Weekly*, 16(52): A118–A128. Retrieved from www.jstor. org/stable/4370525 accessed on 28 December 2018.

Kurmanath, K.V. 2018. *Tenant farmers bear the brunt of agricultural distress.* Retrieved from www.thehindubusinessline.com/markets/commodities/tenant-farmers-bear-the-brunt-of-agri-distress/article24175385.ece?homepage=true accessed on 13 September 2019.

Mani, G. 2016. 'Model agricultural land leasing act, 2016: some observations', *Economic and Political Weekly*, 51(42): 4. Retrieved from www.epw.in/jour nal/2016/42/web-exclusives/model-agricultural-land-leasing-act-2016-some-observations.html accessed on 27 June 2018.

Mearns, R. 1999. *Access to land in rural India: policy issues and options.* Retrieved from www.cpahq.org/cpahq/cpadocs/Access%20to%20Land%20in%20India. pdf accessed on 14 December 2018.

Mokashi, D.S. 1978. 'Agricultural tenancy in Maharashtra: impact on production', *Journal of the Indian Law Institute*, 20(2): 186–218. Retrieved from http://14.139.60.114:8080/jspui/bitstream/123456789/16581/1/007_Agricul tural%20Tenancy%20in%20Maharashtra_Impact%20on%20Production%20 %28186-218%29.pdf accessed on September 10, 2018.

MOSPI Annual Report. 2019. *Periodic labour force survey 2017–18*. Retrieved from www.mospi.gov.in/sites/default/files/publication_reports/Annual%20Report% 2C%20PLFS%202017-18_31052019.pdf accessed on 12 September 2019.

National Institute for Transforming India (NITI Aayog). 2016. *Report of the expert committeee on land leasing: 2016*. Retrived from http://niti.gov.in/writereaddata/ files/document_publication/Final_Report_Expert_Group_on_Land_Leasing.pdf accessed on 27 November 2018.

Newbery, D.M.G. 1977. 'Risk sharing, share cropping and uncertain labor markets', *Review of Economic Studies*, 44: 585–594.

NITI Aayog Report. 2016. *Report of the expert committee on land leasing*. New Delhi: Government of India.

NSSO. 2006. *Report on operational holdings*. 59th Round. Government of India.

Rao, P. and H. Behera. 2017. 'Agrarian questions under neoliberal economic policies in India: a review and analysis of dispossession and depeasantisation', *The Oriental Anthropologist: A Bi-annual International Journal of the Science of Man*, 17. doi:10.1177/0976343020170102. Retrieved from www.researchgate.net/ publication/322570745_Agrarian_Questions_under_Neoliberal_Economic_Poli cies_in_India_A_Review_and_Analysis_of_Dispossession_and_Depeasantisation accessed on 23 August 2018.

Rawal, V. and P. Saha. 2015. 'Women's employment in India – what do recent NSS surveys of employment and unemployment show?', *Society for Social and Economic Research Monograph*, 15(1).

Revathi, E. 2016. *Liberalizing lease market: the Andhra Pradesh land licensed cultivators act*. Centre for Social and Economic Studies Working paper 135, Hyderabad. Retrieved from www.cess.ac.in/cesshome/wp/CESSWorkingPaper- 135.pdf accessed on 21 December 2018.

Singh, N. 1989. 'Theories of sharecropping', in P. Bardhan (ed.), *The economic theory of Agrarian institutions* (pp. 33–72). Oxford: Clarendon Press.

Stiglitz, J. 1974. 'Incentives and risk sharing in share cropping', *Review of Economic Studies*, 41: 219–255.

Thorat, S, M. Mahamallik and N. Sadana. 2011. 'Caste system and pattern of discrimination in rural markets', in S. Thorat and K. Newman (eds.), *Economic discrimination in modern India* (pp. 148–176). New Delhi: Oxford University Press.

6 Customary rights and traditional wisdom

Furthering land governance in Northeast India

Sonali Ghosh and Chandra Bhushan Kumar[1]

> The region is bountifully endowed with bio-diversity, hydro-potential, oil and gas, coal, limestone and forest wealth. It is ideally suited to produce a whole range of plantation crops, spices, fruit and vegetables, flowers and herbs, much of which could be processed and exported to the rest of the country and worldwide. Markets must be developed and problems of transportation, power, infrastructure, finance and services overcome. Its natural beauty, serenity and rich flora and fauna invite trekking and tourism.
>
> (Planning Commission 1997: 2)

For more than two decades, the development deficit of the northeastern region (NER) vis-à-vis mainland[2] India seems to have found attention in the governance discourse.[3] The aftermath of the partition of 1947 impacted the political and economic structure of the region to a great extent not only because it lost out its seamless mobility, but also because it took considerable efforts to redraw political boundaries. The liberalisation era, from the early 1990s, ushered in an era of re-examining the terms of engagement for the mutual benefit of the region as well as of the country (Planning Commission 1997; NEC 2017). Land, the most visible resource of the region, occupied a significant position in designing and advocating a new type of development regime.

The pre-1947 era witnessed a distant frontier policy being adopted in most of the hill areas of the NER by British India. After independence, the new State hesitantly approached the methods of governance using the instrument of schedule areas.[4] Verrier Elwin (1902–1964),[5] an anthropologist, was appointed as a tribal advisor to the first prime minister. Elwin, drawing from his experiences of working in Central India, advocated a middle-path philosophy of least interference in his celebrated book *A Philosophy for NEFA* (1956).[6] This was a departure from the past, yet critics found it insufficient to address the absence of modern development. In 1997, concerned with the presence of insurgency in some pockets in NER and lack of development, the erstwhile Planning Commission of India[7] prepared a report entitled *Transforming the North East*,[8] which claimed the NER 'has vast potential resources but little or no "plan" resources to-day' (Planning Commission 1997: 3). The report further stated that the need to tap the abundant resources was advocated with some caution. It should be ensured that the process of modernisation and development does not subvert the salutary features of the social collectives operating at the grassroots in tribal areas, nor destroy biodiversity through indiscriminate propagation of uniform varieties for the short-term profit of the corporate sector (ibid.: 13). This change in the approach of intervention was not sudden. The debates in the Constituent Assembly during 1946–1949 concerning sixth-schedule governance in NER describe these two diverse strands. In the neoliberal world, modern India thought it necessary to unleash the locked potential of NER.

The newer approach drew its voice from emerging political elites standing on the precincts of formation of legislative bodies in these states, based on electoral representation. Its exposure to a modern way of life and necessity to navigate a modern state started an era of looking at the surroundings as a resource to be harnessed. Aspirations and competitiveness became new drivers to guide the development process. Even as the pace of development in the NER seemed slow, several roadmaps for the future started to appear in the discourse. Instead of community, the State started taking the lead in setting this discourse. However, on ground, it still required, depending upon the power structure, considerable negotiations to facilitate the utilisation of resources, mainly land. Neoliberal ideals had to provide manoeuvring space in this new environment.

The State's public purpose, ranging from schools, health centres, roads, electricity, administrative centres (including official colonies) to large factories, hydropower projects, railways, airports, etc., became obvious grounds for acquiring land in the new regime. Like other regions in the country, the *Land Acquisition Act, 1894*, remained its instrument. But the NER, except for the Assam plains and Manipur valley, was different – politically, socially, and culturally.

Land in NER is dominated by forest, with pockets of shifting cultivation. Out of this, the fact that almost 70 percent is forest cover also complicates the question of acquisition. Ethnic diversity of the region poses another challenge. In Arunachal Pradesh, at least 26 major tribes have practised different patterns of land engagement since time immemorial. Evolution of modern polity in these areas has been sudden which impacted the process of land acquisition. Emergence of a neo-middle class (Walker 2008) in the new digital world of the twenty-first century brought more complexities to the overall development discourse.

Land has diverse connotations within every region. The idea of development in the NER, it seems, never structured around the question of this multiple meaning of land. It was always seen in abundance and available (Dikshit and Dikshit 2014). The initial process of engagement made the realisation of the complexities obvious. Neoliberalism has evolved as an idea with three intertwined manifestations: (1) an ideology, (2) a mode of governance, and (3) a policy package (Steger and Roy 2010). In a society still rooted in a traditional relationship with its natural resources, the neoliberal idea has disrupted the existing relationship and created new arrangements, which are both successful and unsuccessful simultaneously (Igoe and Brockington 2007). Its implications for Northeast India have been appreciated and interpreted by various scholars. Debbarma (2018) views land alienation as a main reason of ethnic conflict. Sitlhou (2015) studies gender biases in Kuki landownership patterns in Manipur. In these appreciations, the focus has been on the consequences of neoliberalism in the transformation of inherent understanding and capacity of the local community in shaping their relationship with the natural resources at various levels. Advancing these arguments further, this chapter uses a specific case concerning evolution of Balpakram National Park from a community-protected forest in the state of Meghalaya and demonstrates that instead of enforcement of the legal instrument of the *Wildlife (Protection) Act, 1972*, the state negotiated with the local community for an arrangement of the declaration of a national park, with a modified relationship of community with the state.

The chapter is divided in five broad sections: first, it outlines Northeast India as a territory; second, it describes patterns of land relationship in various states in the Northeast; third, it opens up the question of forest, which dominates not only the physical space but also the mental space in the region; fourth, it suggests the need to investigate the question of relationship with natural resources from the lens of hybrid neoliberalism; and fifth, it documents the transition of Balpakram from the traditional to the modern era as an example of hybrid neoliberalism.

Northeast India

The NER consists of eight states: Arunachal Pradesh, Assam, Manipur, Meghalaya, Mizoram, Nagaland, Tripura, and Sikkim. These eight states together have an area of 262,185 square kilometres, accounting for 7.98 percent of India's total land area, and have a population of 40 million which accounts for 3.4 percent of India's total population (Census 2011). About 70 percent of the region is hilly, rugged, and generally inaccessible physiographic terrain. With a cultural and ethnic diversity of tribes, the relative historical seclusion and strategic location have combined to turn the region into an important geopolitical unit of the country as well as in the world. The region has remained overwhelmingly rural in seven out of eight states, wherein 84 percent of the population live in rural areas (NIRD 2008). It shares international boundaries with China, Myanmar, Bangladesh, Bhutan, and Nepal.

The NER is the homeland for a rich mosaic of more than 160 Scheduled Tribes belonging to five different ethnic groups and more than 400 distinct tribal and sub-tribal groupings speaking approximately 175 languages along with a large, non-tribal population. Therefore, political progress in each state in the region has followed a different trajectory (Bhaumik 2010). By 1987, all initial seven territories had acquired the status of independent states; Sikkim as a state became part of the NER in 2002. However, variations in the administrative structure continued in the region (Table 6.1). In land matters, this structure plays a critical role in facilitationg the process of acquisition.

The abundance of land as a resource is evident based on the fact that the lower human population density may suggest a favourable land-human ratio compared with other parts of the country. However, a large portion of the region is hilly, and almost 78 percent of farmers are categorised as small or marginal (NIRD 2008). Tenurial patterns and practices are discussed in the next section.

Natural resource conservation is necessarily linked to hills and forests in the NER. Termed as a bio-geographical gateway for much of India's flora and fauna, it is also part of the eastern Himalaya biodiversity hotspot, one of the mega-diverse areas of the world – a meeting ground of temperate east Himalayan flora, the paleo-arctic flora of the Tibetan highland, and

Table 6.1 Constitutional status and administrative structure

States	Special constitutional provisions	Administrative structure
Arunachal Pradesh	Art.371H	No Autonomous Councils, the state has adopted the Panchayati Raj
Assam	Sixth Schedule read with Art. 371B (for Scheduled Areas only)	Three Autonomous Councils: (1) Karbi-Anglong, (2) Dima Hasao, and (3) Bodoland Territorial Areas District
Manipur	Art.371C	The *Manipur (Village Authority in Hill Areas) Act, 1956*, and the *Manipur Hill Areas District Council Act, 1971*
Meghalaya	Sixth Schedule	Three Autonomous Councils: (1) Khasi Hills, (2) Jaintia Hills, and (3) Garo Hills
Mizoram	Sixth Schedule read with Art.371G	Three Autonomous Councils of Pawi, Lakher, Chakma, and other areas without an Autonomous Council
Nagaland	Art.371A	No Autonomous District Councils
Sikkim		No Autonomous District Councils
Tripura	Sixth Schedule	Tripura Tribal Area Autonomous District Council, Khumulwang

Source: Developed by the authors based on data from Planning Commission, 2006

wet evergreen flora of Southeast Asia. It contains more than one third of the country's total biodiversity. It represents an important part of the Indo-Myanmar biodiversity hotspot and is one of the 25 global biodiversity hotspots recognised in the world (Myers et al. 2000). The Northeast has an abundance of two key renewable resources that are significantly linked to development and growth options – water and forests, which are connected to each other in a variety of ways (World Bank 2007).

The NER accounts for one fourth of the country's forest cover and inter-twined with these forests are the livelihood, culture, and societal building blocks of more than 400 tribal and sub-tribal groups with 175 dialects and languages. The altitudinal variation and rainfall patterns of the southwest and northeast monsoon play a significant role in the development of eco-logical niches in this region of India. This reflects the importance of forest resources for the northeastern part of the country (Poffenberger 2006).

The land and forest form an integral part of nature and society where people interact. The land's abundance in the NER facilitated the evolution of a variety of traditional practices, depending on local conditions. Geo-graphical isolation to some extent helped the hill tribes to become inheri-tors and practitioners of these customary practices since time immemorial (Elwin 1957).

Evolution of modern polity within the framework of the Constitution witnessed the emergence of seven distinct states.[9] Earlier, these states were hill tracts and frontiers to be encountered from a distance only. These states attempted to substitute the existing body politics at different layers (village to state). The introduction of the concept of secret voting, development of habitation based on non-farm occupation, and aspiration to acquire mod-ern amenities and way of life collided with the traditional power structure evolved over centuries. The state, gradually, started shaping everyday life. Though clans remained a binding entity to charter the modern polity, there existed an entity to facilitate the forging of new alliances among these clans. Autonomous development councils, local bodies such as panchayats and

Table 6.2 Forest and community control in Northeast India

State	Percent total recorded forest area of state	Percent of forest area under community control
Arunachal Pradesh	82	62
Assam	30	33
Manipur	78	68
Meghalaya	70	90
Mizoram	87	33
Nagaland	85	91
Sikkim*	82.31	7
Tripura	55	41

* Derived from SFR 2005. *Source*: Poffenberger 2006

municipalities, and state legislative bodies became the new centres of power to intervene and influence the way of life.

With the advent of the state, at least three factors brought a paradigm shift in the neoliberal era, especially with reference to people's engagement with land and forest: (1) evolution of modern polity to pursue a common purpose at a different scale; often it is premised on societal development and not limited to a specific tribe; (2) spread of urbanization[10]; and (3) emergence of aspirational culture (*neo*-middle class) in a new digital-age environment. Before examining the implications of these factors for acquisition, it is necessary to understand the landownership and forest questions in the region. The next two sections focus on these.

Landownership and its meaning in neoliberal NER

Two broad patterns of landownership arrangements have emerged in NER: (1) revenue administration under the government operating in the plains and valleys of Assam, Tripura, Manipur, and in the hilly state of Sikkim; and (2) a customary land tenure system under village-level authority operating in the hilly states of Arunachal Pradesh, Meghalaya, Mizoram, and Nagaland, and in the hilly parts of Assam, Manipur, and Tripura, with state and regional variations (MoRD 2009; NIRD 2008). Important categories of the local variants are presented as follows, summarising the existing tenure systems in a respective state:

1 Nagaland: Traditionally and to the present, the land of most Naga tribes is classified broadly into primary or agricultural land and reserved land. The reserved land consists of (a) land kept for public purposes, including forest land under the control of the village council; (b) clan or *khel* land used by clan members; and (c) inherited or acquired, privately owned land (Tamuly 1985).

2 Manipur: Among the *Thadou* tribe of Manipur, land is under the control of the village chief who, after consulting his ministers called *Semang Pachang*,[11] allocates *jhum* plots and ensures all families get an equal share. Each family pays a tax for the land allotted to them (Rajkhowa 1986).

3 Mizoram: For the Mizos, land is under village council controlled by a chief, who allocates land for *jhum* with the advice of experts on shifting cultivation called *Ramhual*.[12] Villagers pay taxes in terms of their share of paddy. Previously the chief's power with regard to land was not touched by the British (Das 1990); however, the Government of Assam abolished the chieftainship in 1954, through *The Assam Lushai Hills District (Acquisition of Chief's Rights) Act, 1954*, and brought land under the control of the state. The present land tenure system in the state of Mizoram is divided into two types: first, temporary land, meaning temporary allotment and use of the land. The state issues a periodic

Patta (ownership document) through which land is allotted tempo-rarily to the users. Periodic *Patta* means a prescribed land settlement document settling the agricultural land periodically under these rules whereby an individual or an organisation has entered into an agreement with the authorities to pay land revenue, taxes, cesses, and rates legally assessed or imposed with respect to the land so settled. Periodic *Patta* holders do not have heritable and transferable rights. Second, landhold-ers, where *Patta* holders of the land are given certificates after having entered into an agreement with the authorities to pay land revenue, taxes, cesses, and rates legally assessed or imposed in respect of the land so settled. A *Patta* holder has heritable and transferable rights of use and sub-letting, subject to payment of land revenue and taxes as stated by the rules (Nongkynrih 2009).

4   Tripura: Tripura had a different regime with *jhum* land allotted by the ruler through his collectors, who in turn were assisted by a village *Choudhury*.[13] Land was classified into six categories: (a) *jhum* land belonging to the community and managed by the village authority and a *Choudhury*: (b) *nal*, fertile land individually owned, inheritable, not alienable; (c) *lunga*, land between hills for permanent cultivation allot-ted to tribals with a yearly tax; (d) *chera*, land situated on both sides of a river that is owned by villagers and allotted for cultivation; (e) *bhiti* and *bastu*, individually owned and heritable but not transferable land (Roy Burman 1986). However, very little remains because tribes are reduced to a minority, and only individual alienable title is currently recognised (Debbarma 2008).

5   Arunachal Pradesh: Landownership in Arunachal Pradesh varied from tribe to tribe. For the *Nyishi* and *Galo* tribes, community land was demarcated and managed by the village council. For the *Adis*, land vested in the community was allotted by the chief to individual house-holds (Agarwal 1991). *Aka* tribals had no tradition of community own-ership, and each family cultivated as much *jhum* or riverbank lands as needed (Fernandes and Bharali 2002).

6   Meghalaya: *Khasis* of Meghalaya have five broad categories of land: (a) *raid*, community land managed by the village council and used only by permanent residents for housing, common facilities, and agriculture; (b) *rykynti*, private land; (c) clan land owned by the respective clans; d) forest land divided into sacred forest, village community forest con-trolled by the village *darbar*, protected forest for domestic use, not for sale, and (e) individual forest used by the owner (Simon 1996; Dutta 2002). In the *Garo* tribe, land was traditionally under the control of the Chief (*Nokma*), while homestead plots were owned by the com-munity (Kar 1982). At present, hilly land, almost 95 percent of the total land, is covered by customary law, while plains lands are governed by the *Assam Land and Revenue Regulation Act of 1886*, adopted by the Garo Hills Autonomous District Council in 1952 (Phira 1991). In

the Jaintia territories of Meghalaya, community land was owned by the Chief, *Syiem*,[14] till the British colonial government acquired all the *rajhali* (*Syiem's* private land), which was subsequently given to tillers against *Pattas* for ten years and subjected to land revenue (Pyal 2002).

7   Assam: The landownership pattern in Assam is vastly different. A total of 30 percent of its land is classified as Revenue Class Land consisting of (a) industrial lands, (b) business class lands, (c) homestead lands, and (d) agricultural lands; another 30 percent of land is Revenue Class (Revenue Department, non-private, and unclassified government lands); and the remaining 40 percent of the state's area consists of forests and community-owned lands (NIRD 2008).

8   Sikkim: A large portion of land in Sikkim is owned by the locals, and the state has prevented transfer to outsiders. The land share of the *Lepcha* and *Bhutia* tribe is 20 percent each, and their land revenue contribution is 16 percent and 19 percent, respectively. Some members of this community still hold more than 100 acres of land (HDR 2005).

However, these broad patterns are not static in nature. With time, the concept of community ownership has given way to individual ownership in a number of tribal communities (Bezbaruah 2007). The inbuilt concept of cash compensation, in the process of acquisition, is one of the prime reasons to influence this transition. In these situations, it may appear that any negotiation for acquisition would be easy. It depends on the purpose for which it is intended to be acquired. However, in theory, in the absence of a cadastral survey in the majority of the far-flung areas, land rights are (at least informally) still entirely community owned. Also, the presence of community in the negotiation process continues. It exists at least at two levels – first, at the level of debating the purpose and second, at the level of stakeholders who need to be compensated. This becomes evident in the case of acquisition for large infrastructure projects such as hydropower projects. Also, land in the Northeast includes forests at most of the locations. Therefore, the purpose and negotiation exercises need to be appreciated in the background of forest and ecology which are intertwined with the lives of the inhabitants. The following section discusses these.

The forest question in the NER – a case for hybrid neoliberalism?

Few landscapes in India have attracted as much attention in terms of social conflict or ecological enquiry as forests (Rangarajan and Sivaramakrishnan 2012). While speaking of land issues in the Northeast, one cannot alienate oneself from the forest issues of the region. Several recent but disjointed studies are available on the critical role of forest ecosystems as building blocks into people's lives, culture, and society (Fernandes and Barbora 2008; Saikia 2011; Sharma 2011; Rangarajan and Sivaramakrishnan 2012,

2014). The challenges in forest land acquisition are discussed in the following three sub-sections.

Inadequate survey, records, and demarcation

Forest conflict in the NER dates back to inter-tribal disputes that have occurred periodically at least as per the recorded history of colonial India for the past 300 years. Tribal resistance to British colonial incursions in the early nineteenth century resulted in special policies enacted to allow customary systems of forest management and respect for traditional systems of governance. This policy reflected recognition by the British colonial government that the hill communities could not be centrally administered and were best allowed to function under their own governance systems. Post-independence, the Indian Constitution also recognised the rights of indigenous communities and has given special rights under the Sixth Schedule of the Constitution.

While the NER boasts of an average forest cover of 70.03 percent (ISFR 2013) of its total geographical area as per the satellite imagery–based assessment of 2013, there is a net loss of 627 square kilometres in total forest cover, compared with the previous assessment done in 2011. While this loss could be primarily attributed to shifting cultivation, commercialisation, and rapid urbanisation, and acquisition of land for major hydropower and non-forestry purposes, it would be worthwhile to analyse the changes that occurred within community-owned forest areas and how existing constitutional safeguards (such as Schedule Six areas) empowering traditional societies to prevent further destruction or degradation of such forests. Other financial incentives to change land use (including corruption and cronyism), political isolation, ruggedness of terrain, and armed conflict have also been a few factors that are likely to impact both government- and community-owned lands. In the case of government-owned forests, the category of Unclassed State Forests (USF; unsurveyed or incompletely surveyed forest areas wherein the rights and concessions allowed to local communities have not been settled) has been a major bone of contention, and several of these areas are now highly encroached or degraded. These USFs become a free-for-all where elite capture from within the local community or by middlemen driven by market forces may occur. The acquired land therefore can neither be put to any legal use (based on local/regional planning missions), nor is it allowed to regrow into its original forest for fear of losing it altogether to the State. Lack of formal government recognition to other types of governance (as in the case of community-owned forests, sacred groves, etc.) and the insistence of forest departments to retain community-managed forests under the category of USF amplifies social tensions with regard to land use and acquisition (NIRD 2008).

Changes in land tenure

There has been marked change in land tenurial systems across Northeast India. For example, the plethora of different systems in force in Meghalaya has led to a complex form of forest management in the state. Although there was little visible change until the 1970s, socio-cultural attitudes have also gradually transformed, and less value is now attached to forests and sacred groves. It is a well-documented fact that the move from traditional community (collective) systems to the State, a faceless entity with an inflexible set of terms of engagement, is unlikely to strengthen communities and may create problems in the future.

Another major issue with land tenure has to do with *jhum*, or shifting cultivation, a form of organic agriculture that is practised by tribal societies in the NER. Earlier termed as primitive and a bane for the region's natural resources by the colonial government (as it involved cyclical clearing and burning of large tracts of forest and bamboo areas), sustained scientific evidence suggests that a more than ten-year *jhum* fallow period of rest after the crop has been harvested, so as to allow natural vegetation such as bamboo to re-grow and the soil to regenerate) is economically and ecologically more sustainable than converting the land for any other form of settled cultivation (Ramakrishnan and Patnaik 1992; Shankar Raman 2001).

Some social scientists confirm that *jhum* has a certain enduring quality which may be interpreted as resistance to change within local communities (Singh 2009). For example, the cultural formation of Mizo community identity is strongly intertwined with *jhum* cultivation. Traditional management of the forest included various forms of regulation, such as limited access, size restrictions, and sacred or protected areas. Such management was based on a strong attachment to land, customary laws, norms, belief systems, and ethical values regarding the environment (Thrupp et al. 1997). The chieftainship institution was also designed to establish a management system and to formulate customary laws regarding the forest (Vanlalhruaia 2012).

It is therefore proven, that in contrast to several other areas, the reason for *jhum*'s persistence is not only to be found in deeply rooted social and cultural tradition, but also rather, in the resilience of the production system itself. This method of agriculture performs the essential function of feeding the rural family, whose occupational options are severely restricted. Although time-consuming, strenuous, and subject to uncertainty, it has the advantage of being self-contained. The shifting cultivator in a remote village needs neither road, nor market, nor government facility to get on with his work (Singh 1996). While *jhum* also leads to open and degraded forests, especially where the fallow period has been reduced to fewer than three years because of increased population pressure and scarcity of land, government land-use policies and horticulture schemes aimed at eradicating *jhum* are likely to cause more harm than benefit in the long run. For example, the primary aim of Mizoram's *New Land Use Policy* (NLUP), 2011, is to develop and give all farmers in the state suitable, permanent, and stable trades.[15] The aims and objectives of NLUP are as follows:

1   To put an end to wasteful Shifting Cultivation.
2   To ensure that all the farmers had land of their own so that they can each pursue a permanent means of livelihood under the Agriculture (and allied sectors), Industry, or Animal Husbandry sectors.
3   To develop all suitable land for Wet Rice Cultivation to attain self-sufficiency in rice and vegetables.
4   To re-afforest the land, save those allocated to the NLUP beneficiaries, so as to regenerate the ecosystem. This will help stabilise the climatic changes wrought by global warming, rejuvenate the flora and fauna, and make Mizoram a better place to live in.
5   To set up a marketing infrastructure so that successful farmers and beneficiaries under NLUP can have a viable commercial outlet for their products.

It is too early to comment on the benefits from the NLUP; however, there is a need to revisit the policy directive on ending wasteful shifting cultivation and the practices being promoted therein, as creating permanent infrastructure and settled agriculture is likely to be counterproductive in this ecologically fragile and seismologically sensitive area.

Similarly, government land-use policies and horticulture schemes aimed at eradicating *jhum* have led to an increase in monoculture plantations such as teak and oil palm in the forested landscape of Mizoram.[16] The Mizoram government has been aggressively promoting oil palm cultivation since 2005 under its NLUP; environmentalists are concerned that this might be a mistake on three counts: excessive water usage, lowered food production, and loss of wildlife diversity. Expansion of oil palm plantations is likely to wean individual farmers away from their traditional practice of subsistence farming, to more economically stable commercial agricultural and livelihood practices. Studies indicate that oil palm plantations are substantially worse from a conservation perspective than the *jhum* landscape as they may actually lead to a greater loss of forest cover because once converted into cultivated land, the forest will never have a chance to grow there again (McCarthy and Cramb 2009; Shankar Raman 2014; Srinivasan 2014).

There are also socio-cultural implications as the conversion of community land to individual holdings is likely to result in elite capture, unequal sharing, and the destruction of the otherwise unique social bonding. The permanence of this shift in the land tenure system will also drastically undermine ecologically conservative traditional land-use practices.

Law and governance

The case of economic underdevelopment of the NER is the result of many factors. The ever-increasing human population is dependent on finite resources and, as a result, per capita uses of all resources are decreasing gradually. Particularly in the case of land resources, where there is a scarcity of arable land in the region (Nandy 2014) following independence in 1947, the Indian Constitution provided a certain degree of autonomy at either the local or regional levels, including the management of natural resources. In reality, successive regulations through centralised administrative mechanisms were introduced. For example, the Chieftainship office in Mizoram was abolished in 1954, and two new administrative categories, Autonomous District Councils and Village Councils, emerged. All land became the property of the government; communal land in its true sense was therefore effectively eliminated.

Enactment of the *Scheduled Tribes and Other Traditional Forest Dwellers (Recognition of Forest Rights) Act, 2006*, was considered to provide a legal framework to recognise the rights of tribal communities. However, the Northeast states, except Assam and Tripura, have approached it cautiously. Arunachal Pradesh and Sikkim considers its applicability non-relevant, citing settled territorial claims among the tribes (Shrimali 2013).

Another significant legal instrument has been the *Wildlife (Protection) Act, 1972*, which intended to provide for the protection of wild animals, birds, and plants. For centuries, tribal communities have formed a symbiotic relationship with their surroundings, primarily forest, hills, and rivers. With the advent of the modern state, armed with codified legal instruments, the existing relationship faced new challenges. However, with the emergence of a new polity, which possessed tribal sensibilities, there has been evolvement of a different kind of arrangement within this legal framework.

Pathway: hybrid neoliberalism in the context of the *Wildlife (Protection) Act, 1972*

Neoliberalism and conservation both seem contradictory to each other in theory (Igoe and Brockington 2016). Neoliberalism thrives on free market with economics as the central topic, whereas conservation thrives on the sustainable harnessing of resources. But, in the real world, both ideas interact frequently as policy makers struggle to find a balance between prosperity and sustainability. They argue that understanding neoliberalism as a process of restructuring the arrangement to maximise the outcome for all stakeholders may be more appropriate. Using the examples from Tanzania, they observed that instead of focusing on deregulation of neoliberalism, one may need to focus on reregulation to tap the untapped potential. A 'hybrid' idea needs to be worked out, and some states in Northeast India have done so; this is especially visible in matters of resource management. Some states have faced challenges too. Realising the challenges of top-down approaches in the implementation of statutory provisions of conservation, the state engaged with the local community to decide a possible future for the areas to be protected. This resulted in a 'hybrid' framework in which both strands – neoliberalism and tradition – find space. Acceptability of this framework allowed the gradual assimilation of conservation laws in community practices of conservation.

In the context of 'hybrid' governance, which includes communities in its ambit, conservation-business partnerships are becoming increasingly common, if not the norm. This can be seen in increased corporate sponsorship of conservation organisations; increased management of protected areas by private for-profit companies (Levine, this issue); and increased emphasis on ecotourism as a means of achieving economic growth, community prosperity, and biodiversity conservation.

Section 35(1) of the *Wildlife (Protection) Act, 1972*, specifies that:

> Whenever it appears to the State Government that an area, whether within a sanctuary or not, is, by reason of its ecological, faunal, floral, Geo-morphological, or zoological association or importance, needed to be constituted as a National Park for the purpose of protection & propagating or developing wildlife therein or its environment, it may, by notification, declare its intention to constitute such area as a National Park . . . all rights in respect of lands proposed to be included in the National Park have become vested in the State Government.

It was not easy for the nascent state to put these provisions into use literally on the ground in Northeast India. It needed to work keeping the traditional practices and culture in view. In one such case, it gradually evolved as a hybrid arrangement, which we prefer calling 'hybrid neoliberalism'.

Celebrating best practices: from coercive conservation to hybrid neoliberalism

The global conservation debate has been for a greater length of time based on the premise that people residing within Protected Areas are a 'problem'. Proponents of state-led conservation have feared that the poverty of people located near National Parks causes them to over-exploit natural resources for subsistence and commercial purposes, threatening the ecological viability of Protected Areas (Dressler and Roth 2011). Strict regulations over resource use and/or removing them altogether from Protected Areas to create 'wilderness' is still considered the most efficient and effective way to preserve nature. Such conservation practice has involved establishing protected areas as per state-led legislations, putting constraints on people's activities, and enforcing a particular vision of nature on rural communities (Agrawal and Redford 2009). In this regard, a unique case in Northeast India, wherein local community came forward for conservation, is a matter of further analysis under the neoliberal lens.

Community-led initiative to create Balpakram National Park, Meghalaya

Located in the South Garo Hills District of Meghalaya State in Northeast India, Balpakram National Park is uniquely important for its rich biodiversity values that have been preserved by the local communities for centuries altogether. The word 'Balpakram' means the 'land of perpetual winds', and the region is blessed with a distinctive topographical feature of deep gorges, lush green tropical forests, and flat table-top mountains (Williams and Johnsingh 1996).

For the local Garo communities, especially the animist *Songsareks*, the gorge is worshipped as the 'land of the spirits' since it is believed that the spirits of the dead live here temporarily before finally embarking on the journey towards their final abode (de Maaker 2007). Garo traditional faith centres on land, nature, *jhum* cultivation, and traditional healing, and is understood by the term 'Songsarek' which encompasses principles, rituals, celebrations, and deities. The entire Balpakram plateau and gorge are believed to be the resting place of spirits of the Garo dead, before their rebirth, and thus sacred to the tribe. Other sites include the *Memang Anti Cha.Ram*, or the Marketplace of the Spirits; *Goera Rong*, *Jaleng*, or The Rock Ledge of Goera, God of Thunder and Lightning; *Mebit-Mebang*, or the Oracle Rock, whose stone pebbles are 'read' to predict harvests; and the *Dikkini Ring*, or Dikki's Canoe, a mound of earth that resembles an upturned canoe (ibid).

Ecologically, the area forms one of the most important remaining habitats for Asian elephants (*Elephas maximus*) in Northeast India (Datta-Roy et al. 2009). The earliest reliable records for elephant numbers in the entire Garo Hills is 1,850, of which 910 were found in the South Garo Hills, although this number has decreased to about 800–840 in the last population census conducted in 2008 (MoEFCC website).[17]

Given its unique ecological importance, scientific explorations began and around the late 1970s, wild-species survey reports were published that highlighted the need to bring the area under the National Protected Area network (Choudhury 2006). Before 1986, Balpakram National Park was a land owned by the local Garo community where they practiced *jhum* (i.e. slash-and-burn shifting agriculture) and lived in small settlements. What is seen in Balpakram today is a mixed-forest type with secondary regrowth of the *jhum* areas as well as primary stands (UNESCO website).[18]

Keeping in mind the biodiversity richness and connectivity of the landscape for regional biodiversity conservation, it was suggested that the area be brought under the 'formal' Protected Area network by declaring it as a National Park, the highest Protected Area category as accorded under the Indian legal system and wildlife laws. Local Forest Department officials worked with local communities and urged them to set aside some area for the National Park. Since the land belonged to local communities, political support at the highest level and compliance by local state actors (such as the Forest Department) was an important factor. It is said, that on the declaration of Meghalaya as a new state in 1972, its first Chief Minister Captain Williamson Sangma, who himself belonged to the Garo tribe, visited *Ganchi Soram* (a series of small hillocks on the Balpakram Plateau – a traditional cremation site) to give thanks and pay respects to ancestors.[19]

His popularity and goodwill ensured that people were motivated to accept Sangma's vision and set aside this area to preserve wildlife. Subsequently, systematic documentation, surveys, and negotiations led to a 'voluntary' sale of community lands and settlements of *jhum* areas. Several of these farming lands that were inside the boundary were relocated to locations on the edges of the current National Park (Karlsson 2011). Finally, on 15 February 1986, Balpakram National Park, with a designated area of 220 square kilometres, was created as per the suitable provisions of the *Wildlife (Protection) Act, 1972*. Compensation was paid for every square metre of land acquired at agreed rates, making it one of the only National Parks in India to be created in such a manner. Thirty-three years later, debate continues on whether the money went to the rightful owners, to instances of alleged corruption (ibid.), but scientific evidence (as obtained through wildlife surveys) establish that since then, Balpakram has grown from strength to strength as one of the last remaining wilderness areas for large mammals such as elephants and hoolock gibbons, as well as lesser-known taxa hitherto unrecorded from India (Kakati and Srikant 2014) in an otherwise highly modified human-influenced landscape. In other areas of the Garo Hills landscape, elephants are greatly impacted because of the non-availability of adequate food resources in sub-optimal habitats and the presence of human-induced developmental structures such as roads, modern settlements; the National Park provides them much-required refuge as they continue with their long migration patterns in the transboundary forested landscape (Aziz et al. 2016).

At the same time, the National Park has indirectly helped preserve the material evidence of animistic beliefs (the grassland plateaus, totem animals among others) of the Songsarek culture where nature is worshipped through intangible spiritual beliefs. Conversion to Christianity since the late 1800s has resulted in 95 percent of the Garos in Meghalaya now identifying as Christian, with the Songsareks being in a minority of 2 percent of Garos or about 17,000 in absolute numbers (de Maaker 2007). The decline has also been marked from 16 percent of Garos in 2001 to 2 percent remaining in 2011 (ibid.). Some attempts have been made at reviving and safeguarding the Songsarek religion in view of its imminent extinction, and with it many associated cultural beliefs and practices of music, dance, dialects, and ethno-medicine.

Discussion and conclusion

This chapter situates neoliberalism as a prism to appreciate the change in the method of governance and to understand the transformation of relationship with resources, particularly land in the setting of the NER in India. Globally, neoliberalism gained momentum as a political response to existing economic crisis. In India, after the hesitancy of the initial decades, the 1980s saw the recognition of this new possibility, and the 1990s announced its arrival in the economy. The neoliberal question in this era has been studied in much detail (Wolford 2007; Kapoor 2009; Desai 2012). In the context of Northeast India, its presence and influence have been different. We argue that this bridging of State-led conservation ideals versus community-based conservation indeed provides a unique model for hybrid neoliberalism.

Since forested land is the most abundance resource in the region, the close-knit tribes and sub-tribes inherited its use within a power structure, which evolved traditionally. Emergence of the State as a super body of politics helped in influencing, and to some extent, altering the traditional power relationship. In the case of *jhum*, it positioned itself as a repository of knowledge and overpowered the age-old practice. Science, as discussed earlier, came to its rescue and forced the State to restore traditional wisdom.

In a secular state, neoliberalism, which values the freedom of the individual and decries the traditional hold on aspirations, has little space for sacredness. As discussed in the chapter, this new order expects that communities must forge a new relationship with their surroundings. However, this requires skilful negotiation respecting local sentiments. Four specific elements help in this negotiation as shown in Figure 6.1:

1   **Compensation element:** How does one compensate the land owned by community? This perennial question poses conflicting situations in the NER. The cases indicate a rupture in the meaning of ownership of a natural resource like land. As acquisition laws are structured on the premise of individual ownership, communities devise ways to seek compensation. The concept of fairness becomes irrelevant as the valuation of ecosystem services does not find any space in the present discourse.

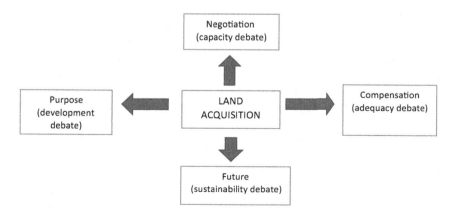

Figure 6.1 Elements of the land acquisition debate in neoliberal Northeast India
Source: Prepared by the authors

2   **Negotiation element:** Negotiation for sharing natural resources is a complex matter. Communities living with nature may lack the capacity to value its worth, to appreciate the trade-offs. The modern state and its apparatus are still grappling with the concept of valuation of ecosystem services. Before coming to the negotiation table, it is imperative to have adequate capacity on both sides to create a win-win situation.

3   **Purpose element:** In the matter of land acquisition, the purpose debate occupies the central position in all settings. Focussed on the end product, this debate creates a dilemma to select between 'development' and 'environment'. The middle path seems missing or compromised. As the capacity to engage in negotiation is limited, 'local' and 'state' have little scope to reconcile in the 'purpose' debate.

4   **Sustainability element:** Does the existing approach of land acquisition address the concerns of sustainability in this resource-abundance territory? As per the current method, the forest (and environment) question remains restricted to afforestation. The bio-culture narrative of engagement has a limited presence.

The complexities of the NER demand patient attention when engaging in debate to appreciate its past, comprehend its present, and visualise its future. The development discourse of this region has to be premised on its one rich resource: 'land'. However, its meaning is not uniform. Multiple meanings of land – a variety of connotations layered with customs, practices, and inheritance shaped by stifling nature – have been the hallmark of this region. Ignorance of these multiple meanings complicates the process of acquisition. These meanings are not static. And thus, they also offer opportunities to create possibilities of engagement.

In these engagements, at most of the locations in the region, the biocultural narrative has to be prominent for two simple reasons: first, sustainability purposes (harmonisation with 'local'), and second, acceptability purposes (possibility of effective negotiation). It is possible to accomplish this, but not quickly. It requires considerable effort to invest in enhancing the capacity of the community as well as the State to engage in four elements: purpose, ownership, sustainability, and capacity.

The NER provides a unique setting to appreciate the complexities of natural resource conservation. Most striking is how neoliberalism and conservation have merged in policy and practice through devolved initiatives, otherwise known as 'hybrid neoliberalism'. New hybrid forms of community-based conservation are built on this discourse by expecting the benefits of markets to 'trickle down' to rural communities (Dressler and Roth 2011). Its developmental status demands the intervention of the modern state to create new physical infrastructures to address the necessary gaps. Its resource richness fuels the desire to harness its resources beyond the local and hence the bigger-sized projects. There has been extensive focus on the purpose of these. There is little debate on the process of this transition. Its near absence in the onslaught of modernity in Northeast India misses an important aspect of current narrative in land acquisition – the bio-cultural narrative.

Notes

1 Both the authors are civil servants who have lived and worked in northeast India and feel deeply connected to the region. Views expressed in this chapter are entirely personal.
2 'Mainland' (*sic*) is popular terminology to distinguish it from the rest of India.
3 www.mdoner.gov.in/content/report-studies-ner lists 24 reports and studies on the Northeast region between 1997 and 2012
4 The Schedule Areas are part of schedule V and VI of the Constitution of India.
5 A prolific writer, Elwin chiefly guided the governance in the current state of Arunachal Pradesh in the 1950s; at that time it was called North East Frontier Administration (NEFA). Ramchandra Guha's book *Civilizing the Savaged* (1999) documents the life and writings of Elwin.
6 Prime Minister Jawahar Lal Nehru, writing the foreword in the book, enunciated five principles, namely, (1) people should develop along the lines of their own genius, and we should avoid imposing anything on them. We should try to encourage in every way their own traditional arts and culture; (2) tribal rights in land and forests should be protected; (3) we should try to train and build up a team of their own people to do the work of administration and development. Some technical personnel from outside, will no doubt, be needed, especially in the beginning. But we should avoid introducing too many outsiders into tribal territory; (4) we should not over-administer these areas or overwhelm them with a multiplicity of schemes. We should rather work through, and not in rivalry to, their own social and cultural institutions; and (5) we should judge results, not by statistics or the amount of money spent, but by the quality of human character that is evolved.
7 The Planning Commission of India was renamed NITI Aayog in 2014. The role and responsibilities of the Commission are redefined along with the name.
8 http://planningcommission.nic.in/reports/genrep/ne_exe.pdf (Accessed on 20 December 2018)
9 Nagaland became a state in 1962; Meghalaya, Manipur, and Tripura in 1972; and Arunachal Pradesh and Mizoram in 1987. Sikkim became a state after its incorporation in Indian union in 1975. Assam, being a seat of administration in British India, did not face transitional challenges.
10 Among the Northeastern states, Mizoram is the most urbanized, with a 51.5 percent urban population. Similarly, Sikkim, which was just 11.0 percent urbanised a decade ago, became almost 25 percent urbanised in 2011. Arunachal Pradesh witnessed proliferation of urban centres in the 1990s (Census 2001).
11 Council of Ministers of the village chief in Manipur
12 Privileged villagers in Mizoram who had the first choice of the *jhum* site, thereby paying more paddy dues to the chief
13 A kind of institution that assisted the village chief in allocation of *jhum* land in Tripura
14 The customary head of the Khasi tribal institution of an administrative area of the United Khasi Jaintia Hills District in Meghalaya
15 Available at http://nlup.mizoram.gov.in/
16 Visit http://news.mongabay.com/2014/10/india-plans-huge-palm-oil-expansion-puts-forests-at-risk/
17 See: http://envfor.nic.in/division/introduction-4 (Accessed on 20 December 2018).

18 See: https://whc.unesco.org/en/tentativelists/6356/ (Accessed on 20 December 2018)
19 Based on a conversation with retired forest officer J. Dutta and Dr Kashmira Kakati, a biologist, who took up a three-year project in Balpakram National Park to study wild carnivores in the region

References

Agarwal, A.K. 1991. 'Towards land reforms in Arunachal Pradesh', in Malabika Das Gupta (ed.), *The impact of land reforms in North East India* (pp. 43–50). Guwahati and New Delhi: Omsons Publications.

Agarwal, A.K. and K. Redford. 2009. 'Conservation and displacement: an overview', *Conservation and Society*, 7(1): 1–10.

Aziz, M.A., M. Shamsuddoha, M. Maniruddin, H.M. Morshed, R. Sarker and M.A. Islam. 2016. 'Elephants, border fence and human-elephant conflict in Northern Bangladesh: Implications for bilateral collaboration towards elephant conservation', *Gajah*, 45: 12–19.

Bezbaruah, M.P. 2007, January–March. 'Land tenure system in North East India: a constraint for bank financing?', *Dialogue*, 8(3): 138–145.

Bhaumik, Subir. 2010. *Troubled periphery: crisis of India's North East*. New Delhi: Sage.

Choudhury, A. 2006. 'The distribution and status of hoolock gibbon, *Hoolock hoolock*, in Manipur, Meghalaya, Mizoram, and Nagaland in northeast India', *Primate Conservation*, 2006(20): 79–87.

Das, J.N. 1990. *A study of the land system of Mizoram*. Guwahati: The Law Research Institute.

de Maaker, E. 2007. 'From the Songsarek faith to Christianity: conversion, religious identity and ritual efficacy', *South Asia: Journal of South Asian Studies*, 30(3): 517–530.

Datta-Roy, A., Ved, N. and Williams, A.C. 2009. 'Participatory elephant monitoring in South Garo Hills: efficacy and utility in a human-animal conflict scenario', *Tropical Ecology*, 50(1): 163.

Debbarma, K. 2018. 'Politics of land alienation and problem of its restoration in Tripura', in Bhagat Oinam and Dhiren A. Sadokpam (eds.), *Northeast India* (pp. 139–149). New York: Routledge.

Debbarma, S. 2008. 'Refugees rehabilitation and land alienation in Tripura', in W. Fernandes and S. Barbora (eds.), *Land people and politics: contest over tribal land in Northeast India* (pp. 88–112). Copenhagen: North Eastern Social Research Centre, Guwahati & International Workgroup for Indigenous Affairs, Denmark.

Desai, M. 2012. 'Parties and the articulation of neoliberalism: from "The Emergency" to reforms in India, 1975–1991', in Julian Go (ed.), *Political power and social theory* (pp. 27–63). Bingley: Emerald Group Publishing Limited.

Dikshit, K.R. and J.K. Dikshit. 2014. North-*east India: land, people and economy*. Dordrecht: Springer.

Dressler, W. and R. Roth. 2011. 'The good, the bad, and the contradictory: neoliberal conservation governance in rural Southeast Asia', *World Development*, 39(5): 851–862.

Dutta, S.K. 2002. *Functioning of autonomous district councils in Meghalaya*. New Delhi: Akansha Publishing House.

Elwin, V. 1957. *A philosophy for NEFA* (reprinted 2009). Delhi: ISHA books.

Fernandes, W. and S. Barbora. 2008. *Land people and politics: contest over tribal and in North East India*. Guwahati: North Eastern Social Research Centre.

Fernandes, W. and G. Bharali. 2002. *The socio-economic situation of some tribes of Bishnupur and Palizi*. Guwahati: North Eastern Social Research Centre (mimeo).

HDR. 2005. *Sikkim human development report*. Sikkim: Government of Sikkim.

Igoe, J. and D. Brockington. 2016. 'Neoliberal conservation: a brief introduction', in Nora Haenn, Richard Wilk and Allison Harnish (eds.), *The environment in anthropology: a reader in ecology, culture, and sustainable living* (pp. 324–331). New York: New York University Press.

Igoe, J. and D. Brockington. 2007. 'Neoliberal conservation: a brief introduction', *Conservation and society*, 5(4): 432–449.

ISFR (India State Forestry Report). 2013. *India state of forestry report 2013*. Dehradun: Survey of India.

Kakati, K. and S. Srikant. 2014. 'First camera-trap record of small-toothed palm civet *Arctogalida trivirgata* from India', *Small Carnivore Conservation*, 50: 50–53.

Kapoor, D. 2009. 'Adivasis (Original Dwellers) "in the way of" state-corporate development: development dispossession and learning in social action for land and forests in India', *McGill Journal of Education/Revue des Sciences de l'éducation de McGill*, 44(1): 55–78.

Kar, P.C. 1982. *The Garos in transition*. New Delhi: Cosmo Publications.

Karlsson, B.G. 2011. *Unruly hills: a political ecology of India's northeast*. New York: Berghahn Books.

McCarthy, J.F. and R.A. Cramb. 2009. 'Policy narratives, landholder engagement, and oil palm expansion on the Malaysian and Indonesian frontiers', *The Geographical Journal*, 175(2): 112–123.

MoRD (Ministry of Rural Development). 2009. *Report of the committee on state Agrarian relations and the unfinished task in land reforms*. New Delhi: Department of Land Resources, Government of India.

Myers, N., R.A. Mittermeier, C.G. Mittermeier, G.A.B. da Fonseca and J. Kent. 2000, 24 February. 'Biodiversity hotspots for conservation priorities', *Nature*, 403: 853–858. doi:10.1038/35002501

Nandy, S.N. 2014. 'Agro-economic indicators: a comparative study of North-East ern states of India', *Journal of Land and Rural Studies*, 2(1): 75–88.

NEC. 2017. *North-eastern council. Regional plan*. Retrieved form http://megplan ning.gov.in/circular/NEC%20Regional%20Plan%202017-18%20to%202019-20.pdf accessed on 11 September 2019.

NIRD Studies. 2008. *Land records in North East: Halloi PK*. Guwahati: North Eastern Regional Centre.

Nongkynrih, A.K. 2009. 'Privatisation of communal land of the tribes of North East India: a sociological viewpoint', in Walter Fernandes and Sanjay Barbora (eds.), *For hearth and home: tribal land alienation and struggles in Northeast India* (pp. 16–36). Guwahati: North Eastern Social Research Centre and IWGIA.

Phira, J.M. 1991. *U Khasi Mynta Bad Ki Riti Tynrai*. Shillong: Government Press of Meghalaya.

Planning Commission. 1997. *Report of the high level commission, transforming the North-East-Tackling backlogs in basic minimum services and infrastructural needs, part I*. New Delhi: Planning Commission, Government of India.

Planning Commission. 2006. *Report of the task force on connectivity and promotion of trade & investment in NE states*. New Delhi: Planning Commission, Government of India.

Poffenberger, M. 2006. *Forest sector review of northeast India*. Background paper no. 12. Community Forestry International.

Pyal, G. 2002. 'Land system in Jaintia hills', in Dr P.M. Passah and Dr S. Sarma (eds.), *Jaintia Hills: A Meghalaya tribe – its environment, land and people* (pp. 23–28). New Delhi: Reliance Publishing House.

Rajkhowa, A.C. 1986. *The customary laws and practices of the Thadou Kukis of Manipur*. Guwahati: The Law Research Institute.

Ramakrishnan, P.S. and S. Patnaik. 1992. '*Jhum*: slash and burn cultivation', in Geeti Sen (ed.), *Indigenous vision: peoples of India, attitudes to the environment* (pp. 215–220). New Delhi: Sage Publication & India International.

Rangarajan, M. and K. Sivaramakrishnan (eds.). 2012. *India's environmental history: from ancient times to the colonial period*. New Delhi: Permanent Black.

Rangarajan, M. and K. Sivaramakrishnan (eds.). 2014. *Shifting ground: people, animals, and mobility in India's environmental history*. Delhi: Oxford University Press.

Roy Burman, B.K. 1986. *Community land and institutional finance with reference to the tribal areas of Manipur and Tripura* (p. 81). New Delhi: Council for Social Development.

Saikia, A. 2011. *Forests and ecological history of Assam, 1826–2000*. Delhi: Oxford University Press.

SFR (State Forestry Report). 2005. *State of forestry report*. Dehradun: Forest Survey of India, Government of India.

Shankar Raman, T.R. 2001. 'Effect of slash-and-burn shifting cultivation on rainforest birds in Mizoram, Northeast India', *Conservation Biology*, 15(3): 685–698.

Shankar Raman, T.R. 2014, 14 May. 'Mizoram: bamboozled by land use policy', *The Hindu*. Retrieved from www.thehindu.com/opinion/op-ed/mizoram-bamboozled-by-land-use-policy/article6005950.ece accessed on 11 September 2019.

Sharma, J. 2011. *Empire's garden: Assam and the making of India*. New Delhi: Permanent Black.

Shrimali, A. 2013, 11 August. 'The forest rights act 2006 is "not relevant" for Arunachal Pradesh, believes state government', *Counterview*. Retrieved from www.counterview.net/2013/08/the-forest-rights-act-2006-is-not.html accessed on 14 August 2015.

Simon, I.M. 1996. *Gazetteer of India, Meghalaya district Gazetteer – Khasi Hills*. Shillong: Directorate of Arts and Culture, Government of Meghalaya.

Singh, D. 1996. *The last frontier: land, forests and people a case study of Mizoram*. New Delhi Tata energy research Institute, India.

Singh, D. 2009. 'The new land use policy: people and forest in Mizoram', in M. Rangarajan (eds.), *Environmental issues in India: a reader* (pp. 298–315). New Delhi: Dorling Kindersley.

Sitlhou, H. 2015. 'Patriarchal bargains and paradoxical emancipation: issues in the politics of land rights of Kuki women', *Indian Journal of Gender Studies*, 22(1): 92–115.

Srinivasan, U. 2014. 'Oil palm expansion – ecological threat to North-East India', *Economic and Political Weekly*, Web edition XLIX(36). Retrieved from www.epw.in/journal/2014/36/reports-states-web-exclusives/oil-palm-expansion.html accessed on 11 September 2019.

Steger, M.B. and R.K. Roy. 2010. *Neoliberalism: a very short introduction* (Vol. 222). Oxford: Oxford University Press.

Tamuly, N.K. 1985. *The customary laws and practices of the Angami Nagas of Nagaland*. Guwahati: The Law Research Institute.

Thrupp, L.A., S. Hecht and J. Browder. 1997. *The diversity and dynamics of shifting cultivation: myths, realities, and policy implications*. Washington, DC: World Resources Institute.

Vanlalhruaia, H. 2012. '*Jhum* cultivation versus the new land use policy: Agrarian change and transformation in Mizoram', in Daniel Münster, Ursula Münster and Stefan Dorondel (eds.), *Fields and forests: ethnographic perspectives on environmental globalization* (pp. 83–89). Munich: RCC Perspectives no. 5.

Walker, K.L.M. 2008. 'Neoliberalism on the ground in rural India: predatory growth, agrarian crisis, internal colonization, and the intensification of class struggle', *The Journal of Peasant Studies*, 35(4): 557–620.

Williams, A.C. and A.J.T. Johnsingh. 1996. 'Threatened elephant corridors in Garo Hills, north-east India', *Gajah*, 16: 61–68.

Wolford, W. 2007. 'Land reform in the time of neoliberalism: a many-splendored thing', *Antipode*, 39(3): 550–570.

World Bank. 2007. *India development and growth in Northeast India the natural resources, water, and environment Nexus*. Report No. 36397-IN. World Bank.

Part 2
Evolving jurisprudence on the land question

7 Land acquisition law in neoliberal India

Old wine in a new bottle?

Rita Sinha

Neoliberalism is an economic system with an ideology, a mode of governance, and a policy package that emphasises deregulation of the economy, liberalisation of trade and industry, and privatisation of State-owned enterprises. In India, neoliberal reforms were launched in the 1990s (Steger and Roy 2010: 11, 14, 91).

The Achilles heel of neoliberal reforms in India proved to be its neglected, creaking land governance system, especially land acquisition. By 2006, countrywide protests against the colonial *Land Acquisition Act, 1894* (LAA) brought land acquisition virtually to a grinding halt, forcing the government to rethink the entire acquisition regimen which resulted in the recently enacted law, the *Right to Fair Compensation and Transparency in Land Acquisition, Rehabilitation and Resettlement Act, 2013* (RFCTLARRA).

State intervention in what should ideally be a purely private transaction between two private parties has given rise to several quandaries and debates in the country. This chapter discusses two issues that have risen to prominence in the neoliberal era: (1) was there justification for the continuity of the colonial land acquisition law well into the neoliberal era, and (2) is the RFCTLARRA in tune with India's neoliberal policies or is it a step backwards towards putting restraints on government from making land available to private enterprises?

Was there justification for the continuity of the colonial land acquisition law well into the neoliberal era?

First, the historical continuity in the land acquisition law from colonial times needs to be established.

Colonial legislative power

By 1807, all three Presidencies – Calcutta, Bombay, and Madras– under the East India Company (EIC) were empowered to function as local legislatures and were self-sufficient in the matter of making laws, for the mofussil and for the Presidency Town, the latter being subject to the veto of the concerned Supreme Court (Jain 2014: 452, 487).

The *Charter Act, 1833*, ended the system of enactment of Regulations by the Presidency Governments and instead brought in the Legislative Council. However, the EIC retained veto power through its Court of Directors. While all laws made by the various governments before 1833 were called *Regulations*, the enactments of the Legislative Council were termed *Acts of the Government of India* and had the same force and effect as an Act of Parliament and were binding on all Indian courts. The veto power of the Supreme Court was removed (ibid: 488). After the 1857 rebellion, *The Government of India Act, 1858*, deprived the EIC of the Indian government. The Secretary of State for India supplanted the President of the Board of Control, and a Council of India was set up. The Governor General was added on the honorific of Viceroy as the personal representative of the Crown (Smith 1958: 673, 676, 683). The *Indian Councils Act, 1861*, separated the legislative and executive functions of the Governor General's Council. However, all legislation required the assent of the Governor General before being enacted as law, and certain matters required his prior sanction (De 2016: 24).

Controversy regarding the status of private property

There was uncertainty regarding the legal status of immovable property in the territorial acquisitions of the EIC. Around 1784, Warren Hastings claimed that absolute powers of property rights to land should be vested in the Company-State as the successor to the Mughal Empire on the grounds that property rights existed even under Mughal despotism. One view is that a consensus emerged in the Parliament that all lands in Bengal should be considered the estate and inheritance of native landholders and families. (Smith 1958: 522) argues that Pitt[1] chose to leave the issue of sovereignty over the EIC's possessions in India an open question. The amending *Act of 1793* gave statutory recognition to the personal laws of Indians regarding inheritance and succession to lands (De 2016: 22). If the EIC had acquired property rights in lands under its possession, the course of land appropriation in India would, perhaps, have taken a different course.

Evolution of land acquisition law

Having rented land for establishing the Madras Presidency Town and bought land for establishing the Calcutta Presidency, the EIC now opted for land acquisition as a mode of obtaining land to create infrastructure required for its commercial expansion. Since most of the infrastructure needed was linear, such as roads, railways, canals, and tramways, which entailed obtaining small pieces of land in perpetuity over long distances from numerous landowners, many of whom may have had unclear titles to the land; acquisition seems to have been the preferred mode to purchase and renting.

The first land acquisition law enacted in the country by the EIC was *Regulation I of 1824* (Ray and Patra 2009: 41). It applied throughout the whole of the provinces immediately subject to the Presidency of Fort William. It provided rules for enabling the officers of government to obtain, at a fair valuation, land or other immovable property required for roads, canals, or other public purposes (Law Commission of India 1958: 1). *Land acquisition by the State for a public purpose was retained as section 4(1) of the LAA and forms section 2(1) of the RFCTLARRA.*

In Bombay Province, the *Building Act XXVIII of 1839* provided the machinery for acquisition of land for widening or altering any existing public road, street, or other thoroughfare or drain or for making such new ones within the islands of Bombay and Colaba. This Act was extended by the *Act XVII of 1850* to taking lands for railways within the Presidency (Law Commission of India 1958: 2). The Act also provided that compensation should be determined by a jury of 12 (Sarkar 2012: 1).

In the middle of the nineteenth century, the railway network was being developed, and legislation was needed for acquiring lands for it. The *Act XLII of 1850* declared railways to be public works which enabled the provisions of *Regulation I of 1824* to be used for acquiring lands for the construction of railways. The *Act I of 1850* also extended some of the provisions of Regulation I of 1824 to Calcutta town, with the object of confirming the title to lands in Calcutta taken for public purposes (Law Commission of India 1958: 1).

The *Madras Presidency Act XX of 1852* enabled the EIC to acquire land in the Presidency of Fort St. George for public works in general. As per the Act, compensation was to be settled by the Collector or if the parties disputed it, by arbitration. Simultaneously, the *Bengal Act XLII of 1850* was extended to the Madras Presidency. Both these Acts were extended by *Act I of 1854* for acquisition of land in Madras Town (Sarkar 2012: 1). *Settlement of the compensation by the Collector was included in the LAA as section 11 and forms section 27 of the RFCTLARRA.*

After the 1857 rebellion, the British Crown took over the EIC's Indian possessions. All previous enactments were repealed by *Act VI of 1857*, which enacted one general law for the acquisition of land for public purposes in all the territories under the EIC. Under this Act, the Collector was empowered to fix the amount of compensation by agreement, if possible; but if there was no such agreement, the dispute had to be referred to arbitrators whose decision was final and who could not be impeached, except on the grounds of corruption or misconduct (Law Commission of India 1958: 2–3). The *Act VI of 1857* was further amended by *Act II of 1861*, dealing mainly with temporary occupation of land (Sarkar 2012: 1). *The provisions for temporary occupation of land were retained as section 35 in the LAA and from section 81 of the RFCTLARRA.*

Then came *Act XXII of 1863*, which was significant because it empowered the government to acquire land for private companies but only for works of public utility, which were defined under the Act as any bridge, road, railroad, tram road, canal for irrigation or navigation, work for the improvement of a river or harbour, dock, quay, jetty, drainage work or electric telegraph, and all works subsidiary to any such work (*R.L. Aurora vs. State of U.P. [Uttar Pradesh]*, dated 1.12.1961, equivalent citations: *1962 AIR 764, 1962 SCR Supl.(2)149*). *Acquisition of land for private companies for works of public utility, now public purpose, was retained as section 40 (1)(a) in the LAA and has been incorporated as section 2 (2)(b) of the RFCTLARRA.*

The method of settlement of compensation by arbitrators proved to be unsatisfactory, as they were incompetent and, sometimes, even corrupt, and there was no provision for appeal against their award (Law Commission of India 1958: 2–3). The *Act X of 1870* repealed earlier acts; land acquisition for public purpose and for companies were consolidated under this Act. Acquisition for companies, brought in as Chapter VII, was introduced into the Act for the first time (*R.L. Aurora vs. State of U.P.*, dated 1.12.1961). *The LAA retained Parts II and VII for land acquisition for public purpose and land acquisition for companies, respectively. The RFCTLARRA has done away with two separate Parts and brought both kinds of acquisition under section 2.*

The *Act of 1870* also provided for reference to a civil court for the determination of compensation if the Collector could not settle it by agreement. It laid down a detailed procedure for the acquisition of land and also provided definite rules for the determination of compensation (Law Commission of India 1958: 2–3). *The reference to the civil court for the determination of compensation was retained as section 18 of the LAA. The RFCTLARRA has substituted the Land Acquisition, Rehabilitation and Resettlement Authority (LARRA) for the civil court and reference to it is made vide section 64. Sections 23 and 24 of the LAA included the rules for determination of compensation in the form of 'Matters to be considered on determining compensation' and 'Matters to be neglected in determining compensation', respectively. The RFCTLARRA has retained only 'Parameters to be considered by Collector in determination of award' as section 28 and omitted those which are to be neglected.*

The *Land Acquisition Act, 1894*, replaced the *1870 Act*. This Act was slowly fine-tuned by amendments in 1914, 1919, 1920, 1921, 1923, 1933, and 1938 (Law Commission of India 1958: 3). The *1923* amendment was significant because it introduced the provision of providing an opportunity to persons interested in the lands proposed to be acquired to state their objections to the acquisition and to be heard by the authority concerned in support of their objections (*op. cit.*). *This provision was retained as section 5A of the LAA and has been included as section 15 of the RFCTLARRA.*

By the amendment effected in 1933, besides works of utility, particularly railways, acquisition was also permitted for the erection of dwelling houses for workmen employed by the Company or for the provision of amenities directly connected therewith (Standing Committee on Rural Development (2011–2012): Para 3.3). *This provision was retained as section 40(1)(a) in the LAA but has been omitted in the RFCTLARRA.*

The *Government of India Act, 1935*, provided, in section 299, that no person shall be deprived of his property in British India save by authority of law. This clause embodied the fundamental principle of the common law that the Executive may not extinguish property rights without the authority of the Legislature. The Act also provided that no land acquisition law, either federal or provincial, could be enacted without making provision for payment of compensation; and any bill seeking to provide for land acquisition or extinguishment or modification of rights and privileges in land or in land revenue could be introduced only with the previous sanction of the Governor General in his discretion or in the case of provincial legislation, with the previous sanction of the Governor in his discretion. This provision safeguarded vested interests, notably those of *zamindars, taluqdars, inamdars*, and *jagirdars*[2] (Wahi 2016: 945).

Post-independence: colonial continuities in land acquisition laws

The end of colonial rule in 1947, and the Republican Constitution of 1950, did not bring about any significant change in the land acquisition law. The Constitution of India, by Article 372, allowed all colonial laws to remain in force unless they were explicitly repealed (Ray and Patra 2009: 41). Vide the *Indian Independence (Adaptation of Central Acts and Ordinances) Order, 1948*, The *Land Acquisition Act, 1894*, was amended and made applicable to the Provinces of India instead of to 'the whole of British India'. Under the *Adaptation Order of 1950*, after the adoption of the Constitution, the Act became applicable to 'the whole of India except Part B States'. Under the *Adaptation of Laws No. 2 Order, 1956*, which was promulgated after the *States Re-organization Act, 1956*, the Act became applicable to 'all the territories which immediately before 1st November, 1956 were comprised in Part B States' (Law Commission of India 1958: 3–4).

The *Land Acquisition Act, 1894*, was amended in 1962, 1967, and 1984 (Standing Committee on Rural Development 2008–2009: 1). The 1962 amendment was necessitated by a judgment passed by the Apex Court in the case *R.L. Aurora vs. State of U.P.*, dated 1.12.1961, where in a strongly worded judgment the Court, opposing land acquisition for companies as a public purpose, ruled that it could not have been the intention of the Legislature to make the government a general agent to acquire lands for companies in order that their owners are able to carry on their activities for private profit (*R.L. Aurora vs. State of U.P.*). This judgment restricted the government's power to acquire land for companies as public purpose. Hence, the government amended the law retrospectively through the *Land Acquisition (Amendment) Act, 1962* (Ray and Patra 2009: 42). There was also a fear that past cases would be reopened, with landowners demanding restoration of acquired lands or payment of damages (World Bank, Urban Resettlement–Legal Report 2007: 10). *This amendment was incorporated as sub-section 4A of section 41 in the LAA and forms section 2 (2)(b) of the RFCTLARRA.*

The 1967 amendment to the LAA

Initially, under the *Act of 1894*, no time limit was prescribed for making the declaration under section 6 after the publication of the notification under section 4(1) of the Act. This led to unreasonable delays which disadvantaged the owner because the market value of the land was determined on the basis of the notification published several years earlier. This was pointed out by the Supreme Court in *State of Madhya Pradesh vs. Vishnu* Prasad *Sharma AIR 1966 SC 1593*. The *Land Acquisition (Amendment and Validation) Ordinance, 1967*, was promulgated which laid down a time frame of three years for making the declaration from the date of publication of the notification under section 4(1) (Law Commission of India 2002: 7).

In the same case, the Supreme Court also expressed the view that only one declaration could be made for a notification under section 4(1) (World Bank, Urban Resettlement–Legal Report 2007: 10). The Ordinance of 1967 provided that, if necessary, more than one declaration could be made from time to time in respect of different parcels of land covered by the same notification under section 4(1) of the Act. The provisions of the Ordinance were later incorporated into the *Amending Act of 1967* (Law Commission of India 2002: 7–8). *This provision was retained as section 6(1) of the LAA and forms section 19(1) of the RFCTLARRA.*

The 1984 Amendment to the LAA

The *Amending Act of 1984* introduced payment of 12 percent per annum interest for the period commencing from the date of the intention and ending with the date of the Collector's award, and payment of solatium at the rate of 30 percent of the market value of the acquired land. It also provided for an opportunity to those who were dissatisfied with the Collector's award to apply to him for a re-determination of the compensation from the Reference Court (World Bank, Urban Resettlement–Legal Report 2007: 10). *Payment of 12 percent per annum interest for the period from the date of the notification till the date of the Collector's award/possession was retained as section 23 (1A) in the LAA and forms section 69(2) of the RFCTLARRA. Payment of solatium at the rate of 30 percent of the market value of the acquired land was retained as section 23(2) of the LAA. An enhanced solatium of 100 percent of the compensation amount is included as section 30(1) in the RFCTLARRA. The provision to apply through the Collector to a Reference Court for re-determination of the compensation award was incorporated as section 28A in the LAA and forms section 73(1) of the RFCTLARRA except that LARRA has replaced the Reference Court.*

The 1984 Amendment in the LAA reduced the period for making the declaration under section 6 to within one year from the date of publication of the notification under section 4(1), instead of the three years introduced by the *Amending Act of 1967*, failing which the section 4(1) notification would lapse. It also inserted an Explanation below section 6(1) to the effect that if the court had granted a stay order on any action or proceeding taken in pursuance of section 4(1) notification, the period covered by the stay order would be excluded while computing the period of one year allowed for the declaration to be made (Law Commission of India 2002: 9). *These provisions were retained in the LAA as Proviso to section 6(1) and Explanation 1 of section 6(1), respectively, and form Third Proviso to section 19(2), and First Proviso to section 19(7), respectively, of the RFCTLARRA, with powers to extend the period in the Second Proviso.*

The *National Policy for Resettlement and Rehabilitation for Displaced Persons* was drafted by the Ministry of Rural Development, Government of India, in 1998 along with a Land Acquisition (Amendment) Bill, 1998, which came in for sharp criticism when circulated for public opinion (Pal 2017: 161). It was not tabled in Parliament. The *National Policy on Rehabilitation and Resettlement, 2003*, introduced by the Bhartiya Janta Party (BJP), was replaced by the *National Rehabilitation and Resettlement Policy, 2007*, by the Congress-led Central Government; possibly influenced by the Singur episode of 2006. This Policy, being advisory in nature, was largely ignored by the states and Union Territories (UT), necessitating legal backing to it. Hence, the Land Acquisition (Amendment) Bill, 2007, and the Rehabilitation and Resettlement Bill, 2007, were introduced in December 2007, and, after due procedure, were re-introduced in and passed by the Lok Sabha on 25 February 2009. Because of objections from the BJP and the CPI (M) (Communist Party of India–Marxist), the bill could not be included in the Agenda of the Rajya Sabha the next day and, with the lapse of the Fourteenth Lok Sabha, both the Bills lapsed.

The Land Acquisition, Rehabilitation and Resettlement Bill, 2011, was presented in the Parliament in September 2011, which after due procedure, was passed as the *Right to Fair Compensation and Transparency in Land Acquisition, Rehabilitation and Resettlement Act, 2013, (RFCTLARRA)*. This Act became effective from 1 January 2014, after bringing the curtain down on the 119-year-old *Land Acquisition Act, 1894* (LAA) which stood repealed.

The NDA government (National Democratic Alliance) attempted to amend the nascent RFCTLARRA in 2015. The proposed amendments included removing the consent clause and removing the mandatory social impact assessment (SIA) in five areas, viz., defence, rural infrastructure, housing, industrial corridor, and social infrastructure. They also would have changed the term 'private company' to 'private entity' and the definition of public purpose to include private hospitals and educational institutions. They would have made using or returning acquired land within five years flexible by replacing that with the duration of the project or within five years, whichever was later. The proposed amendments would have made compensation and R&R applicable to the 13 acts exempted under the RFCTLARRA (Singh 2016: 67–68). Unable to go through with the Amendments in Parliament because of lack of a majority in the Rajya Sabha, the NDA left it open to state governments to make necessary amendments utilising the provisions of Article 254(2) of the Constitution (Ramesh and Khan 2016).

Five states, namely, Tamil Nadu, Gujarat, Telengana, Haryana, and Jharkhand, received Presidential assent to amendments to the RFCTLARRA till June 2018.[3]

Colonial continuity in land acquisition laws established

From the foregoing account, it is evident that the land acquisition law was brought into the country by a 'Company-State' – the EIC – with the objective of creating infrastructure that would enhance its trade and profits. By giving such acquisitions the label of 'public purpose', it skewed the definition of 'public purpose' in the context of a private entity.

Acquisition of land by the State for private profit-making companies has been with India since 1863 in the form of *Act XXII of 1863*. In *Act X of 1870*, the first part, which was used for land acquisition by the 'state', was drafted *by* a company, viz., the EIC. Part VII, which accommodated *Act XXII of 1863*, was drafted for acquiring land *for* private companies. The *1894 Act* inherited both these parts, which explains why the tenor of the colonial land acquisition law, such as speedy acquisition, payment of low compensation, and lack of concern for the land losers beyond monetary compensation, echoed the mindset of traders out to make quick profits rather than that of a welfare state acquiring land for the public good.

It is evident that several provisions in the LAA hark back to colonial times, and the RFCTLARRA has also retained some of them. The RFCT-LARRA has also retained a good deal of the procedural arrangement and schematic layout[4] of the LAA and has primarily added on welfare measures to assuage irate land losers and also some features that promote the neo-liberal policies of the State. For example, in preliminary investigation, the RFCTLARRA includes preparation of the SIA Study and R&R Scheme; Miscellaneous Provisions contain several new insertions for prevention of un-utilisation and mis-utilisation of acquired land; and, public purpose includes acquisition of land for private companies and PPP projects, fulfilling the government's neoliberal agenda.

The RFCTLARRA stands at the political fault line of a changing India, undergoing significant transitions: political, economic, social, environmental, and spatial. A deepened democracy attempts to find room for dissenting voices, including civil society, marginalised castes, Scheduled Tribes, as well as for powerful regional political parties (Goswami 2016: 4).

Post-independence persistence by the State with a colonial law

Though the LAA was a colonial law, its real abuse took place in the postcolonial Nehruvian era when it was used to acquire vast tracts of land to jump start an ambitious industrialisation agenda. The colonial state never had such an industrial vision for India; rather, it was antithetical to it (Chakravorty 2016: 50).

By 1991, a financial crisis loomed large over the country with India's national debt approaching 50 percent of the GDP (gross domestic product). Dr Manmohan Singh, by then India's finance minister, ushered in neoliberal reforms to rescue India out of the financial crisis. As prime minister in 2004, he carried the neoliberal reforms further and linked the Indian economy to globalisation (Steger and Roy 2010: 92–93). The liberalisation of the Indian economy ushered in a new phase of conflict over land acquisition, since land was increasingly being acquired for private investors. This became a major source of agitation for civil society and subaltern movements (Nielson and Nilsen 2014).

Opposition to this regressive regimen of land acquisition gathered momentum in the country from 2005 onwards. Major trouble spots erupted – Govindpura in Punjab; Jaitapur and Maval in Maharashtra; Greater Noida and Noida Extension, Tappal, Aligarh, Bajna, Dadri, and Karchana in Uttar Pradesh; Kalinganagar, Puri, Narayanpatna, Angul, and Paradeep in Orissa; and Nandigram and Singur in West Bengal (Editorial, *The Times of India* 2011). The Singur episode of 2006 became a watershed in the history of resistance to land acquisition. It politicised the land acquisition issue which forced governments to mull over the entire acquisition regimen (Pal 2017: 170). According to Chakravorty (2016: 57, 60), in Singur, land acquisition was used as a 'wedge issue' to topple the communist government in West Bengal which had been continuously in power for 34 years. This success turned land acquisition into a 'wedge issue' in many parts of the country. As a result, the old acquisition system began to fail. Despite so much opposition to land acquisition instead of abolishing it, the State enacted a new, 'reformed' law in the hope that it would revive the moribund land acquisition process.

Examining reasons for State persistence with land acquisition in the neoliberal age

A major land governance issue which compels the State to persist with land acquisition is lack of clear, 'conclusive' titles to property. The country follows the system of 'presumptive' titles based on land revenue records, which are mostly outdated and unreliable, and on the Deeds system of Registration of land transfers. Till land revenue was the mainstay of the State economy, land revenue records were updated and maintained meticulously and formed a reliable source of information about 'presumptive' ownership of land, so much so that sections 32 and 35 of The *Indian Evidence Act, 1872*, attached special importance of evidentiary value to them (Wadhwa 1989: 4). However, by the 1980s, when the land tax ceased to be an important source of revenue and it became uneconomical to collect it, several states abolished it. With the abolition of land revenue, the upkeep of the records was neglected making them obsolete and unreliable as a source of determining landownership. Land acquisition, a cruel and inhuman solution, was used to counter the deeper malady of poorly maintained land records and weak land rights (Ramesh and Khan 2015: 133).

The State attempted to rectify the upkeep of land records in the country. The scheme of the National Land Records Modernization Programme (NLRMP), built upon two earlier schemes – Strengthening of Revenue Administration & Updation of Land Records (SRA&ULR), and Computerization of Land Records (CLR), which were launched in 1987–88 and 1988–89, respectively – was launched in 2008, and aimed at building up a real-time, comprehensive, and integrated land record system through use of modern technology, with the ultimate goal of ushering in the system of Conclusive Titles (Sinha 2010: 59–60). The NLRMP now forms part of the 'Digital India' programme, but progress has been so slow that land revenue records still remain unreliable in several states. Till 2015, only four state governments were following the programme guidelines (Ramesh and Khan 2015: 133).

The 'Deeds' system, following the principle of *caveat emptor*, or buyer beware, part of British common law based on a maxim of Roman law, puts the entire onus for making a legally valid purchase on the buyer (Belisle 2011). Obviously, it is unsuitable for brisk and large-scale private land transfers which neoliberalism requires. To rectify the situation, in 2008, the DoLR took approval of the Cabinet to introduce Conclusive Titling based on the Torrens system as an alternative to the Deeds system and made a draft National Titling Act, 2008. After several rounds of discussions with state governments, stakeholders, and international experts, a draft of the National Titling Act, 2011, was prepared in 2010 in the hope that the new system would first be introduced in Union Territories by 2011, since the states were unresponsive.[5] In 2013, the DoLR constituted an Expert Committee to prepare a Road Map for Titling. In January 2014, this Committee recommended a new type of titling system more suitable for India, viz., Systematic Selective Titling (Department of Land Resources 2014: 8). Finding very little response from state governments and UTs, in 2018, according to the then Secretary of the DoLR, the Department decided to close the chapter of attempting to introduce Titling in the country.

Litigation from unrecorded interests in land is a grave risk for private purchasers, whereas when land is acquired, all such disputes stand terminated and the land vests in the government free from all past encumbrances. This is one of the most compelling reasons for companies to root for acquisition of land, especially when fairly large chunks of land are required involving several landholders.

Rural India typically has a large number of landholders with small holdings. Sarkar (2009: 6) estimated that as many as 261 families can be involved in a land parcel of just 4.3 hectares. The private sector finds it difficult to negotiate with small landholders because of the sheer numbers involved, the lack of legal titles, and the reluctance of farmers to give up land because of a lack of exit options from agriculture (Singh 2016: 70–71). Land acquisition, on the other hand, puts the onus of conclusive negotiation on the Collector.

Related to the problem of large numbers of landholders is the 'hold-out' problem, where a few landowners whose land is located within the pro-posed project area or near the main road refuse to sell their lands, thereby causing fragmentation and discontinuity of the project site or disconnection with the main transport route. The buyer is left with no option but to seek help from the State to acquire such lands. In the case of cent percent land acquisition there is no scope for a 'hold-out'.

Land acquisition over-rides laws in many states, which prohibit sale of agricultural lands to non-cultivators. Moreover, there is an automatic change in land use obviating the need to obtain non-agricultural use clear-ance from the government which is mandatory before agricultural land can be diverted to other uses. Mutation in the Record of Rights after Registra-tion, by which rights in the purchased property actually accrue to the buyer, is often delayed in private purchases, leaving the buyers at risk to frauds.

'Suitability' is a factor in land acquisition; certain types of lands are 'un-substitutable', as for example, lands suited for mineral extraction or for strategic use (Morris and Pandey 2009: 14). When owners of such lands are reluctant to sell, the State's intervention is needed for compulsory acquisi-tion for 'development' purposes. This is a major cause of land acquisition in tribal areas which are rich in natural resources.

Another attraction of land acquisition under the LAA was the low market value ascribed to the land by the State, making it a more economical way of accruing land for both the State and the private sector. It allowed the State to indulge in a patronage system to lure private industry which is not pos-sible when the land market functions freely.

It becomes clear that the State had 'compulsion' to continue with the land acquisition regime in the neoliberal era but little 'justification', since it remained lackadaisical towards attempts to reform land governance.

RFCTLARRA: old wine in a new bottle?

The RFCTLARRA is an amalgamation of colonial inheritance, pacifist wel-fare measures, and tenets of a neoliberal state. The primary 'pacifist' pur-pose of enacting the RFCTLARRA is to reduce social tensions (Singh 2016: 71). It, therefore, seeks to negotiate a compromise equilibrium between sub-altern groups, vulnerable to marginalisation and capable of mobilisation, and dominant groups, who stand to gain from the liberalised economy. This equilibrium is ultimately intended to facilitate India's process of neoliberali-sation (Nielsen and Nilsen 2014).

Two factors seem to have played a predominant role in moulding the pacifist measures in the RFCTLARRA, namely, lessons learnt from land conflicts against land acquisition – primarily the agitation in Singur – and agitations against the government's SEZ (special economic zone) policy and removal of the major defects in the LAA. The moot point is whether these pacifist reformatory measures restrain the State from acquiring land for its neoliberal agenda.

Lessons learnt from land conflicts: Singur and SEZ policy

The major error in Singur was of acquiring highly fertile multi-crop land instead of less fertile mono-crop agricultural land (Nielsen and Nilsen 2014). This has probably brought the 'special provision to safeguard food security' into the RFCTLARRA. Acquisition in Singur was done without substantial consultations with local stakeholders (Ibid 2014). The RFCTLARRA includes the consultative process at several stages of the acquisition – at the initial stage under section 4 sub-section (1) when the government decides to acquire land for public purpose; in the preparation of the SIA study; in the discussion of the draft R&R Scheme; in the preparation of the R&R Scheme in Scheduled Areas; and for carrying out social audits when the land acquired is, or exceeds, 100 acres.

In Singur, the outdated land records, on the basis of which compensation was calculated, did not record the massive conversion of unirrigated *sali* land to irrigated, multi-crop *suna* land which received higher compensation, resulting in many landowners being grossly under paid (Nielsen and Nilsen 2014). The RFCTLARRA mandates updation of land records between the issue of the preliminary notification and the publication of the declaration.

According to Jenkins, the triggering factor for bringing in the new Act was the UPA (United Progressive Alliance) government's SEZ policy (Jenkins 2014: 4). The SEZ regimen brought several evils with it. It initiated large-scale acquisitions as a multi-product SEZ required as much as 1,000 hectares of land. According to the International Labour Office (2012), acquisition of land for notified SEZs is likely to displace approximately 1.14 million people, a figure 18 times higher than the number of people officially likely to get direct employment in these notified zones (Parwez 2016: 138, 139, 142).

The RFCTLARRA has incorporated processes to examine land requirements in the SIA study and in section 8 sub-section (1)(c) by the government before issue of the preliminary notification.

The RFCTLARRA recommends the fixation of limits or ceiling for private purchase of land beyond which R&R provisions become automatically applicable. For acquisitions of 100 acres or more, an R&R Committee is mandated to monitor and review the progress of the R&R and to carry out post-implementation social audits in consultation with the relevant local bodies. The issue of livelihoods is addressed at the time of undertaking the SIA and when it is evaluated by the independent multi-disciplinary Expert Group (IMEG), as well as at the time of preparation of the R&R scheme.

Of the total land notified for the SEZ, only 42.59 percent was utilised and approximately 215 square kilometres were left vacant even as industry complains of a shortage of land to set up factories and plants. Of the total land notified in six major states, 14 percent was later de-notified and diverted to other profitable purposes not related to the SEZ (Parwez 2016: 142–144). The RFCTLARRA requires the government to ascertain if there is unutilised acquired land available and to utilise the same before proceeding to acquire land afresh. The Miscellaneous Provisions provide that if acquired land remains unutilised for a period of five years from the date of taking over possession, the same must be returned to the original owner or owners or their legal heirs, as the case may be, or to the Land Bank of the concerned government. Change in the original public purpose is disallowed and if this original public purpose cannot be achieved then the appropriate government can utilise such land for some other public purpose.

Removal of major defects in the LAA

Factoring Singur and SEZ policy learning, major changes were introduced to the RFCTLARRA.

Change in the compensation regimen

A major flaw in the LAA was provision of inadequate compensation for land losers (Wahi et al. 2017: 10). The LAA provided neither 'value of the land' nor 'just compensation', but merely 'reasonable' compensation (Singh 2016: 69).

Perhaps the single most impactful transformation brought about by the RFCTLARRA is the change in the compensation regimen. Compensation has been enhanced manifold in monetary terms, as the market value arrived at is to be multiplied by a factor of one to two in rural areas, based on the distance of the project from urban areas, and a factor of one in urban areas. Solatium has been enhanced to 100 percent of the compensation amount from 30 percent of market value. State governments are empowered to enact laws to further enhance the entitlements. The Act has curtailed the power of the Central Government to reduce the compensation and R&R benefits when amending the Schedules to the Act.

In many areas, agriculture is no longer remunerative, and farmers were basically not averse to land acquisition but held back because of the abysmally low compensation paid under the LAA. For example, in Uttar Pradesh, where land acquisition was opposed virulently, viz., the Greater Noida and Noida Extension, Tappal, Aligarh, Bajna, Dadri, and Karchana areas, 80 percent of farmers owned one hectare or less of land and 40 percent of farmers wanted to give up farming as it was not sustainable (Editorial, *The Times of India*, 2011). The jump in the compensation package is likely to bring them on board with parting with their lands. The experience of Powergrid, a central PSU (public sector undertaking), shows that land-owners in the Rajahaat area of Calcutta, in Agra, Uttar Pradesh, and in Jharkhand state, who were contesting the Collector's awards under the LAA, are now willing to sell their lands to Powergrid as per compensation provisions made in the RFCTLARRA (Srivastava 2014: 2).

However, negative reactions to the enhanced compensation have also come in. Singh (2016: 68) mentions that the cost of acquisition will become prohibitive for the government. The larger the area acquired, the higher will be the cost per acre because of R&R for a higher number of landowners. Chakravorty (2016: 57) maintains that the new compensation regime reverses the distributional impact of acquisition from a deeply regressive one that frequently devastated land and livelihood losers to one that creates a windfall for land losers (not livelihood losers) and generates a tax on the rest of the population. Chakravorty's conclusions about the unsustainability of the compensation provisions have been refuted by Wahi et al. (2017: 12) on the grounds that, because of evasion of registration fees, most lands are undervalued, so that government usually pays less compensation than the market value of the land. Hence, the compensation provisions in the RFCT-LARRA are not only sustainable but also realistic.

Overall, higher compensation is likely to remove the current major road-block in land acquisition in most areas and revive the neoliberal agenda.

Introduction of R&R for affected families

The LAA regimen lacked concern regarding the fate of land losers beyond providing low monetary compensation and provided no R&R at all for landless families who were critically dependent on the acquired land for their survival but were not entitled to any compensation for loss of live-lihoods. Consequently, both land losers and the affected landless families often made common cause to oppose land acquisition, as happened in Sin-gur, as stark impoverishment stared them in the face in the aftermath of the acquisition.

Sections 16–18, along with The Second Schedule of the RFCTLARRA not only provide R&R for all 'affected families', both land owning and landless, but also make R&R a justiciable right. R&R has also been made applicable in the case of private purchases, and partial private purchase and partial acquisition of land for private companies beyond the prescribed area. In the latter case, R&R becomes applicable for the entire area, including that which has been purchased through private negotiations.

However, there is a dichotomy about the preparation of the R&R Scheme in the Act. While section 16 makes it appear as if the preparation of the R&R Scheme is a consultative process since the draft R&R Scheme is required to be discussed with the relevant local bodies and also discussed in a public hearing, section 43 sub-section (3) states that the Administrator is responsible for the formulation, execution, and monitoring of the R&R

Scheme 'subject to the superintendence, directions and control of the appropriate Government'. The R&R Scheme would have had greater credibility had its preparation been left in the hands of expert, independent agencies rather than those of governments known for their penchant for displacement rather than for rehabilitation.

Moreover, the land size when R&R becomes applicable will also be decided by the appropriate government, most likely to be the state governments (Goswami 2016: 13). This leaves scope for 'adjustments' to accommodate private companies.

The RFCTLARRA, like the LAA, does not debar large-scale acquisitions and consequential large-scale displacements. It merely provides R&R for the affected families. The neoliberal agenda, thus, remains undisturbed, although larger acquisitions will now come at much higher costs.

Curtailment of activities under public purpose

The vague definition of public purpose under the LAA and liberal interpretation given to it by the courts enabled the justification of virtually every land acquisition as serving a public purpose. Moreover, once land acquisition for a company was declared to be a public purpose, the State could misuse its urgency powers for the acquisition.

Although the RFCTLARRA, too, does not define public purpose, it has abridged the list of activities considered as public purpose and curtailed powers of state governments to add to public purposes at will, through centralisation of activities hitherto more decentralised under the LAA, such as restricting land acquisition for infrastructure projects to items listed in the Central Government notification of the Department of Economic Affairs dated 27 March, 2012, and restricting acquisition of land for industrialisation to provisions made in the Central Government's National Manufacturing Policy. Any addition to infrastructure facilities requires notification by the Central Government after tabling such notification in Parliament. The RFCTLARRA restricts use of urgency powers to the minimum area required for the defence of India or national security or for any emergencies arising out of natural calamities or any other emergency with the approval of Parliament.

Under the LAA there was opacity regarding the issue of notification and declaration, which led not only to asymmetry of knowledge between requirers and land losers, but also enabled the government to abuse its power by changing the purpose of the acquisition from public purpose to acquisition for private industry after the issue of the notification/declaration. A classic example is the case involving the Greater Noida Industrial Development Authority (GNIDA), located in District Gautam Buddh Nagar of U.P., where after the issue of the notification, on 10.6.2009, and the declaration, on 9.11.2009, for acquisition of land for GNIDA in village Shahberi for the public purpose of integrated planned industrial development as per the approved Development Plan, the state government, in connivance with GNIDA, illegally changed the land use in March 2010 and handed over the acquired land to private builders for constructing a multi-storied residential complex. The Supreme Court held this to be a colourable exercise of power by the state (*Greater Noida Industrial Development Authority vs. Devendra Kumar & Ors.*).[6] Under the RFCTLARRA the government is required to state clearly in the notification the nature of the public purpose involved, reasons necessitating the displacement of affected persons, summary of the SIA Report, and particulars of the Administrator appointed for R&R. Similarly, in the declaration, the state is required to give information about the resettlement area and a summary of the R&R Scheme. There is, thus, less opacity and better symmetry of information about the acquisition and R&R and a curb on abuse of state power.

The new Act restricts land acquisition to the government's own usage, for PSUs, for PPP (public-private partnership) projects, and private companies which fulfil the public purposes listed under the Act. As a result of lessons learnt from past protests against land acquisition for private companies, the RFCTLARRA has added the rider of consensual acquisition of land for private companies and PPP projects. Prior consent of 80 percent and 70 percent of affected families is mandatory for acquisition of land for PPP projects and private companies, respectively.

The restricted list of public purposes in the RFCTLARRA includes industrialisation and creation of infrastructure which form the cornerstone of neoliberalism. By offering the carrot of land acquisition, the government can channel the resources of all eligible agencies to fulfil its neoliberal agenda and the curtailment of activities under public purpose may actually help to focus resources on it since land will not be diverted to other public purposes. One view of this consent clause is that it has been included merely to circumvent the hold-out problem faced by private companies (Pal 2017: 163).

The process for carrying out the consensus for acquisition of land for PPP projects and private companies is the sole responsibility of the government. It is a well-known fact that in the past when consent has not been forthcoming, the legal owners have been forced out of their lands and compensation denied to them (ibid:162). There is evidence that fake documents purporting to show consent of the Gram Sabha were produced to get clearance from the government (Bhattacharya et al. 2017: 190). Hence, leaving the consensus process entirely in government hands causes a sense of unease.

Social impact assessment

The LAA was criticised for lacking provisions for people's participation in the government decision to take over their land (Wahi et al. 2017: 10). The consultative processes introduced in the new Act have already been enumerated. The RFCTLARRA has also introduced an SIA Study for the first time in the land acquisition law to:

> Establish clearly the public purpose of proposed acquisition, to prevent diversion of acquired land from stated public purpose from taking place, not acquiring land in excess of actual requirement, no acquisition of multi-crop irrigated land unless as a last resort and identification of losers of livelihood and others entitled to compensation.
>
> (Singh 2016: 71)

On the one hand, the SIA is slated to be prepared in a consultative and participatory manner through a public hearing. On the other hand, the government has been assigned an over-arching role in the preparation of the SIA – deciding the procedure for carrying out the SIA, arranging the consultative process with the local bodies, getting the Social Impact Management Plan (SIMP) prepared, organising the public hearing with affected families, and giving publicity to the SIA and the SIMP. This is likely to cast a shadow over the neutrality of the SIA Study and the SIMP.

Although an IMEG is empowered to veto the SIA Study on the grounds that the project does not serve any public purpose or that the social costs and adverse social impacts of the project outweigh the potential benefits, the government retains the right to over-rule it and go ahead with the project despite the veto. Thus, while giving voice to the demand for greater public participation in the decision-making process of land acquisition, the RFCTLARRA leaves enough muscle with the State to ensure that the neoliberal agenda is not derailed.

Special provisions for Scheduled Tribes

Unlike the LAA, the RFCTLARRA pays special attention to the Scheduled Tribes (tribals or Adivasis), considering that the tribal belt has erupted in violent protests against land acquisition. More than 80 districts in the heartland of India, most of them with a concentrated Adivasi population, have been declared Left Wing Extremism–affected areas by the Government of India (Bhattacharya et al. 2017: 192). A major triggering factor for frequent use of eminent domain powers in the Scheduled Areas (SAs) is the presence of rich natural resources for which there is a humungous appetite in both the public and private sectors. The SAs are rich in coal, iron ore, bauxite, and chromite (*op. cit.*). Further, 38 percent of all dams lie within the SAs, and 27 out of the 50 major mining districts are part of SA districts, yielding almost 90 percent of the royalty accruals to the central and state governments (Wahi and Bhatia 2018: 36–37). The tribals have a non-commodity view of land so that the land market in SAs are not just imperfect but nonexistent as there are virtually no 'willing sellers' of Adivasi lands (Pal 2017:

162). This necessitates frequent use of land acquisition to access the natural resources.

Sections 41 and 42 of the RFCTLARRAA make a wide range of provisions to address various concerns of the Adivasis, especially that, as far as possible, no land should be acquired in SAs, and even where it is acquired it should be done only as a demonstrable last resort and that no land should be transferred by way of acquisition in the SAs in contravention of any prevailing law or final judgment of a court relating to land transfer, thereby restricting transfer of land to 'outsider' private companies.

These provisions are mere placebos because the rich natural resources of these areas make them 'unsubstitutable' lands, and the neoliberal state is likely to continue acquiring tribal lands to access these resources. It remains to be seen whether the Adivasis consider the major sops of the RFCT-LARRA – higher compensation and R&R – adequate recompense for what they lose culturally when they lose their land.

In conclusion

It may be said that the State had 'compulsions' rather than 'justification' to continue with colonial land acquisition laws in the neoliberal era, because of its indifference towards land governance reforms. The RFCTLARRA has retained some colonial features and the schematic layout of the LAA but has added new reformatory features so that it is more of a blended wine in the old bottle of land acquisition. Overall, the RFCTLARRA has imbued the State with overwhelming powers to control virtually every stage of the acquisition process, so that, despite the reformative processes which empower affected people and restrict abuse of State power, it retains the vitality to compulsorily amass land, the basic raw material for neoliberalism, and is an effective tool to accomplish the neoliberal agenda of the State.

Notes

1 William Pitt the Younger was the youngest British prime minister. The *Pitt's India Act, 1784*, established the dual system of control by the British government and the EIC. The EIC's political functions were differentiated from its commercial activities.
2 All of them were aristocrats – large landholders.
3 This information was obtained from the DoLR.
4 They are as follows: *Definitions*, *Preliminary Investigation* (which included the preliminary notification, hearing of objections, making of declaration, marking out of land, enquiry by Collector, Report by Collector); *Reference to the Court* (which included Award of Court, calculating costs of acquisition, and redetermination of compensation); *Apportionment of Compensation; Payment of Compensation* or deposit of it in court followed by investment of the sum deposited in the court; and *Miscellaneous Provisions*.
5 Based on first-hand information as Secretary of the DoLR 2008–2010
6 Special Leave to Appeal (Civil) No(s). 16366/2011, dated 6 July 2011, along with batch of 36 SLPs

References

Belisle, Lindsay L. 2011. 'Deeds registration and the principle of "Caveat Emptor"', *Amandala*. Retrieved from http/amandala.com.bz/news accessed on 24 January 2013.

Bhattacharya, Rajesh, Snehashish Bhattacharya and Kaveri Gill. 2017. 'The Adivasi land question in the neoliberal era', in Anthony P. D'Costa and Achin Chakraborty (eds.), *The land question, India-State, dispossession and capitalist tradition* (pp. 176–196). New Delhi: Oxford University Press.

Chakravorty, Sanjoy. 2016. 'Land acquisition in India: the political economy of changing the law', *Area Development and Policy*, 1(1): 48–62. doi:10.1080/2379 2949.2016.1160325. Retrieved from https://doi.org/10.1080/23792949.2016.11 60325 accessed on 5 September 2019.

De, Rohit. 2016. 'Constitutional antecedents', in Sujit Choudhry, Madhav Khosla and Pratap Bhanu Mehta (eds.), *The Oxford Handbook of the Indian Constitution* (pp. 17–37). New Delhi: Oxford University Press.

Department of Land Resources. 2014. *Land titling-road map: report of the expert committee*. New Delhi: DOLR, Ministry of Rural Development, Government of India.

Editorial. 2011, 7 September. 'The pot boils-in the line of fire', *The Times of India*, New Delhi.

Goswami, Amlanjyoti. 2016. 'Land acquisition, rehabilitation and resettlement: law, politics and the elusive search foe balance', *Journal of Land and Rural Studies*, 4(1): 3–22.

Greater Noida Industrial Development Authority vs Devendra Kumar & Ors. Special Leave to Appeal (Civil) No(s). 16366/2011, dated 6 July 2011, along with batch of 36 SLPs.

Jain, M.P. 2014. *Outlines of Indian legal and constitutional history*. Gurgaon: LexisNexis.

Jenkins, Rob. 2014. *The federal politics of responding to LARRA: state-level adaptation to, and national efforts to amend, India's right to fair compensation and transparency in Land Acquisition, Rehabilitation and Resettlement Act, 2013* (LARRA). Paper prepared for Berkeley/Kings/IGIDR Conference on The Political Economy of Contemporary India, 20–21 November 2014, Mumbai.

Law Commission of India. 1958. *Tenth report: the law of acquisition and requisitioning of law*. New Delhi: Ministry of Law and Justice, Government of India.

Law Commission of India. 2002. *One hundred eighty second report on amendment of section 6 of the Land Acquisition Act, 1894*. New Delhi: Ministry of Law and Justice, Government of India.

Morris, Sebastian and Ajay Pandey. 2009. 'Land markets in India-Distortions and issues', in *India infrastructure report 2009* (pp. 13–19). New Delhi: Oxford University Press.

Nielson, K.B. and A.G. Nilsen. 2014. 'Law struggles and hegemonic processes in neoliberal India: Gramscian reflections on land acquisition legislation', *Globalizations*. doi:10.1080/14747731.2014.937084. Retrieved from www.researchgate.net/publication/272122251_Law_Struggles_and_Hegemonic_Processes_in_Neo liberal_India_Gramscian_Reflections_on_Land_Acquisition_Legislation accessed on 11 September 2019.

Pal, Malabika. 2017. 'Land acquisition and "Fair Compensation" of the "Project Affected", scrutiny of the law and its interpretation', in Anthony P. D'Costa and

Achin Chakraborty (eds.), *The land question, India – state, dispossession and capitalist tradition* (pp. 151–175). New Delhi: Oxford University Press.

Parwez, Sazzad. 2016. 'A study on special economic zone implicated land acquisition and utilisation', *International Journal of Development and Conflict*, 6: 136–153.

Ramesh, Jairam and Muhammad Ali Khan. 2015. *Legislating for justice: the making of the 2013 land acquisition law*. New Delhi: Oxford University Press.

Ramesh, Jairam and Muhammad Ali Khan. 2016, 2 November. 'Winking at the states', *The Hindu*. Retrieved from www.thehindu.com/opinion/lead/Winking-at-the-States/article16086906.ece accessed on 8 September 2018.

Ray, Sanjukta and Shreemoyee Patra. 2009. 'Evolution of political economy of land acquisition', in *India infrastructure report 2009: land – a critical resource for infrastructure* (pp. 41–43). New Delhi: Oxford University Press.

R.L. Aurora vs. State of U.P., dated 1.12.1961, equivalent citations: 1962 AIR 764, 1962 SCR Supl. (2) 149.

Sarkar, P.K. 2012. *Law of acquisition of land in India*. New Delhi: Eastern Law House.

Sarkar, Runa. 2009. 'Overview of the report', in *India infrastructure report 2009: land – a critical resource for infrastructure* (pp. 1–9). New Delhi: Oxford University Press.

Singh, Sukhpal. 2016. 'Land acquisition in India: an examination of the 2013 act and options', *Journal of Land and Rural Studies*, 4(1): 66–78.

Sinha, Rita. 2010. 'Modernizing India's land records management system', *The Administrator: Journal of the LBSNAA*, 51(1): 59–64.

Smith, Vincent A. 1958. *The oxford history of India*, edited by Percival Spear (4th Edition). New Delhi: Oxford University Press.

Srivastava, R.K. 2014. *Land purchase policy of powergrid*. Unpublished paper. Gurugram: Powergrid Corporation of India Limited.

Standing Committee on Rural Development. 2008–2009. 'Fourteenth Lok Sabha, Thirty-Ninth report. 2008', The *Land Acquisition (amendment) Bill, 2007*, prepared by Department of Land Resources, Ministry of Rural Development, Government of India. New Delhi: Lok Sabha Secretariat.

Standing Committee on Rural Development. 2011–2012. 'Fifteenth Lok Sabha, Thirty-First report, May 2012', The *Land Acquisition, Rehabilitation and Resettlement Bill, 2011*, Ministry of Rural Development (Department of Land Resources). New Delhi: Lok Sabha Secretariat. Retrieved from www.indiaenvironmentportal.org.in/files/file/31st%20Report%20Complete.pdf accessed on 3 September 2019.

State of Madhya Pradesh vs Vishnu Prasad Sharma, AIR 1966 SC 1593.

Steger, Manfred B. and Ravi K. Roy. 2010. *Neoliberalism, a very short introduction*. New York: Oxford University Press.

Wadhwa, D.C. 1989. *Records-of rights-guaranteeing title to land-a preliminary study*. New Delhi: Planning Commission, Government of India.

Wahi, Namita. 2016. 'Property', in Sujit Choudhry, Madhav Khosla and Pratap Bhanu Mehta (eds.), *The oxford handbook of the Indian constitution* (pp. 943–963). New Delhi: Oxford University Press.

Wahi, Namita and Ankit Bhatia. 2018. *The legal regime and political economy of land rights of scheduled tribes in the scheduled areas of India*. New Delhi: Centre for Policy Research.

Wahi, Namita, Ankit Bhatia, Dhruva Gandhi, Shubham Jain, Pallav Shukla and Upasana Chauhan. 2017. *Land acquisition in India: a review of supreme court cases from 1950 to 2016*. New Delhi: Centre for Policy Research. Retrieved from http://cprindia.org/news/5978 accessed on 23 December 2018.

World Bank, Urban Resettlement – Legal Report. 2007, January. Urban resettlement and law-land acquisition, R&R and slum improvement – case studies of Maharashtra (Mumbai), Tamil Nadu (Chennai) and Andhra Pradesh (Hyderabad)-A report submitted to the World Bank for the Urban Resettlement Workshop, Bangkok, Thailand, 10–13 September 2006.

8 Land acquisition for economic development

A comparative analysis of some landmark court judgments of the United States of America and India

Malabika Pal

The use of *eminent domain* for the acquisition of land has been very controversial in the two largest democracies of the world, the United States of America (USA) and India. In India, the issue has come in for greater scrutiny in the context of the neoliberal design of development. The power to acquire land and property was vested in governments with two major limitations: that the power be used only for public use and that just compensation must be paid. In the USA, the Fifth Amendment to the federal Constitution gives the takings clause which states: '(N)or shall private property be taken for public use without just compensation'. It is through the interpretation of the terms that the scope of the power has expanded over the years. One major contentious issue is acquisition of land and property on behalf of the private sector for economic development or what has been termed 'economic development takings'. This has come into focus after the landmark case of *Kelo vs. City of New London*[1] (*Kelo*) decided by the US Supreme Court. In India, the Land Ordinance promulgated on 31 December 2014 was seen as a determined attempt to alter the land acquisition legislation to legitimise the large-scale acquisition of land for 'private entities' for the 'public purpose' of economic development.

There has been no guidance in the Constitution regarding the specific meanings of the two terms 'public purpose' and 'just compensation' both in India and the USA. Courts and legal scholars have spent enormous efforts in the USA to interpret the two terms. In India, the terms have been used to suit the development paradigm of the time. In the Nehruvian period, State-led industrialisation was the public purpose for which large tracts of land were acquired using the *Land Acquisition Act, 1894* (LAA). The dispossession that resulted was termed 'development – induced-displacement'. In recent decades, using the neoliberal economic model, land acquisition takes place for purposes which may involve just transfer of land from one private party to another under the garb of development.

The scrutiny of the issue is important since development is a legitimate goal of the State. In a detailed book on *Kelo*, Somin (2015) has gone into the historical and constitutional background of the use of eminent domain and concluded that there should be a ban on economic development takings. In this context, it is important to analyse what interpretation the courts have employed. While there have been thorough analyses of the reasoning of landmark decisions regarding economic development takings in the USA, there has hardly been any examination of the reasoning in Indian court judgments.[2] While in the USA the justification of public use is subject to judicial review, in India after the 44th Constitutional Amendment, the only restraint that remained was Article 6 (3) of the LAA whereby any declaration of the government that the land was required for public purpose is conclusive evidence unless shown to be a colourable exercise of power.

This chapter begins with some important developments in India and the USA to provide a background to the interpretation of 'public purpose' as economic development. This is followed by a section which goes deeper into the nature of the neoliberal economic development paradigm adopted in India which has focussed mainly on efficiency and ignored equity, inclusiveness, and sustainability. The next section gives the influential standard in takings discourse by Frank Michelman (1967) which has the unique feature of incorporating 'justice' along with efficiency. The next section examines a few landmark judgments from the two countries to see how the reasoning regarding economic development takings has evolved. In the United States, *Berman vs. Parker*[3] (*Berman*) is said to have opened the 'floodgates of economic development takings'.[4] In India, the successive constitutional amendments and landmark judgments such as *Somavanti and Others vs. State of Punjab and Others (And connected Petitions)*[5] (*Somavanti*) have created conditions favourable for large-scale acquisitions for economic development. The more recent judgment in *Kedar Nath Yadav vs. State of West Bengal and Ors*[6] (hereafter Singur Case) merits a separate section to highlight the significant position taken with regard to the question of public purpose. This is followed by a comparative analysis and the relevance of Michelman's framework. A final section gives the concluding remarks.

Judicial and legislative views on compulsory acquisition for economic development

The decision in *Kelo* upholding the use of eminent domain for the purpose of economic development was important because just a year earlier in the landmark ruling in *County of Wayne vs. Edward Hathcock*[7] (*Hathcock*), the Supreme Court of Michigan had reversed the oft-cited case of *Poletown Neighborhood Council vs. City of Detroit*[8] (*Poletown*) on the ground that the economic development justification does not serve a valid public purpose. The majority opinion in *Kelo* was milder, with suggestions for 'a national debate' or 'state legislation' coming from Justice John Paul Stevens. Sharp dissents were put forward by two of the judges, Justice Sandra Day O'Connor and Justice Clarence Thomas. The reasoning employed in the judgment was scrutinised, and there was huge 'political backlash'. According to Somin (2015: 60): 'In the ten years prior to Kelo, four state Supreme Courts – Illinois, Michigan, Montana, and South Carolina (which reaffirmed its earlier stance) – held that their state constitutions forbade economic development takings that transfer property to private parties'. The post-*Kelo* legislations vary in their effectiveness in restricting the power of eminent domain. Somin concludes that 'the *Kelo* decision was a major error that the Court should eventually overrule' (Somin 2015: 4). There have been calls for a constitutional amendment to ban economic development takings altogether (Cohen 2006).

In India, there was large-scale acquisition under the *Special Economic Zones Act, 2005*, which allowed compulsory acquisition of land for the setting up of industries in enclaves. However, this was stalled because of fierce opposition by farmers' organizations, civil society, and particularly the electoral debacle of the left-front government in West Bengal. Thereafter, the focus shifted to equity or fairness, with policies being drafted at the national level to make rehabilitation legally enforceable. Just a few months before the general elections in 2014, new legislation entitled the *Right to Fair Compensation and Transparency in Land Acquisition, Rehabilitation and Resettlement Act, 2013* (RFCTLARR) was notified. It is interesting to note that during the process of consultations, the Standing Committee of Parliament in its Report on Rural Development dated 17 May 2012 had recommended that the government should refuse to acquire land for private parties (Ramesh and Khan 2015: 4). The Act brought in many new provisions, notable among which were the consent clause by which 70 percent consent was required for purely public projects and 80 percent for public-private partnership (PPP) projects. An elaborate process of social impact assessment (SIA) was specified which included consultation with the affected land losers. It was explicitly incorporated that Urgency Clause was to be used only for national defence and in cases of natural calamities (section 40 (1) of the RFCTLARR). The compensation amount was increased to four times the market value in rural areas and twice the market value in urban areas along with enhanced solatium taking into account the compulsory nature of the acquisition.

On 31 December 2014, the Land Ordinance was promulgated which included four broad categories – industrial corridors, infrastructure, rural infrastructure, and affordable housing along with national defence for which consent and SIA would not be needed, effectively putting them under the category of the Urgency Clause. The unwritten justification was that the urgency route was imperative for economic development to occur. The broader 'private entity' was substituted in place of 'private company' throughout the Act.[9] Although the bill incorporating these and other changes was passed in the Lok Sabha in the budget session in February 2015, it failed to gather the requisite numbers in the Rajya Sabha. Thereafter, the Ordinance was re-promulgated twice, and a second bill with some further changes was introduced in Parliament again in the monsoon session and sent to a Joint Parliamentary Committee. When it became difficult to get political muster to pass the bill, most of the contentious provisions were deleted and the bill deferred to the winter session of Parliament. There was a call to the states to incorporate provisions of the Land Ordinance, which later led to competitive dilution in state land acquisition laws.[10]

This entire sequence of events has raised important issues: the attempt to expand the scope of eminent domain beyond recognition through legislation in the name of economic development; facilitate the urgency route for large-scale acquisition without consent, SIA, and consultation; and expand the use of the coercive power of compulsory acquisition on behalf of the private sector. The process of economic development involves changes in land use, and conditions need to be made such that a land market develops which will channel the resource to its highest valued use.

Neoliberal context of land acquisition for economic development

Since the mid-1980s, India has adopted what has been termed 'neoliberalism' which broadly refers to an economic model built upon the classical liberal ideal of the self-regulating market. The public policies that characterise this paradigm include deregulation of the market, liberalisation of trade and industry, and privatisation of State-owned enterprises.[11] Although there is a shared belief across the globe on the power of self-regulating markets to create a better world, neoliberalism has been adapted in different countries according to their particular social contexts.

The nature of neoliberal economic development adopted in India has been described in a lucid way by Bhaduri (2009). He emphatically points out that economic growth must be seen as an outcome of employment growth. In contrast, three features, among many, militate against this. One, the State has abdicated its role as a key player in industrialisation. Federal and state governments, of all political hues, have been extending various privileges to large corporations, mostly private, as incentives for promoting corporate-led development. The composition of output produced is oriented towards the rich minority. Two, the increasing openness of the Indian economy to international finance and capital flows rather than to trade in goods and services has the effect that the foreign exchange reserves are mostly due to accumulated portfolio investments and short-term capital inflows from various financial institutions. Finally, the fiscal restraint adopted by the State to comply with the interests of financial markets has adverse consequences for expanding public expenditures in basic health, education, and public distribution. This, coupled with the low capacity of industries to generate employment, leads to widening inequality.

The most visible aspect of this process of industrialisation is land acquisition by the State for the 'public purpose' under the major heads of mining, industry, and special economic zones (SEZs). Most of those displaced by force are Adivasis or tribals, who constitute 40 percent of those displaced in the name of development, although they comprise only 8 percent of the population. Bhaduri (2009: 37) writes: 'The public purpose such violence serves is handing over to private corporations the possession of the iron-rich land in Chhattisgarh, Jharkhand and Madhya Pradesh, the bauxite-rich land of Orissa, the diamond mines in Bastar and so forth'. The State also provides supporting infrastructure to these corporations at public cost by providing cheap sources of water, transport, and tax concessions. This leads to rapid growth of corporate profit and wealth. Even the common lands that traditionally provided supplementary income to the poor are systematically encroached upon. Bhaduri contends that this forcible acquisition of land and dispossession leads to internal colonisation of the poor. The poorest face the terror that is 'development'.

Incorporating both efficiency and equity considerations

The costs of the neoliberal strategy of development have led to coercive redistribution which needs to be reversed. The dispossession that has resulted in this phase of India's economic growth has been far less developmental since they are mostly for real estate compared with the earlier Nehruvian state which acquired land for public-sector industrial projects that generated high-quality employment and had ancillary linkages and generated revenue for the State.[12]

One framework that can be useful in this context is the standard provided by Michelman (1967). To bring in justice into the cost-benefit calculation of projects, he introduced 'demoralization costs' – property ownership gives a sense of security and people can then invest for future enjoyment of product. Any uncertainty involving redistributions destroys this sense of security and causes demoralisation. These are costs which are psychological in nature and distinct from the usual economic costs incorporated in the cost-benefit calculation. Michelman distinguishes among three factors: efficiency gains, demoralising costs, and settlement costs. Efficiency gains (B – C) are:

> The excess of benefits produced by a measure over losses inflicted by it, where benefits are measured by the total number of dollars which prospective gainers would be willing to pay to secure adoption, and losses are measured by the total number of dollars which prospective losers would insist on as the price of agreeing to adoption.

Demoralisation costs (D) consist of:

> The total of (1) the dollar value necessary to offset disutilities which accrue to losers and their sympathizers specifically from the realization that no compensation is offered, and (2) the present capitalized value

of lost future production (reflecting either impaired incentives or social unrest) caused by demoralization of uncompensated losers, their sympathizers, and other observers disturbed by the thought that they themselves may be subjected to similar treatment on some other occasion.

(Michelman 1967: 1214)

Settlement costs (S) are 'measured by the dollar value of time, effort, and resources which would be required in order to reach compensation settlements adequate to avoid demoralization costs'. According to Michelman, positive efficiency gains (B − C > 0) are not enough to go forward with a project; settlement costs and demoralisation costs also need to be taken into account. The standard helps to answer two questions: one, which projects should go forward and two, when should compensation be paid to losers. A project for which the dollar benefits exceed costs should not be adopted if the net efficiency gains are less than both demoralisation costs (D) and settlement costs (S). Symbolically, a project should not be undertaken if (B − C) < min (D, S). Regarding compensation, we first consider those projects which pass the test, that is, for which (B − C) > min (D − S). For these, the lower of the two, D or S, should be incurred. That is, if D > S, then compensation should be paid but if S > D, then compensation should not be paid.

USA and Indian court judgments in economic development takings cases

The objective of this section is to examine the reasoning employed in some landmark judgments to bring out certain common threads such as justification of public purpose when the actual interest involved is a private one, the end justifies the means, justification of bolstering the economy either through an increase in employment or tax revenue, and distribution of the burden of development. Since the verdict in *Kelo*, the discourse in the two countries has been very different, but in both countries, judicial deference to legislative determination has meant that it is only through legislation that a more equitable framework can be reached.[13]

In *Berman*, the US Supreme Court in a unanimous decision, delivered by Justice William O. Douglas, upheld the use of eminent domain for a comprehensive redevelopment plan covering a large area of the District of Columbia in the 1950s. It was held to satisfy public purpose since there was widespread blight which was injurious to public health, safety, morals, and welfare. The appellant had argued that his property was not blighted by any standards to which the Court reasoned: 'community development programs need not, by force of the Constitution, be on a piecemeal basis – lot by lot, building by building'. It was within the authority of the Congress to decide what values it thinks are in the public interest and could authorise the lease or resale to private parties. As for the justice part, the Court stated:

'The rights of these property owners are satisfied when they receive the just compensation which the Fifth Amendment exacts as the price of the taking'.

In the 5–2 decision in *Poletown*, many of the important principles enunciated in *Berman* came in for close scrutiny. The Detroit Economic Development Corporation proposed to acquire a large tract of land to be given to General Motors Corporation (GMC) for the establishment of an assembly plant. Under the *Economic Development Corporation Act*, the state of Michigan was empowered to assist industries and commercial enterprises to strengthen and revitalise the economy in the early 1980s. The plaintiffs, who consisted of a neighbourhood organisation that would lose 4,200 homes, challenged 'the constitutionality of using the power of eminent domain to condemn one person's property to convey it to another private person in order to bolster the economy'. They argued that whatever incidental benefits may accrue to the public, the primary benefit from assembling land for GMC would be as profits to the corporation and thus did not constitute a public use.

The Supreme Court of Michigan upheld the acquisition by relying on the *Berman* reasoning that when a legislature speaks, the public interest has been declared as 'well-nigh conclusive' and that the right of an individual was secondary to general benefit. The benefit to be received by the municipality was a 'clear and significant one' in terms of alleviating unemployment and revitalising the economic base of the community. Justice Fitzgerald in his dissent highlighted that Michigan cases show a 'limited construction' of the term 'public use' for condemnation purposes and reasoned that it cannot be such that the evolution has 'eroded our historic protection against the taking of private property for private use to the degree sanctioned by this Court's decision today'. He argued:

> The decision that the prospect of increased employment, tax revenue, and general economic stimulation makes a taking of private property for transfer to another private party sufficiently 'public' to authorize the use of eminent domain means that there is virtually no limit to the use of condemnation to aid private businesses.

Further, the condemnation placed the 'burden of aiding industry on the few, who are likely to have limited power to protect themselves from the excesses of legislative enthusiasm for the promotion of industry'. Justice Ryan in his dissent attested to this by stating that the decision disregarded the rights of the few in pursuit of the 'disastrous philosophy that the end justifies the means'. The 'quick take' statute of Michigan was used because of the deadline of 1 May 1981 imposed by GMC, and this did not 'afford adequate time for sufficient consideration of the complex constitutional issues'. Although the projected public cost of preparing the site for GMC was more than $200 million, the site was sold to GMC for $8 million along with a 12-year tax abatement clause. In his opinion, 'the unintended jurisprudential mischief' which had been done, if not rectified, would have 'echoing effects' far beyond the case at hand. The unwavering rule of the state for over a century was that the power of eminent domain could be used for private corporations only in cases falling within 'the instrumentality of commerce exception'. These were: (1) public necessity of the extreme sort – those private enterprises generating public benefits whose very existence depends on the assembly of land by government coordination. The production of automobiles does generate public benefits, but it cannot be argued that the existence of a new assembly plant for GMC requires the use of eminent domain; (2) continuing accountability to the public; and (3) when the land is selected using criteria not in the interest of the private corporation but in public interest. In the case of GMC, the factors that determined the location were matters of private significance. He thus concluded that with this case 'the Court has subordinated a constitutional right to private corporate interests'.

In the oft-cited case of *Hawaii Housing Authority vs. Midkiff*[14] (*Midkiff*), the US Supreme Court unanimously upheld the acquisition in the mid-1980s, relying heavily on *Berman*. In *Midkiff*, the attempt was to reduce the perceived social and economic evils of land oligopoly and thus was taken as a valid public use. To the question using eminent domain for transfer of property for private use, it was argued that the Court had long ago rejected the literal requirement that property should be put for use by the general public.

After 23 years, the Supreme Court of Michigan reversed its verdict in *Poletown*, the case that had been regarded as a 'visible symbol of the abuse of eminent domain' (Somin 2004) and quashed the acquisition in *Hathcock*. Reversing the judgment in *Poletown*, the majority held: 'In this case, Wayne County intends to transfer the condemned properties to private parties in a manner wholly inconsistent with the common understanding of "public use" at the time our Constitution was ratified'. The majority reasoned that the three distinguishing factors that Justice Ryan had highlighted in *Poletown* described the understanding that prevailed in Michigan's pre-1963 eminent domain jurisprudence, and that must have been the meaning when the Constitution was ratified. Apart from *Poletown*, Wayne County could not find a single case in which it was held that a vague economic benefit accruing from a private-profit maximizing enterprise is a 'public use'. It added: 'To justify the exercise of eminent domain solely on the basis of the fact that the use of that property by a private entity seeking its own profit might contribute to the economy's health is to render impotent our constitutional limitations on the government's power of eminent domain'.

Although the reversal of *Poletown* was hailed as the landmark, shortly after, the US Supreme Court held in *Kelo* that the use of eminent domain for the acquisition of private property to increase tax revenue and to revitalise an economically distressed city constitutes 'public use' within the takings clause. The Supreme Court of Connecticut, which relied heavily on *Berman* and *Midkiff* had ruled in favour of the city of New London's economic development plan which included a $300 million plant by the pharmaceutical giant Pfizer. Nine of the 15 privately owned condemned properties brought an action claiming that the taking violated the Fifth Amendment's public use restraint. The majority held that the city had invoked a state statute that specifically authorised the use of eminent domain to promote economic development; that the city was trying to coordinate various commercial, residential, and recreational uses of land with the aim of creating greater value; and that the carefully formulated plan carried out in a comprehensive manner would provide appreciable benefits to the community.

They also held that promoting economic development was a traditional and long-accepted function of the government, and there was no way of distinguishing economic development from other public purposes. Even though conditions of blight were not present, the area was 'sufficiently distressed' to justify a programme of economic rejuvenation. The US Supreme Court did not require a 'reasonable certainty' that public benefits would actually materialise and refused to 'second-guess' as to which particular lands were required for plan implementation. Finally, it argued that the Fifth Amendment did not constrain the states from placing further restrictions on the exercise of takings power. It relied on *Berman* in its ruling that the challenges of individual owners must be resolved not on an individual basis but in light of the entire plan.

Justice Sandra Day O'Connor, who was joined in her dissent by Justice Antonin Scalia, the Chief Justice, and Justice Clarence Thomas, gave a sterling dissent which became the basis of an enormous amount of debate.[15] She began by quoting Justice Chase who in *Calder v Bull*[16] decided just after the Bill of Rights was ratified, stated:

[A] law that takes property from A and gives it to B; It is against all reason and justice, for a people to entrust a Legislature with such powers; and, therefore, it cannot be presumed that they have done it.

She went on to argue that the Court has abandoned this long-held limitation and under the banner of economic development made all private property vulnerable to a taking provided they can be shown to yield greater benefits. If the incidental public benefits are considered enough, it effectively means that the 'for public use' part of the takings clause no longer exists. The petitioners' contention was one of principle: that the property can be taken for building roads or railroads but not for private use and profit making. She argued that the case at hand presents a fundamental question: 'Are economic development takings constitutional?' Her conclusion was that they are not. She argued that the takings in *Berman* and *Midkiff* removed harm and thereby directly benefitted the public even though they were turned over to private parties. She argued:

The trouble with economic development takings is that private benefit and incidental public benefit are, by definition, merged and mutually reinforcing. In this case, for example, any boon for Pfizer or the plan's developer is difficult to disaggregate from the promised public gains in taxes and jobs.

Implicit in the Court's decision is that eminent domain may be used to upgrade property which means that the 'specter of condemnation hangs over all property'.

Justice Clarence Thomas in his dissent argued that the change in phraseology has occurred so that 'a costly urban renewal project whose stated purpose is a vague promise of new jobs and increased tax revenue' and which is agreeable to the private corporation Pfizer is approved as 'public use'. This erases the Public Use Clause from the Constitution, and that is something the Court cannot do given that these were originally ratified liberties. After going through a series of cases, he argued that the questionable application of *Berman* and *Midkiff* shows that the 'public purpose' standard is 'not susceptible to principled application'. He concluded: 'Allowing the government to take property solely for public purposes is bad enough, but extending the concept of public purpose to encompass any economically beneficial goal guarantees that these losses will fall disproportionately on poor communities'.

This dissent of Justice Thomas is very significant for India since the neoliberal design of development has meant that costs have fallen disproportionately on the poor. One important reason is the valuation method arising out of the colonial LAA followed for 119 years, with two amendments in 1962 and 1984, to suit successive models of development. It is no wonder that the relevant sections 23 and 24 have been the most contentious. Section 23 stated that, in determining the amount of compensation to be awarded for land acquired under the LAA, the Court must take into consideration the market value of the land on the date of publication of notification under section 4(1), the damages sustained on account of standing crops or trees on the land, and severance of the land from the land loser's other lands or because the acquisition injuriously affects the land loser's other property at the time of the Collector's taking possession of the land. Section 24 specified that the Court shall not take into account the degree of urgency which led to the acquisition, any disinclination of the land loser, and any post-acquisition increase in the value of the land likely caused by changed land use.

The Indian scenario between the 1930s and 1980s

The interpretation of these clauses by the courts has been crucial for determining the final value of land.[17] One landmark case decided in pre-independent India (in 1939) in which the reasoning has been discussed in detail is *Sri Raja Vyricherla Narayana vs. The Revenue Divisional Officer*.[18] We discuss this case in detail to highlight that the interpretations in colonial times of various aspects of sections 23 and 24 adopted without much change in post-independent India. This case concerned an appeal regarding the appropriate quantum of compensation for the acquisition by the Vizagapatnam Harbour Authority of his land known as Lova Gardens adjoining the harbour. These gardens were formed by a valley, the upper portion of which consisted of a shallow basin in the hills which formed a catchment area of a spring of water yielding even in the dry season an average flow of 50,000 gallons a day of excellent drinking water. Started in 1920, the construction of the Vizagapatnam Harbour had made considerable progress by 1926, with the possibility of it being ready for opening in 1929. The Harbour Authority allocated the harbour site to oil companies and other industrial concerns. On 5 January 1929, the appellant filed his compensation claim, saying that the potentiality of Lova Gardens as a building site would be destroyed if he were deprived of the spring. He claimed Rs. 2,50,000 on account of 'damages sustained by severance', Rs. 1,200 per acre for the land, and Rs. 16,050 as the value of the masonry structures, roads, and trees on the land; the total claim amounted to Rs. 3,96,730. The Land Acquisition Officer on 18 January 1929 awarded Rs. 17,745–1–3, including 15 percent solatium as prescribed by section 23(2) of the LAA. For the spring, he awarded Rs.5,000; for the trees and buildings, Rs. 4,493; and the land at partly Rs.50 per acre and partly at Rs.300 per acre.

The appellant argued before the subordinate judge of Vizagapatnam that the matter should be referred to the Court for determination under section 18 of the LAA, claiming that the spring could be used by the appellant or as a source of water supply for the Harbour Authority or the oil companies and others carrying on their business in the harbour area. The judge found that, as of 13 February 1928, the value to the vendor of the potentiality of his land could be assessed even though there were no other potential purchasers other than the Harbour Authority. The contingent possibility of the user had to be taken into account and not the realised possibility as the basis of valuation, and the use to which the acquiring authority has actually put the property would be strong evidence to show that property acquired could be put to such use by the owner on the date of acquisition. He accordingly made a total award of Rs. 120,750, including solatium and interest. The respondent Harbour Authority appealed to the Madras High Court. Wadsworth and Stodart JJ allowed the appeal on 4 May 1937 on the grounds that the owner on his own could not have made profitable use of the land and carry out a water supply scheme in the malaria-infested area, and the acquisition was meant to make the area fit for development. There could not be any value for the special adaptability of the land to supply drinking water to the Harbour Authority or anyone else, and the value of the spring arose entirely because of the anti-malarial scheme carried out by the Harbour Authority. The award of the Land Acquisition officer was restored.

The landowner then appealed to His Majesty in–Council. Justice Romer stated:

> The general principles for determining compensation that are specified in these sections differ in no material respect from those upon which

compensation was awarded in this country under the *Land Clauses Act, 1845*, before the coming into operation of the Acquisition of Land (Assessment of Compensation) Act of 1919. . . compensation must be determined, therefore, by reference to the price which a willing vendor might reasonably expect to obtain from a willing purchaser.

Any sentimental value far in excess of its 'market value' should not be taken into account to increase the compensation.

Justice Romer, in his detailed discussion of what constitutes 'the market price' in section 23 of the LAA, argued that unlike commodities, there is no market for land and therefore the prices of similar plots cannot be ascertained. Thus, prices quoted in past deals for land of similar quality and position could be taken as the 'market value'. If the land possesses some unusual or unique features, then there will be no market value to guide them and it will have to be determined as best as possible from the materials before the Court. He cautioned:

> [I]t is equally plain, however, that the land must not be valued as though it had already been built upon, a proposition that is embodied in Section 24 (5) of the Act and is sometimes expressed by saying that it is the possibilities of the land and not its realised possibilities that must be taken into consideration.

The total price on 13 February 1928 would be Rs. 40,000, which along with solatium amounts to Rs.46,000.

The determination of the value of land is fraught with contention because of the variation in valuation which can be the case even when the same method is used throughout in a single case of successive litigation. In the case of *Prithiviraj Taneja vs. State of Madhya Pradesh and Others*,[19] the Land Acquisition officer awarded Rs.7,616, including solatium; the District Judge enhanced it to Rs.32,285 plus 6 percent interest. The owner petitioned the land should be valued at Rs.10 per square yard before the Madhya Pradesh High Court which valued it at Rs.1 per square yard and, adding loss of earnings, solatium, and interest, the award amounted to Rs.88,381. In the Supreme Court of India, the owner's counsel argued that the small plots adjoining the land had been sold for Rs.8 and Rs.9 per square yard. The Supreme Court, however, held that Rs.1 represented a 'fair market value' for the land in dispute and stated: 'We agree with the High Court that the price paid for small plots of land cannot provide a safe criterion for determining the amount of compensation for a vast area of land'. Dismissing the appeal, it concluded:

> There is an element of *guess-work* inherent in most cases involving determination of market value of the acquired land. But this in the very nature of things cannot be helped. The essential thing is to keep in view the relevant factors prescribed by the Act. If the judgment of the High

Court reveals that it has taken into consideration the relevant factors, the assessment of the market value of the acquired land should not be disturbed.

[Italics added]

We note that it is also because of the guess work involved that the compensation awarded can be fixed at a level far below what the land loser would be happy to accept.

Although the valuation of land has been the most contentious issue, there have been other points of contention. In *R L Arora vs. The State of Uttar Pradesh*,[20] the petitioner owned land in the village of Nauraiya Khera in the district of Kanpur, Uttar Pradesh, out of which nine acres were sought to be acquired through eminent domain for an industrialist. Later, the Supreme Court quashed the acquisition[21] on the grounds of inadequate consideration of how the product would be sufficiently useful to the public to justify the acquisition for a company. In 1962, by amending sections 40, 41, and 7 of the LAA, impediments were removed which had come in the way of the earlier acquisition, and the validity of the acquisition was upheld.

The stage for large-scale acquisition without much judicial scrutiny was set when the Supreme Court of India stated in *Somavanti*:

Now whether in a particular case the purpose for which land is needed is a public purpose or not is for the State Government to be satisfied about. If the purpose for which the land is being acquired by the State is within the legislative competence of the State the declaration of the Government will be final subject, however, to one exception. That exception is that if there is a colourable exercise of power the declaration will be open to challenge at the instance of the aggrieved party.

The majority opinion was that the declaration made by the government under the *Land Acquisition Act, 1894*, was conclusive evidence of public purpose and open for judicial scrutiny. The allegation of contravening Art.14 was also dismissed on this ground. It was further argued by the majority that the expression 'partly out of public revenues' in the proviso section 6(1) of the Act did not necessarily mean that the State's contribution must be substantial and would depend upon the facts of the case and therefore was not a colourable exercise of power. Justice Subba Rao, in his dissent argued that the interpretation 'wholly or partly' could only mean substantial part of the estimated compensation and Rs. 100 in this case cannot be taken as a substantial part.

In *Indrajit C Parekh of Ahmedabad . . . vs. State of Gujarat And Ors*,[22] the acquisition of 5,632 square yards of private land for setting up dispensaries for the Employees State Insurance Scheme, Ahmedabad was upheld by the Supreme Court of India and the contribution of Rs. 1 by the state of Gujarat fulfilled the public purpose requirement. The allegation of colourable exercise of power was quashed on the grounds that a nominal contribution was sufficient.

Continuity of judicial precedents in the neoliberal era

Two trend-setting cases – of 2003 and 2008 – are discussed here to show the continuity of reasoning from the 1960s and 1980s.

In *Pratibha Nema & Ors vs. State of M.P. & Ors*,[23] the acquisition of 73.3 hectares of dry land located in Rangwasa village of the Indore District to establish a diamond park became the contentious issue. The Industries Department and/or Madhya Pradesh Audyogik Kendra Vikas Nigam Ltd. would add another 44.8 hectares of government land and would then allot the same to private industrial units for setting up diamond-cutting and polishing units with modern technology. It was expected that 'prestigious exporters from India as well as foreign countries were likely to establish their units in this park which would generate good deal of foreign exchange and create employment potential'. The petitioners argued that the acquisition of land was for 'the Company and not for public purpose' and hence was a colourable exercise of power. This was quashed by the Supreme Court on the grounds that 'the acquisition was thought of with the earnest objective to achieve industrial growth of the state in public interest'.

Another landmark case for acquisition for economic development was *Sooraram*[24] in which the allegation was that the Government of Andhra Pradesh sought to acquire land to develop a 'Financial District and Allied Projects' 'with mala fide intention and oblique motive to transfer valuable land of small farmers to a foreign company and few selected persons with vested interest'. It was, therefore, a colourable exercise of power. The attempt to use the Urgency Clause was quashed by the High Court of Andhra Pradesh as being 'illegal, unlawful and unwarranted'. The appellants argued that in the era of globalisation, if foreign companies wanted to set up business, eminent domain must not be used to facilitate their establishment.

In the Supreme Court, some American cases, including *Berman*, *Midkiff*, and *Kelo*, were cited as precedents. Pointing out that the present case was similar to *Kelo*, the Supreme Court relied on the majority reasoning and argued that when the 'legislature's purpose is legitimate and the means not irrational' the courts cannot debate about the 'wisdom of socio-economic legislation'. Also, the public ends can be better served 'through an agency of private enterprise'. A series of Indian cases[25] were referred to, to finally conclude that what is important is whether the acquisition is for the general interest of the community as opposed to the private interest of an individual. It held: 'If the project taken as a whole is an attempt in the direction of bringing foreign exchange, generating employment opportunities and securing economic benefits to the State and the public at large, it will serve public purpose'. However, it added that not all cases are above judicial scrutiny.

The landmark interpretation of public purpose in the Singur judgment

In a significant development, the Supreme Court of India quashed the acquisition of land in Singur decided on 31 August 2016. Tata Motors Ltd. (TML) had proposed to build a factory on 1,000 acres of land which was acquired by the West Bengal Industrial Development Corporation and would employ 1,800 people through direct employment and 4,700 employees through vendors and service providers, thus serving the public purpose of alleviating the unemployment problem in the state.[26] However, this argument did not hold up to judicial scrutiny because it was held that after the 1984 Amendment to the LAA, acquisition of land for a company is no longer covered under 'public purpose' under section 3(f)(viii) but would have to be done under Part VII. Also, it was held by Justice Gowda that many objections were filed by the owners under section 4 of the LAA. These should have been considered under section 5-A (2) of the Act. That was not done by the Land Acquisition collector. Thus, the acquisition was quashed on grounds of procedure, and the Supreme Court of India ordered that the land be returned to the original owners within ten weeks of the judgment.

Regarding whether the acquisition satisfied the grounds of public purpose, Justice Mishra relied heavily on *Sooraram* to justify that the acquisition served the public purpose of economic development. However, Justice Gowda argued against the conclusion reached by the Calcutta High Court that it was for a public purpose. Apart from the unanimous verdict of quashing the acquisition, this challenge to the justification of public purpose should constitute a landmark judicial intervention even though the final verdict was not based on it.

A comparative analysis

A comparison of the two sets of cases show that while in the United States we find a weakening of the stand expressed in *Berman*, in India judicial support for acquisition for economic development has been as strong as it was in *Somavanti*. The Singur judgment seems to have turned the trend somewhat but has gone largely unnoticed, perhaps because it remains one of the lone voices[27] against the neoliberal trend of expansively defining public purpose.

While the decision was unanimous in *Berman* and none of the principles enunciated were explained in detail, in *Kelo* it was a close 5–4 verdict arrived at after detailed reasoning by both the majority and the dissenters. Further, even within the majority, Justice Kennedy stated that a 'demanding level of scrutiny' was required to guard against 'the risk of undetected impermissible favouritism of private parties'. In India, however, the judgments have been unequivocally in favour of acquisition for economic development, and even transfer to private parties had been made easy with the interpretation of the

1984 Amendment to the LAA that even a paltry sum of one rupee would suffice the 'public use' requirement. The foregoing analysis attests to the argument that the Indian courts have applied a more liberal interpretation than their American counterparts (Ramesh and Khan 2015: 26).

The purported efficiency rationale often given by the State and held in deference by the judiciary is that the act of acquisition often involves transfer to a higher valued use. In this case, the 'value' involved was determined by the neoliberal paradigm of development. Since the land losers are being paid the market price and economic development will ultimately benefit all, the transfer is said to be justified on equity grounds as well. It is sometimes emphasised that the economic benefits are 'clear and significant' (*Poletown*) or that the area was 'sufficiently distressed' (*Kelo*) without providing any definitive benchmark. In *Berman*, evidence was presented that 64.3 percent of the buildings in Area B were beyond repair. To the allegation that the public benefit mentioned in *Kelo* was 'vague', the US Supreme Court held that as long as the legislature had made the determination of benefits, it was out of judicial scrutiny. The costs of acquisition have been ignored by courts in both countries. Somin (2015: 78–79) notes how the economic harm imposed by the General Motors plant in Detroit far outweighed the economic benefits.

We find that *Berman* and *Midkiff* were taken as precedents in *Kelo* as well as in *Sooraram*, although the contexts were very different. There was similarity between *Hathcock* and *Sooraram*, since in both an effort was being made to attract domestic and international investors to the region to enhance employment and tax revenue. However, the outcomes in both the cases were different. While in *Hathcock* the majority quashed the acquisition, in *Sooraram* the acquisition was upheld. In fact, in *Sooraram*, there was no mention of *Hathcock*, but the majority opinion in *Kelo* was quoted.

Also, Justice Stevens had argued in *Kelo* that the risk of favouritism in economic development takings is minimized so long as it is part of an integrated plan. By this logic, the petitioners' allegation of discrimination in *Somavanti* would hold more weight than what the Supreme Court of India was willing to concede. In *Berman*, the court had held that although the plaintiff's property was not blighted, economic development projects could not be implemented on a piecemeal basis but would have to be conceived of as a whole. This reasoning, which was relied upon in *Kelo* and *Sooraram*, would effectively preclude any owner from raising objections if his land falls within a designated comprehensive plan even if his land did not obstruct its execution. In both the countries one finds that those who have to part with their lands are often those with less political and economic strength.

Among the cases analysed, it was only in *Hathcock* that the majority held that economic development takings do not pass constitutional muster. In India, at the time of ratification of the Constitution, the right to property was a fundamental right. Successive Constitutional Amendments took away the status and eventually only Article 300A protects it by the provision that property cannot be taken away without the sanction of law. In the USA, the 'original intent' and 'original meaning' of the takings clause have been differentiated; the former refers to the interpretation of the Constitution in accordance with the intentions of the framers, and the latter relates to interpretation according to public understanding at the time of framing (Somin 2015: 63–65). In India, there is almost complete silence on the need to bring in constitutional limitations on economic development acquisitions. Exceptionally, Agarwal (2014) draws attention to the 'original will' of 'India's founding fathers' by putting together the constitutional debates that preceded the ratification of the Constitution.

Incorporation of Michelman's framework

Neoliberal design of economic development enhances demoralisation through the six sources outlined by Michelman, namely: (1) when the efficiency gains are doubtful and indicate unprincipled redistribution; (2) when losers feel they are having to take a disproportionate share of the burden; (3) when settlement costs are low but compensation is not forthcoming; (4) when the loss is unlikely to be recouped by benefits linked to the project; (5) when the losers cannot expect to gain in the future from similar projects; and (6) when they lack the political influence to do so (Michelman 1967: 1217–1218).

An examination of the reasoning employed by the majority in the cases reveals that, except in *Hathcock* and Singur, all concentrated on the efficiency aspect only. The concept of economic development is much broader than just increase in tax revenue, generating employment, or incidental economic benefits which are captured by the narrower term of economic growth. Since the public purpose of economic development mostly has been left to legislative discretion, it becomes imperative for the legislature to incorporate a stricter welfare standard for economic development takings to be perceived as legitimate. Under the Michelman standard, first, those acquisitions which are undertaken on behalf of private enterprises potentially generating incidental public benefits would get ruled out because of the huge demoralisation costs they would generate.

Second, it is important to distinguish strategic holdouts and those who genuinely do not want to part with their property at any price. Small successful businesses may find relocation unprofitable. Often some parcels are left out of the purview of acquisition because of the influential nature of the owners as with the Italian Dramatic Club in Fort Trumball (*Kelo*) and actress Smt. Vijay Nirmala (*Sooraram*), while the land belonging to weaker sections is attached for acquisition, creating demoralisation because of the feeling that economic development disproportionately harms those less influential.

Third, the calculation of settlement costs would ensure that those are factored in while considering the viability of any enterprise. Estimates of displaced people who were not rehabilitated in India in the post-independence period (1947–2000) are around 50 million (Fernandes 2004), for the USA (1953–1980) about three million (Somin 2015). The broad interpretation given by both *Berman* and *Somavanti* have made it easy to disregard the settlement costs that are so crucial for any equitable resource reallocation.

Fourth, demoralisation could be reduced if eminent domain were used only in those cases falling within 'the instrumentality of commerce exception' emphasised by Justice Ryan in his dissent in *Poletown*. There are instances in which a consultative process yielded results so that the community was convinced that they were giving up their land for the larger public purpose of development. The case of farmers in 100 villages in Karnataka who agreed to give up their land willingly is a case in point (Aji 16 August 2015).

Fifth and finally, it is important to incorporate these demoralisation costs in the cost-benefit analysis like SIA laid down in the RFCTLARR. There must be transparency to ensure that the comprehensive process is carried out in a manner so that even the less politically influential get fair compensation. Fischel (1995) has rightly emphasised that Michelman's framework provides 'an indispensable vocabulary for analysing the takings issue'. Ignoring these costs can lead to political instability and jeopardise the very purpose of economic development for which the land was acquired in the first place.

Conclusion

The comparative analysis points towards balancing both efficiency and equity for achieving holistic development. In India, it is important to look at the nature of the development process itself. Industrial development needs to be in consonance with agricultural development and modernisation. This is important to reduce instances of acquisition on the grounds that agriculture is no longer remunerative and that the transfer will increase value. Productive assets need to be created which will help generate employment on a long-term basis rather than give rise to some one-time profits for real estate developers. It would indeed be regrettable if millions more are displaced and private interest groups continue to dictate the acquisition process for decades to come. India could draw lessons from the tribute Robert Post, the dean of Yale Law School, paid Michelman for being a champion of socio-economic rights: 'If we had listened to Frank, we would be a kinder, gentler nation now' (quoted from Rice 2012).[28]

Notes

1 545 US 469 (2005)
2 Gonzalves (2010) and Singh (2012) are two exceptions.
3 348 US 26, 32–34 (1954)

4 Justice Sandra Day O'Connor in her dissenting opinion in *Kelo*
5 AIR 1963 SC 151
6 2016 SCC SC 885
7 684 Mich NW2d 765 (2004)
8 410 Mich 616; 304 NW2d 455 (1981)
9 The term 'private entity' was defined as 'any entity other than a Government entity or undertaking and includes a proprietorship, partnership, company, corporation, non-profit organization or other entity under any law for the time being in force'.
10 Many states have adopted the provisions of Land Ordinance, 2014. Gujarat and Telengana have adopted it almost verbatim.
11 For a concise introduction to neoliberalism, see Steger and Roy (2010).
12 See Levien (2011).
13 Agarwal (2014: xii) warns: 'Violation of a basic human right on a large scale may lead to unrest that can only put a spoke in the giant wheel of India, slowing it down, or even bringing it to a grinding halt'.
14 467 US 229 (1984)
15 Somin (2015: 135) argues: 'The *Kelo* backlash led to more new state legislation than that generated by any other Supreme Court decision in history'.
16 3 Dall. 386 1 L Ed. 648 (1978)
17 Pal (2013) has discussed these sections and the interpretation by the courts in independent India in order to determine the compensation award in the final verdict.
18 (1939) 41 BOMLR 725
19 1977AIR 1560, 1977 SCR (2) 633
20 AIR 1962 SC 764
21 AIR 1964 1230
22 AIR 1975 SC
23 AIR 2003 SC 7133
24 [1] *Sooraram Pratap Reddy and Others*; [2] *Suraram Krishna Reddy and Another*; [3] *V. Krishna Prasad*; [4] *A.L. Sadanand*; [5] *Malla Reddy And Others*; [2] *District Collector, Land Acquisition and Others*; [3] *Government of Andhra Pradesh and Others*; [4] *District Collector and Others* 2008 (9) SCC 552
25 Among the many landmark cases cited, two important cases which dealt with the issue under discussion were *Pandit Jhandulal & Ors vs. State of Punjab & Ors. (1961) 2 SCR 459* and *Aflatoon & Ors vs. Lieutenant Governor of Delhi & Ors (1975) 4 SCC 285.*
26 This acquisition and the protests that followed generated many academic writings. A summary is provided in Pal (2017).
27 It is important to note that there were three Supreme Court judgments in 2011 in which land acquisition was quashed on procedural grounds. They are *Dev Sharan and Others vs. State of Uttar Pradesh and Others* [(2011) 4 SCC 769], *Radhey Shyam vs. State of Uttar Pradesh* [(2011) 5-SCC-533], and *Greater Noida Industrial Development Authority vs. Devendrakumar and Others[*(2011) 12- SCC-375].
28 Quoted from Rice, Lewis (2012), A Career of 'Reflective Equilibrium': Celebrating Frank Michelman. Harvard Law School Posts.

References

Agarwal, S. 2014. *The Indian federalist: the original will of India's founding fathers.* Chennai: Notion Press.

Aji, Sowmya. 2015, 16 August. 'Does Karnataka's Narasupara industrial town offers lessons in land acquisition? Not quite', *The Economic Times*, ET Bureau. Retrieved from http://economictimes.indiatimes.com/news/politics-and-nation/does-karnatakas-narasapura-industrial-town-offer-lessons-in-land-acquisition-from-farmers-not-quite/articleshow/48497030.cms accessed on 10 October 2015.

Bhaduri, A. 2009. *The face you were afraid to see: essays on the Indian economy.* New Delhi: Penguin Books India Limited.

Cohen, C.E. 2006. 'Eminent domain after Kelo v city of new London: an argument for banning economic development takings', *Harvard Journal of Law and Public Policy*, 29(2): 491–568.

Fernandes, W. 2004. 'Rehabilitation policy for the displaced', *Economic and Political Weekly*, XXXIX(12): 1191–1193.

Fischel, W. 1995. *Regulatory takings: law, economics and politics.* Cambridge: Harvard University Press.

Gonzalves, C. 2010. 'Judicial failure and land acquisition for corporates', *Economic and Political Weekly*, XLV(52): 37–42.

Levien, M. 2011. 'Rationalising dispossession: the land acquisition and resettlement bills', *Economic and Political Weekly*, XLVI(11): 66–71.

Michelman, F.I. 1967. 'Property, utility, and fairness: comments on the ethical foundations of "Just Compensation" law', *Harvard Law Review*, 80: 1165–1258.

Pal, M. 2013. 'Rehabilitation of the "project affected": eminent domain and just compensation', in S. Gangopadhyay and V. Santhakumar (eds.), *Law and economics, volume 2: practice* (pp. 1–18). New Delhi: Sage Publications India Pvt. Ltd.

Pal, M. 2017. 'Land acquisition and "Fair Compensation" of the "Project Affected"-scrutiny of the law and its interpretation', in Anthony P. D'Costa and Achin Chakraborty (eds.), *The land question in India: state, dispossession, livelihoods and contestation in India's capitalist transition.* Oxford: Oxford University Press.

Ramesh, J. and M.A. Khan. 2015. *Legislating for justice: the making of the 2013 land acquisition law.* New Delhi: Oxford University Press.

Rice, Lewis. 2012. *A career of 'reflective equilibrium': celebrating frank Michelman.* Harvard Law School Posts. Retrieved from https://today.law.harvard.edu/a-career-of-reflective-equilibrium-celebrating-frank-michelman/ accessed on 28 March 2020.

Singh, Ram. 2012, 12 May. 'Inefficiency and abuse of compulsory land acquisition: an enquiry into the way forward', *Economic and Political Weekly*, XLVII(19): 46–53.

Somin, I. 2004. 'Overcoming Poletown: county of Wayne v. Hathcock, economic development, takings and the future of public use', *Michigan State Law Review*, (4): 1005–1039.

Somin, I. 2009. 'The limits of backlash: assessing the political response to *Kelo*', *Minnesota Law Review*, 93(6): 2100–2178.

Somin, I. 2015. *The grasping hand: Kelo v city of New London and the limits of eminent domain.* Chicago: Chicago University Press.

Steger, M.B and R.K. Roy. 2010. *Neoliberalism: a very short introduction.* New York: Oxford University Press.

9 Neoliberalism, environmental protection, and regulation of land

Shiju Mazhuvanchery

India has been a frontrunner among developing countries in the enactment of environmental laws. From the 1970s onwards, several laws intended at curbing pollution, conserving natural resources, and regulating technology have been adopted. One major reason for such an interest in environmental issues has been the commitment by top political leadership to the cause. It was during the prime ministership of Indira Gandhi that many of these laws were enacted. Her biographers like Frank (2001) and Ramesh (2017) have noted her affinity towards nature and the steps that she had taken, including the launching of Project Tiger, towards this end. Her participation in the United Nations Conference on Human Environment in 1972 held at Stockholm (she was one of two heads of states who attended the event) had a ripple effect on the legislative field back home.

The legislative path that India took was not a blind imitation of the West. From the beginning, it was made clear that environmental protection and development had to go hand in hand. There was a clear understanding that technological progress is necessary for alleviation of poverty and protection of the environment. In her speech at the Stockholm Conference, Indira Gandhi was stressing this point when she said, 'The environment cannot be improved in conditions of poverty. Nor can poverty be eradicated without the use of science and technology'. Though this may sound close to a neoliberal attitude towards environmental regulation, it is far from the truth. The development and technological progress that she mentioned was not the one that neoliberal ideologues propagated. In the same speech, she makes that distinction very clear: 'The inherent conflict is not between conservation and development, but between environment and reckless exploitation of man and earth in the name of efficiency'.

Judicial activism is yet another feature of Indian environmental laws, wherein land-related concerns are selectively addressed. The head start given by the Legislature and the Executive was carried forward by an active judiciary. It employed many concepts like the 'precautionary principle', 'polluter pays principle', 'public trust doctrine', etc., to ensure that the laws were enforced in their letter and spirit. This was achieved by an expansionist interpretation of Article 21 of the Indian Constitution that guaranteed right to life and personal liberty. Holding that it was human life with dignity that was protected under Article 21, the courts in India interpreted Article 21 to include the right to a healthy environment. Dam and Tewary (2005) identify three distinct phases in the development of environmental jurisprudence by the Indian judiciary. In the first phase – the creative phase – the courts were involved in expanding the scope of fundamental rights by reading new rights into Article 21, including the right to a clean environment. In the second phase – the law-making phase – the courts were busy framing norms and evolving principles for the protection of the environment. The third phase saw the Judiciary entering the domain of the Executive and being involved in the policy-making arena. It may be also noted here that the Executive seems to be lacking in effective implementation of concepts mentioned earlier in the context of the land question. Judiciary responded to the inaction by the Executive by devising its own implementation mechanisms like the creation of monitoring committees (Sahu 2014). But judicial activism in the field of environmental law has been subjected to critical scrutiny by many (Chowdhury 2014; Rosencranz and Lele 2008).

Environmental laws can be broadly divided into two categories, viz., laws that protect the environmental media and laws that regulate activities that may have an adverse impact on the environment. Laws that protect wetlands, lakes, forests, etc., are examples of the first category, whereas laws that regulate genetically modified organisms, the nuclear industry, hazardous substances, etc., are examples of the latter. Environmental laws that regulate land fall under the first category. Indian laws view regulation of land as an important tool for environmental protection, and many of them contain prescriptions on land use. In developed countries, land regulation is considered as the weakest link in environmental protection (Tarlock 2007). This is due to the constitutional protection of private property in those jurisdictions. But India is not constrained by these limitations as right to property is no longer a fundamental right under the Indian Constitution. A later part of this chapter looks at some of these laws.

The 1980s saw fundamental changes in global economic policy. US President Ronald Reagan and UK Prime Minister Margaret Thatcher changed the fundamentals of the world economy by giving more importance to market forces. This had a distinct impact on the field of regulation, especially environmental regulation. Environmental regulation till that time was based on a 'command and control' approach and contained prescriptions as to what could be done and what could not be. This type of regulation is gradually giving way to regulations based on market instruments like cap and trade and information-based instruments like labelling.

In this larger context, this chapter is an attempt to look at the Indian environmental laws that affect land use, including land pollution, and how these laws are faring in the neoliberal era of regulation. The second part of the chapter looks at some of the laws that impose restrictions on land use for environmental protection directly or indirectly. The third part chronicles the change in regulatory approach towards the environment from a prescriptive one to one that uses neoliberal instruments. An attempt is also made to examine whether Indian laws are also undergoing a similar shift in their regulatory approach. The fourth part examines the role of judiciary in environmental regulation and sustainable development, and whether land-related concerns are addressed, such as valuation, land use, land acquisition, and so on. Two cases decided by two High Courts are analysed to find out whether the judiciary is influenced by neoliberal principles like cost-benefit analysis (CBA) and whether 'cost' related to land has been addressed or not. The fifth part concludes.

Land use and environmental protection

Air, water, and soil are the three basic inter-related natural resources of the planet. All these basic resources must be protected for the survival of life on the planet. For the success of environmental protection initiatives, sustainable use of land is crucial (Tarlock 2007). Regulating land use can have a significant impact on human health and environment. However, land-use regulation is considered to be the weakest link in environmental law (ibid). This is mainly due to the private ownership of land as opposed to air and water, both of which are considered to be common property. Right to property is considered to be an important constitutional right in many jurisdictions, including the USA. But it remains a fact that State control over private land is increasing. Zonal and planning regulations were the first to impose restrictions on exclusive use of land by the owners (Morris 1973). The finite nature of land and the increasing need of land both for economic development and conservation are causing immense pressure on it. This in turn has resulted in a three-cornered conflict. First, the owner of the land views it as a commodity from which maximum profit must be extracted. Second, the neighbours do not want their environment threatened by activities on the land, thereby reducing the value of their land. Third, the community at large has a stake in the land, in the sense that such land can be put to more productive use such as low-income housing or open space (ibid). It is in this contested terrain that land-use regulations must operate for the protection of the environment.

Though constitutional protection of private property poses challenges to the use of land regulation for environmental protection in most of the developed world, that was not a major hindrance in the case of India. Two reasons explain this contradiction. First, colonialism in India ensured that there was no fundamental constitutional guarantee for the private ownership of land. The State had the ultimate say in land use. The doctrine of eminent domain enforced through various land acquisition laws gave ultimate authority over land to the State. Second, even though the Constitution adopted after independence guaranteed right to property as a fundamental right under Article 31, successive constitutional amendments diluted it.

These amendments ensured that private property rights were subservient to public interest. Starting with the First Constitutional Amendment in 1951, limits were imposed on the enjoyment of this right. The 44th Constitutional Amendment in 1977 finally took away this fundamental right. It meant that by the time Indian environmental laws started evolving in the 1970s, the State did not have constitutional hurdles to overcome for imposing restrictions on land use. It remains a fact that Article 300A grants a constitutional right to property. But as right to environment is recognised as a fundamental right through judicial interpretation, any challenge on the ground of violation of right to property is bound to fail.

When one goes through the Indian laws, both environmental and otherwise, several of them impose restrictions on land use for environmental protection. Some of these laws are analysed here.

The Indian Forest Act, 1927

Environmental protection through land-use regulation has been a feature of Indian law from British colonial time onwards. The *Indian Forest Act, 1927*, was undoubtedly drafted as a draconian legislation imposing absolute State control over forests to further the commercial interests of the British Empire. The impact of the 1927 legislation and the Acts that preceded it on the local communities has been aptly summarised by Gadgil and Guha (1992: 134): 'By one stroke of the executive pen (the Act) attempted to obliterate centuries of customary use by rural populations all over India'. The 1927 Act categorised forests into four types, viz., reserved forest, protected forest, village forest, and other forests; State control gradually reducing with each type. 'Other forests' were in private hands, and the Act gave power to the State to regulate the activities in them in certain cases. Section 35 of the Act authorised the State to regulate and prohibit certain activities such as breaking up or clearing of land for cultivation, pasturing of cattle, and the firing or clearing of vegetation, even in private forest land. However, this was not a blanket power vested on the State. These prohibitions could be imposed only if they were necessary for certain purposes mentioned in the said section. A perusal of these purposes reveals that many of them are in one way or the other connected with environmental protection. Protection against storms, winds, rolling stones, floods, and avalanches; preservation of the soil in the ridges and slopes and in the valleys or hilly tracts; prevention of landslips; maintenance of water supply in springs, rivers, and tanks; and preservation of public health are purposes that have a direct bearing on the protection of the environment. This law considers landslides and effect on soil, but not land aspects per se.

With the enactment of The *Forest (Conservation) Act, 1980*, that imposed restrictions on the use of forest land for non-forest purposes and 'de-notification' of reserved forests by state governments without the prior approval of the Central Government, has converted the 1927 Act into an environmental protection legislation. The spate of directions given by the Supreme Court in *Godavarman Tirumulpad vs. Union of India* (1997) over a period of two decades have further consolidated the nature of this Act as a conservation law. Seen in that light, The *Indian Forest Act, 1927*, and the various other state laws that operate in many states in its place are powerful tools available with the state governments to regulate land use for conservation purposes.

The Wildlife (Protection) Act, 1972

The *Wildlife (Protection) Act, 1972*, can rightly be described as independent India's first legislative attempt at conservation. The legislative approach to protect wildlife adopted in this Act is twofold. By imposing a complete ban on hunting, the Act ensures that wildlife is protected wherever it is found (section 9). In addition to this, the Act adopts an ecosystem approach and designates a series of protected areas where human activity is restricted. The protected area network as provided in the Act consists of the following: National Parks, Sanctuaries, Conservation Reserves, Community Reserves, and Tiger Reserves. Restrictions on land use are imposed by the provisions of the Act in these protected areas. When one goes through the provisions of the Act, it is clear that except for Community Reserves, all other protected areas comprise government land and as such do not affect private property rights. However, the Indian reality is something different from what is portrayed in the statutory provisions. Millions of people live in protected areas and areas designated as reserved forests and protected forests under the forest laws. Most of these people have been living there for generations, and their continued stay in these areas is technically illegal; consequently, their land rights are not recognised. To correct this The *Scheduled Tribes and Other Traditional Forest Dwellers (Recognition of Forest Rights) Act, 2006*, was enacted. This Act grants limited land rights (manage and conserve forest land) to the people who have been staying in these areas.

The Environment (Protection) Act, 1986

The *Environment (Protection) Act, 1986* (EPA) was enacted in the wake of the Bhopal Gas Disaster. The Act gives immense power to the Central Government to take any measure to protect the environment. Exercising this power, the Central Government has issued notifications declaring certain areas as Ecologically Sensitive Areas (ESA) or Ecologically Fragile Areas. These notifications are issued to protect certain areas because of their environmental importance and impose restrictions on land use such as the prohibition on setting up polluting industries, use of pesticides in agriculture, etc. Murud-Janjira[1] was the first instance when the EPA route was used to impose restrictions on land use. The Notification was issued in the backdrop of the state government's consideration of a proposal to set up a ship repair yard in the region that could have destroyed the mangroves (Kapoor et al. 2009). The Notification issued by the Ministry of Environment and Forests in 1989 prohibited the location of industries in the region except those connected with tourism. Doon Valley[2] (1989), Dahanu[3] (1991), Aravalli[4] (1992), etc., are examples of such notifications imposing restrictions on land use.

Eco-Sensitive Zones are declared by the Central Government using the same powers under the *Environment (Protection) Act, 1986.* These areas are located around the protected areas declared under the *Wildlife (Protection) Act, 1972.* The extent of the area varies from place to place, extending up to a 10-kilometre radius in certain cases. These notifications typically impose land-use restrictions in alignment with conservation objectives. A list of prohibited and regulated activities is normally given in the Notification. Prohibited activities include mining, establishment of hazardous industries, wood-based industries, etc. Construction activities, setting up of hotels, etc., are regulated. In addition, state governments are required to prepare a Zonal Master Plan for the area. Most master plans allow infrastructure projects and change in land use that augment economic growth, such as setting up hotels as part of eco-tourism.

Coastal Regulation Zone Notification, 2019, is another step taken under the *Environment (Protection) Act, 1986,* that imposes restrictions on land use in coastal areas. India, being one of the major coastal states, realised the importance of protecting its coastlines from an environmental angle and introduced this Notification as early as 1991. The Notification has been amended many times and is one of the major tools of land-use restriction for environmental protection. It imposes restrictions on land use on 500 metres from the coastline (coastal regulation zone). Some of the activities prohibited in the 'coastal regulation zone' are setting up of industries, handling of hazardous substances, land reclamation, bunding, and disturbing the natural course of water. Coastal areas are categorised into different zones for conservation and protection.

Master plans under town and country planning laws

Master plans are prepared for the organised and structured growth of the cities. The Town and Country Planning Laws and the Development Authority Laws give the statutory base for master plans. In that way these plans impose restrictions on land use. One can see that recent master plans give importance to environmental protection and conservation of natural resources. The Revised Master Plan 2015 of the City of Bangalore is one such example. Concerned about rampant construction taking place around the lakes and surrounding areas, the master plan imposes severe restrictions on building activities. These restrictions are imposed in areas falling within 30 metres around the lakes, 50 metres from the middle of the primary rajkaluves, 25 metres from the middle of secondary rajkaluves, and 15 metres in tertiary rajkaluves. Rajakaluves are stormwater drains that carry water to the lakes. Similar restrictions can be seen in the master plan for Hyderabad City.

The foregoing analysis shows that there are a number of environmental and other laws that impose restrictions on land use for the purpose of environmental protection. These laws are prescriptive in nature, imposing restrictions and prohibitions, and controlling land use. With the advent of globalisation and liberalisation, doubts have been expressed about the utility of prescriptive laws for environmental protection in general in the discourse on sustainable development. One can observe changes taking place in the nature and approach of environmental regulations as a response to these concerns. The next section is an attempt to analyse this shift in the nature of environmental regulation from one that adopts prescription to one that adopts market-based tools.

Neoliberalism and environmental regulation

Environmental movements and environmentalism in general have been viewed as a counter-hegemonic struggle and as a critique of the expansionist logic of capitalism (Tulloch and Neilson 2014). Environmental movements in the 1970s attacked the capitalist mode of production and the culture of consumption that fuelled it. Carson's *Silent Spring* (Carson 1962) and Club of Rome's influential report *Limits to Growth* (Meadows et al. 1972) are examples of how environmentalists viewed capitalism as posing a serious threat to the natural environment. This is true even of Indian environmental movements. The much written-about struggle by the Narmada Bachao Andolan is a prime example. TWAIL[5] (Third World Approaches to International Law) scholar Balakrishnan Rajagopal presents the fight by the indigenous people in the Narmada valley as a counter-hegemonic struggle against globalisation (Rajagopal 2005). Booker Prize winner-writer and a familiar face of the Narmada struggle, Arundathi Roy has also presented it as one against capitalism and the agenda of 'development' presented by it (Roy 1999). Similarly, the Niyamgiri struggle by the Kondh tribals is also seen as an opposition to the 'neoliberal economy rut by globalization and promoted by the state'. Many see Niyamagiri as 'a site of resistance of forces unleashed by capitalist neoliberal economy and the state run by upper caste elites' (Pandey 2017: 47). These struggles are studied by many scholars from the perspective of land rights.[6]

However, a dramatic shift in this attitude happened at the global level with the Rio Conference and its most influential concept, sustainable development, which focuses on environment concerns that would make development 'sustainable'. It is argued that sustainable development neutralised the critique of capitalism as posing a threat to ecology and effectively gave a clean chit to it (Tulloch and Neilson 2014). This was achieved by putting economic growth, eradication of poverty, and ecological integrity on an equal footing and emphasising the viability of markets in environmental protection (ibid). Thus, capitalism has become green (Colombo 2014). This change in attitude towards capitalism and markets had its influence on environmental policy and regulation as well. The central tenet of this new regulation was assigning value to nature. Commodification of carbon through the Kyoto Protocol was the first instance of such an approach at the international level (Swyngedouw 2010). Assigning economic value to ecosystem services is another example of the neoliberal shift in environmental policy.

When it comes to environmental law and policy, a distinction is made between traditional and neoliberal regulation. The traditional regulation, prescriptive in nature, adopted a command and control approach. It prescribed what could be done and what could not be done (Salzman 2013). Environmental regulations of this genre set standards and imposed bans. Neoliberal regulations, on the other hand, adopted market- and information-based instruments to achieve environmental protection (Czarnezki and Fiedler 2016). These instruments are broadly defined as 'instruments or regulations that encourage behaviour through market signals rather than through explicit directives' (Stavins 2000: 1). In this context, it is noteworthy that capitalism (including multinational corporations) considers 'land' as a factor of production, which reinforces the argument of using land as a commodity in neoliberal India. Moreover, air and water pollution as a by-product of increasing industrialisation are dealt with by pollution laws, but India has yet to enact land pollution regulations/law.

Reagan's presidency is credited with having heralded the neoliberal era in environmental regulation (Czarnezki and Fiedler 2016). The mandatory 'Regulatory Impact Assessment' before introduction of a new regulation was a major step towards market-based approaches. The successive Republican and Democratic presidents have followed neoliberal approaches. The neoliberal approach to environmental regulation mainly takes two different forms (ibid). The first one relies on market-based instruments such as cap and trade, subsidies, taxes, etc. It is for the industry to act with these types of instruments/options available to them. The second set of instruments is based on information. Labelling, environmental audit reports by the industry, etc., fall in this category, and it is for the society/consumer to take necessary action through their purchasing decisions (Sullivan 2013).

Cost-benefit analysis (CBA) is a major policy tool in the neoliberal environmental regime (Czarnezki and Fiedler 2016). In its simplest formulation, CBA mandates that agencies should adopt regulations only when the likely benefits exceed the likely costs, and if there are many regulatory options satisfying this test, the one that maximises benefit should be adopted (Sunstein 2005). CBA is projected as a model of rationality (OECD 2018) as opposed to the precautionary principle (Sunstein 2005). However, emphasising the importance of valuation of natural resources and availability of reliable data in this type of regulation, Czarneski and Fiedler argue that prescriptive regulation is still required and cannot be completely ruled out (Czarnezki and Fiedler 2016).

But neoliberal regulation at any point does not mean that everything is left to market forces and the State is completely absent from the scene. The State must play an active role to create a 'market' that will facilitate environmental protection. For this, neoliberal states are required to come out with rules both for the institutional and for individual behavioural change (Nikula 2017). This can be in the form of incentives and burdens. In this way of functioning, there is negligible scope for land issues in the measures for environment protection; neither the Judiciary nor the Executive consider land aspects as a co-factor of environment protection, despite land being the most valuable resource/asset.

Even at the international level, environmental governance has become more pluralistic and transnational as a result of globalisation (Kutting 2004). Multinational corporations play an important role in this context. The internal rules of many of these corporations deal with environmental concerns. These internal rules force the corporations to adopt environmental standards that may be higher than what is provided for in the national laws of the host country. There can be many reasons for inclusion of environmentally friendly measures in their internal conduct. Global image of the corporation can be one of them.

When it comes to Indian environmental law and policy, one is yet to notice a definitive shift towards the neoliberal approach. But there are signals of such a change in some of the laws and policies. The *Water (Prevention and Control of Pollution) Cess Act, 1977*, introduced for the first time incentives and deterrence as a means for controlling pollution. The Act imposed a cess on the utilization of water by the industry, and huge rebates were provided for those industrial establishments that took measures for pollution control in the form of setting up treatment plants. On the other hand, those industries that polluted water sources paid an enhanced cess. There are many incentives in the form of subsidies that are provided by the government for environmentally friendly products such as installation of solar panels, etc. The mandatory rating and labelling of certain products like air conditioners and refrigerators based on energy efficiency under the *Energy Conservation Act, 2001*, is an example of information-based instruments directed at environmental protection. The Clean Energy Cess imposed on coal was another example of using taxation as a means for environmental protection.[7] However, no such step is taken when it comes to land regulation. But an analysis of some of the judicial decisions reveal that neoliberal regulatory instruments like CBA are frequently used by the judiciary in adjudicating disputes involving land regulations intended at protection of natural resources. The concept of 'sustainable development' has become the most used tool by the Indian judiciary when confronted with the question of environment versus development. The next section attempts to analyse two such judgments where such an approach has been adopted.

Indian judiciary and neoliberal environmental regulation: two case studies in land regulation

This part looks at whether the Indian judiciary is influenced by neoliberal notions of environmental regulation when presented with issues relating to restrictions on land use, including land pollution. Indian judiciary is famed for its zeal for environmental activism. Concepts like the precautionary principle have been invoked by the Indian Supreme Court in several cases. For this analysis, cases wherein the issues of 'development' and environmental protection have come in direct conflict have been taken. In both these decisions, the question revolved around whether violations of land-use restrictions intended at environmental protection were justified or not. Two High Court decisions have been chosen for this analysis. The choice of High Court decisions has been done intentionally. In the Indian context, most of the environmental conflicts are decided (as opposed to resolved) at the local level. The High Courts exercising writ jurisdiction and supervisory powers under Articles 226 and 227 of the Constitution becomes the venue for the adjudication of these disputes. This is true in many of the cases even after the establishment of the National Green Tribunal and its regional benches. Two decisions, one by the Goa bench of the Bombay High Court and another by the then Andhra Pradesh High Court, are analysed here. In both these disputes, Public Interest Litigations have been filed against mega developmental projects on the grounds of adverse impact on the environment and violation of environmental protection laws. In both these cases, objections on the environmental front were raised on the grounds of violations of laws that imposed land-use restrictions. These objections were rejected, and the decisions were based on what can be described as cost-benefit analysis. The rationale behind both these judgments was that the benefits of these projects far outweighed the adverse impact on the environment.

Goa Foundation vs. Konkan Railway corporation

In *Goa Foundation vs. Union of India* (1992), the Goa Bench of the Bombay High Court was approached to determine the apparent violations of environmental protection laws in the Konkan Railway project. This 741-kilometre rail line connects the coastal regions of the states of Maharashtra, Goa, Karnataka, and Kerala with Mumbai. With 1,880 bridges and 91 tunnels, the rail line passes through the Western Ghats and the coastal regions of Goa. The Goa Foundation, an environmental action group dedicated to the conservation of Goa's natural environment, filed the writ petition on many grounds. The major legal challenges were the following: an Environmental Impact Assessment had not been conducted and environmental clearance had not been obtained, forest clearance under the *Forest (Conservation) Act, 1980,* had not been obtained, and the provisions of the *Coastal Regulation Zone Notification, 1991,* had been violated. It may be noticed here that the last two contentions were based on violations of land-use restrictions imposed by environmental laws. In a short judgment, the Court rejected all of these arguments and cleared the project. The opening lines of the judgment itself reveal the attitude of the judges towards environmental protection involving mega developmental projects:

> Very few people are fortunate to see their dreams fulfilled and people residing on the west coast saw fulfilment of their dreams when the Central Government decided to provide a broad-gauge railway line from Bombay to Mangalore and thereafter to extend to the State of Kerala. It was a long-standing demand of the people to improve the economic conditions and to make accessible the hinterlands in the State of Maharashtra, State of Goa and State of Karnataka.

These opening lines remind one of evangelist Matthew's presentation of Jesus as the long-awaited redeemer of the Israelites.[8] The only difference here is that 'development' is seen as the redeemer, and 'land' is not valued despite being a highly valued resource. One can notice that these are the major premises behind this judgment.

The first objection to the project was that necessary clearances had not been obtained under the *Forest (Conservation) Act, 1980*. This short piece of legislation is intended to curb the utilisation of forest land for non-forest purposes. As per section 3 of this Act, prior approval of the Central Government is necessary for such conversion of forest land. Popularly called 'forest clearance', this permission is given by the Ministry of Environment, Forest and Climate Change after satisfying many conditions, including compensatory afforestation. The court brushed aside this objection by observing that it was the Central Government which had cleared the project, and the Railway ministry which was executing the project was part of the Central Government. Anyone familiar with the workings of the various ministries in the Central Government and their functions clearly knows that project clearance does not mean that forest clearance is also automatically given. It may also be noted here that forests were originally in the State List of the Constitution, thereby vesting the legislative and executive powers over forests to the state governments. It was through the *42nd Constitutional Amendment Act, 1976*, that the item 'forest' was shifted from the state list to the concurrent list, thereby conferring concurrent power to the Central Government.

Another objection raised was based on the alleged violation of the *Coastal Regulation Zone Notification, 1991*. Petitioners contended that construction of rail lines on the ecologically fragile Khazan land violated the Notification. Khazan lands are 'reclaimed wetlands, salt marshes and mangrove areas, where tidal influence is regulated by the construction of embankments and sluice gates' (Sonak 2014: v). These areas are now facing environmental degradation mainly because of saline intrusion, and it is attributed to the socio-economic changes brought out by the process of globalisation (Rubinoff 2011). The Court rejected the argument on the grounds that what were prohibited under the Notification were industrial activities and all the restrictions in the Notification had to be read in that context. Approaching the Notification that way, construction of a railway line was not a prohibited activity.

However, the main reasoning given by the Court for rejecting all the objections on the environmental front was one based on a CBA. The Court was swayed by the apparent benefits of the project to turn a blind eye to the ecological damage of a project of such magnitude. The Court held:

> (E)ven otherwise, the extent of damage is extremely negligible and a public project of such a magnitude which is undertaken for meeting the aspirations of the people on the west coast cannot be defeated on such considerations. It is not open to frustrate the project of public importance to safeguard the interest of few persons. It cannot be overlooked that while examining the grievance about adverse impact upon a small area of 30 hectares of Khazan lands, the benefit which will be derived by large number of people by construction of rail line cannot be brushed aside. The Courts are bound to take into consideration the comparative hardship which the people in the region will suffer by stalling the project of great public utility. The cost of the project escalates from day to day. . . . No development is possible without some adverse effect on the ecology and environment, but the projects of public utility cannot be abandoned and it is necessary to adjust the interest of the people as well as the necessity to maintain the environment.

The underlying rationale expressed in the foregoing paragraph brings out certain points worthy of consideration. First, in mega infrastructure projects the decision should always be based on a CBA, which does not include valuation of land as an important component. This is because a project of such magnitude inevitably would adversely affect the environment. Second, when one calculates the environmental costs, it is treated as the interest of a 'few' and the impact is negligible from the point of view of the geographical area/land affected. Third, the Court assumes that the interest of the people lies in 'developmental' projects, and it must be balanced against the interest of the few, that is, the environment. The concluding paragraph aptly summarises this sentiment:

> We hope and trust that unnecessary obstructions are not raised to the project of such huge public utility and which will herald the prosperity for the poor people on the western coast. It should be remembered that the project of such gigantic magnitude has become available after the people fought for over a century and the petty interest of a local area should not defeat the project in respect of which the Central

Government has already spent a huge amount. We decline to exercise our writ jurisdiction in such cases because the writ jurisdiction is meant to advance the cause of justice and not to defeat exercises undertaken by the Government for the public benefit. The machinery of the Court should not be used for subserving the private interest or the interest of a local area to the detriment of the public at large.

This judgment is not an isolated one. Divan and Rosencranz (2002) chronicle a couple of such cases decided by the Supreme Court in which a similar approach was adopted. The Supreme Court in those cases, including the *Narmada* (2000), effectively uses the concept of 'sustainable development' as a balancing principle to give a go-ahead for the project. Here too, consideration of the land is absent, the much discussed 'public purpose' and 'eminent domain' is linked closely to value, and limited availability of land as a resource and consequent displacement costs are completely ignored by the Court.

Forum for a better Hyderabad vs. Government of Andhra Pradesh

Forum for a Better Hyderabad vs. Government of Andhra Pradesh (2003) is a decision rendered by the High Court of undivided Andhra Pradesh. Petitioners in this case challenged the permission granted for the construction of a new airport at Hyderabad. The challenge was on the grounds that it was proposed to be set up in the catchment area of Himayatsagar Lake. A Government Order issued in 1996 had prohibited the setting up of polluting industries, major hotels, residential colonies, etc., within a 10-kilometre radius of Himayatsagar and Osmansagar lakes in the city of Hyderabad. Petitioners argued that many parts of the new airport, including one runway, fell within the prohibited zone.

Discussions on the environmental laws of India often revolve around legislation passed by the Union Parliament and decisions by the Supreme Court of India. A closer look at the Constitution reveals that most of the subjects that directly deal with the environment, such as land, water, etc., are in the domain of states. Various state governments have adopted laws and other regulations intended to protect the environment. Government Order (G.O.Ms.No.111 MA dated 08.03.1996) is one such measure adopted by the Andhra Pradesh State Government.

Himayatsagar and Osmansagar lakes are two major sources of drinking water for the twin cities of Hyderabad and Secunderabad. These lakes had been meeting the drinking water needs of the twin cities since the 1930s onwards, and protection of these water sources was a priority for successive governments. G.O. No. 50 issued in 1989 was the first attempt at regulating land use around these lakes. It was issued to protect the hydrological regime of the catchment areas. The main restrictions imposed by this G.O.

were: prohibition of the interception of any inflows of water into the lakes, removal of unauthorized check dams, prohibition of unauthorised tapping of ground water in the catchment areas, prohibition of the construction of anicuts, and prevention of unauthorised occupation of the land. G.O. No. 192 issued in 1994 replaced the 1989 G.O. and imposed further restrictions. G.O. No. 192 was issued based on the Interim Report submitted by the Expert Committee constituted by the Hyderabad Metropolitan Water Supply and Sewerage Board (HMWSSB) to monitor the quality of water in these two lakes. The significance of this G.O. lies in the introduction of an area-wide prohibition. The said G.O. prohibited the establishment of any polluting industries, major hotels, and residential colonies within a radius of 10 kilometres from full tank level (FTL) of the two lakes. It further mandated that, to carry out developmental activities beyond 10 kilometres within the catchment area, a no objection certificate (NOC) should be secured from different agencies. G.O.Ms. No. 111.M.A. dt. 8–03–1996 was issued based on the second report submitted by the Expert Committee. It prohibited polluting industries within a radius of 10 kilometres both upstream and downstream. In addition, it imposed a complete ban on the setting up of any industry within the prohibited zone.

The validity of this G.O. was examined by the Supreme Court in two *A.P. Pollution Control Board* cases (1999 and 2000). After referring to various studies by different agencies, the Court upheld the validity of the G.O. The Court employed the precautionary principle in reaching its decision. Further, the Court cautioned against granting any exemption to polluting industries within the prohibited zone. It is in this context that permission was granted by both the Central and State governments for the construction of a new airport, parts of which, including one runway, fell within the prohibited zone. The court upheld the decision of the government, holding that 'Airport' is not a 'polluting industry' and hence did not come within the prohibition of the G.O. It completely ducked the issue relating to the prohibition of setting up any industry within the prohibited zone. The Court adopted a hands-off approach and observed that:

> It is well-settled that this court in exercise of the jurisdiction under Article 226 cannot sit in appeal over expert bodies as appellate authority and give opinion unless authorities failed to discharge statutory duty cast upon them under the relevant statutes.

Even though this judgment does not explicitly refer to the cost-benefit analysis as in the Konkan Railway case, scrutiny reveals that the rationale for both the decisions is the same. The Court mentions the need for a new airport at Hyderabad and notes with approval the decision of the Government to set one up: 'It is to be noted that the Government of A.P. decided to develop a new International Airport due to various constraints faced in the existing Begumpet Airport and cater to the growing needs of air traffic'.

The Court also mentions the development of new airports in other cities like Bangalore. The Court refers to the balancing principle (the same principle adopted by the Goa Bench in the Konkan Railway case) in finally disposing off the petition. The Court concludes:

> In the circumstances, and particularly keeping in view the need to strike a balance between the process of technological development of the society and the Environment, we are of the view that the matter does not warrant interference of this court in exercise of the discretionary jurisdiction under Article 226 of the Constitution of India.

An analysis of this judgment shows that the Courts are employing cost-benefit analysis, balance test, concept of sustainable development, etc., when confronted with explicit prohibition contained in regulations regarding land use. The underlying rationale behind such an approach is the belief that 'development', the ultimate redeemer to lift millions out of poverty, cannot be sacrificed at the altar of the environment. Neoliberal tools become handy in that process. What is to be noted here is that the Courts are deciding cases against clear prohibitions contained in the regulations.

These two judgments are not isolated examples of the judiciary swayed by the 'benefits' of large infrastructure projects. As mentioned earlier, Divan and Rosencranz (2002) analyse a couple of such cases that adopted a similar approach. The difference in judicial approach towards large infrastructure projects and individual pollution-related cases is noted (Upadhyay 2000). In the former type of cases, the courts take a 'hands-off' approach and do not interfere in executive actions. *Worli Koliwada Nakhwa Matsya Vyavasay Sahkari Society Ltd vs. Municipal Corporation of Greater Mumbai* (2019) recently decided by the Bombay High Court may be an exception to this trend. In this case, a coastal road project in the city of Mumbai had to be stopped because of illegalities in the granting of environmental clearance and clearance under the Coastal Regulation Zone (CRZ) Notification.

Conclusion

Land-use regulation is an important component of environmental law. Unlike air and water, the other two basic natural resources that are subject to common ownership, land held under private ownership presents legal hurdles in regulation. This has been particularly evident in many developed countries because of the constitutional protection of private property. However, in India this is not the case because of the subjection of right to property to public interest in the constitutional framework. Thus, there are several laws both at the national and local levels which impose restrictions on land use with an aim to protect the environment. These laws protect coastal areas to the hilly regions and forests from the pressures of development.

Neoliberal tenets have influenced the way in which regulations are shaped in the past two to three decades in all realms of life. The field of environmental regulation has not been an exception. Prescriptive regulation in the form of prohibitions and standards is giving way to market-based instruments such as cost-benefit analysis and cap and trade. Information-based instruments like labelling and audit reports are also used as regulatory tools. This in a way is putting the onus of environmental protection on individuals by forcing them to alter their purchase decisions. In the larger framework, concepts like sustainable development have helped capitalism to co-opt environmental protection, thus making it in turn ethical and green, which undermines the importance of land. As such, land is an essential, limitedly available resource, but capitalism considers it as a factor of production, that is, merely a commodity.

A unique feature of Indian environmental jurisprudence is the active involvement of the judiciary in environmental protection. The Indian judiciary has adorned many mantles in its zeal for environmental protection. Public educator, policy maker, super administrator, etc., are some of the roles that judiciary plays in environmental matters. But a very different picture emerges when one analyses the role of the Courts in 'developmental' projects. As demonstrated in the two judgments discussed previously, neoliberal instruments like CBA comes to the rescue of the Court in condoning violation of land-use regulations, including land pollution, valuation of land, and absence of a land governance mechanism. Thus, it can be concluded that neoliberal precepts are yet to find a foothold in environmental and land laws in India. Especially, land-use regulations are still couched in a prescriptive language of prohibitions and restrictions. It is through judicial decisions that these concepts are entering into environmental jurisprudence; the Legislature and the Executive have yet to comprehend the need for land protection through effective land governance.

But even when the courts are using neoliberal tools like cost-benefit analysis and sustainable development, the value of the environment and particularly that of land is not adequately appreciated. The environmental value of land depends on several parameters. The ecosystem services provided by wetlands and forests are not taken into consideration in the cost-benefit analysis employed by the judiciary. On the other hand, as was demonstrated in the Konkan Railway case, the environmental value of land was reduced to that of the interest of a few environmentalists and the benefit derived from the project as that of the entire population. Even cases decided in recent years such as the Kudankulam[9] judgment demonstrate a similar approach. Such an approach by the judiciary raises serious questions about the viability of neoliberal tools in the adjudication of environmental disputes, especially those involving land-use regulation.

Notes

1 Murud–Janjira is a coastal village in Maharashtra famous for its seventeenth-century fort. The proposal to set up a ship repair yard was met with stiff opposition by environmentalists. They objected to the large-scale destruction of mangroves

around the island. The Central Government decided to protect the area by imposing restrictions on land use, including setting up of industries.
2 Located in the state of Uttarakhand, Doon Valley's ecological significance is very
high, with Rajaji National Park being part of it. Rampant limestone mining rang
alarm bells for the valley that led to a series of protests finally culminating in the
issuance of the Notification. The 1989 Notification imposed restrictions on location of industries, mining, tourism, grazing, and land use.
3 The proposal to set up a thermal power plant in this coastal city of Maharashtra
led to protests and issuance of the Ecologically Sensitive Area notification. Restrictions were imposed on change in land use and setting up of hazardous industries
by the Notification.
4 The Aravallis is a range of mountains that runs through the western states of
Rajasthan and Haryana. Developmental activities taking place in the mountain
ranges led to the issuance of the Ecologically Sensitive Area notification.
5 TWAIL can be broadly defined as a methodology to understand the history, processes, and institutions of international law from a Third World perspective. For
more, see: Chimni (2006).
6 See: Bhagat-Ganguly (2016) for details.
7 Both these taxes, water cess and clean energy cess, have been abolished by the
introduction of the Goods and Service Tax in 2007.
8 'The people living in darkness have seen a great light; on those living in the land
of the shadow of death a light has dawned' (New Revised Standard Version, Matthew 4: 16). Those who are interested in eco-theology may note that these verses
were written by the evangelist as a fulfilment of the prophesy of Isaiah. And the
irony lies in the fact that Isaiah is often seen as a prophet who spoke about the
environment and the need to protect it (Leal 2006: 128–133).
9 *Sundarrajan vs. Union of India* (2013)

References

A.P. Pollution Control Board vs. M. V. Nayudu I (1999) 2 SCC 718
A.P. Pollution Control Board vs. M. V. Nayudu II (2001) 2 SCC 62
Bhagat-Ganguly, Varsha. 2016. *Land rights in India*. New Delhi: Routledge India.
Carson, Rachel. 1962. *Silent spring*. Boston: Houghton Mifflin.
Chimni, Bhupinder. 2006. 'Third world approaches to international law: a Mani-
festo', *International Community Law Review*, 8(1): 3–27.
Chowdhury, Nupur. 2014. 'From judicial activism to adventurism – the *Godavar-
man case* in the supreme court of India', *Asia Pacific Journal of Environmental
Law*, 17: 177–189.
Colombo, Dario. 2014. 'Environment and neoliberalism: a critical discourse analy-
sis of three Italian cases', *ESSACHES Journal for Communication Studies*, 7(1):
63–82.
Czarnezki, Jason J. and Katherine Fiedler. 2016. 'The neoliberal turn in environmental regulation', *Utah Law Review*, 2016(1): 1–40.
Dam, Shubhankar and Vivek Tewary. 2005. 'Polluting environment, polluting constitution: is a "Polluted" constitution worse than a polluted environment', *Journal
of Environmental Law*, 17(3): 383–393.
Divan, Shyam and Armin Rosencranz. 2002. *Environmental law and policy in India:
cases, materials and statutes*. New Delhi: Oxford University Press.
Forum for a Better Hyderabad v. *Government of Andhra Pradesh* (2003), MANU/
AP/1257/2003

Frank, Catherine. 2001. *Indira: the life of Indira Nehru Gandhi*. London: Harper Collins.

Gadgil, Madhav and Ramachandra Guha. 1992. *This fissured land: an ecological history of India*. New Delhi: Oxford University Press.

Goa Foundation v. Union of India, AIR 1992 Bom. 471.

Godavarman Tirumulpad v. Union of India, AIR 1997 SC 1233.

Kapoor, Meenakshi, Kanchi Kohli and Manju Menon. 2009. *India's notified ecologically sensitive areas: the story so far*. New Delhi: Kalpvriksh.

Kütting, Gabriela. 2004. 'Globalization and the environment: moving beyond neoliberal institutionalism', *International Journal of Peace Studies*, 9(1): 29–46.

Leal, Robert Barry. 2006. *Through ecological eyes: reflections on Christianity's environmental credentials*. Strathfield: St. Paul's Publications.

Meadows, Donella H., Dennis L. Meadoes, Jorgen Randers and William W. Behrens 1972. *Limits to growth*. New York: Universe Books.

Morris, Eugene J. 1973. 'Regulation of land use', *Real Property, Probate and Trust Journal*, 8: 509.

Narmada Bachao Andolan v. Union of India (2000) 10 SCC 664.

New Revised Standard Version. 1993. *The Holy Bible*. Nashville: Catholic Bible Press.

Nikula, Ilari. 2017. *Neoliberal environmentalism*. Retrieved from http://web.isanet.org/Web/Conferences/HKU2017-s/Archive/ceb6c473-5cb9-4308-9e23-efe6157f7785.pdf accessed on 10 April 2019.

OECD. 2018. *Cost-Benefit analysis and the environment: further developments and policy use*. Paris: OECD Publishing. Retrieved from http://dx.doi.org/10.1787/9789264085169-en accessed on 2 April 2019.

Pandey, Annapurna Devi. 2017. 'The challenges of neoliberal policies and the indigenous people's resistance movement in Odisha, India', *e-cadernos ces*, http://journals.openedition.org/eces/2340 accessed on 31 March 2019.

Rajagopal, Balakrishnan. 2005. 'The role of law in counter-hegemonic globalization and global legal pluralism: lessons from the Narmada valley struggle in India', *Leiden Journal of International Law*, 18: 345–387.

Ramesh, Jairam. 2017. *Indira Gandhi: a life in nature*. New Delhi: Simon & Schuster India.

Rosencranz, A. and S. Lele. 2008. 'Supreme court and India's forests', *Economic and Political Weekly*, 43(5): 11–14.

Roy, Arundhati. 1999, May. 'The greater common good', *Outlook*.

Rubinoff, Jante Ahner. 2011. 'Pink gold: transformation of backwater aquaculture on Goa's Khazan land', *Economic and Political Weekly*, 36(13): 1108–1114.

Sahu, Geetanjoy. 2014. *Environmental jurisprudence and the Supreme Court: litigation, interpretation, implementation*. Hyderabad: Orient Blackswan.

Salzman, James. 2013. 'Teaching policy instrument choice in environmental law: the five P's', *Duke Environmental Law & Policy Forum*, 23(Spring): 363–376.

Sean, P. Sullivan and P. Sean. 2013. 'Empowering market regulation of agricultural animal welfare through product labeling', *Animal Law Review*, 19(2): 391–422.

Sonak, Sangeeta M. 2014. *Khazan ecosystems of Goa*. Dordrecht: Springer.

Stavins, Robert N. 2000, January. *Experience with market based environmental policy instruments*. Resources for the Future Discussion Paper, No. 0009.

Sundarrajan v. Union of India (2013) 6 SCC 620.

Sunstein, Cass R. 2005. 'Cost-benefit analysis and the environment', *Ethics*, 115(1): 3051–3385.

Swyngedouw, Erik. 2010. 'Apocalypse forever? Post-political populism and the spectre of climate change', *Theory, Culture & Society*, 27(2–3): 213–232.

Tarlock, Dan A. 2007. 'Land use regulation: the weak link in environmental protection', *Washington Law Review*, 82(2): 651–666.

Tulloch, Lynley and David Neilson. 2014. 'The neoliberalisation of sustainability', *Citizenship, Social and Economic Education*, 13(1): 26–38.

Upadhyay, Videh. 2000. 'Changing judicial power: courts on infrastructure projects and environment', *Economic and Political Weekly*, 35(43/44): 3789–3792.

Worli Koliwada Nakhwa Matsya Vyavasay Sahkari Society Ltd v. *Municipal Corporation of Greater Mumbai* (2019). Writ Petition (L) 560 of 2019. Retrieved from https://indiankanoon.org/doc/148877812/ accessed on 20 August 2019.

Index

Note: page numbers in **bold** indicate a table.

Printed in the United States
By Bookmasters